Lying and Insincerity

Lying and Insincerity

Andreas Stokke

OXFORD
UNIVERSITY PRESS

Great Clarendon Street, Oxford, OX2 6DP,
United Kingdom

Oxford University Press is a department of the University of Oxford.
It furthers the University's objective of excellence in research, scholarship,
and education by publishing worldwide. Oxford is a registered trade mark of
Oxford University Press in the UK and in certain other countries

First Edition published in 2018
Impression: 2

Published in the United States of America by Oxford University Press
198 Madison Avenue, New York, NY 10016, United States of America

British Library Cataloguing in Publication Data
Data available

Library of Congress Control Number: 2018931635

ISBN 978-0-19-882596-8

Printed and bound by
CPI Group (UK) Ltd, Croydon, CR0 4YY

Contents

Detailed Contents

Preface

I started thinking about lying and its relation to deception in 2010, while I was working as a postdoctoral research fellow at the Centre for the Study of Mind in Nature (CSMN) at the University of Oslo. I wrote a paper responding to work by Don Fallis on the topic, and later I organized a workshop held in April 2011 at the CSMN on those themes with participation by Don Fallis, Jenny Saul, Liz Camp, Roy Sorensen, and myself. Although I had no premonition of this at the time, this early work was to prove the start for a long-term project of thinking about insincerity in speech.

When starting to work on these issues in Oslo in 2010–11, I was greatly encouraged by, among many others, Herman Cappelen, Nick Allott, Olav Gjelsvik, Timothy Chan, and Torfinn Huvenes, all of whom provided me with thoughts and ideas of immense value. Many central strands in this book stem from these early conversations. I am very grateful to all of those who helped this project get underway.

Later in 2011 Herman Cappelen and Patrick Greenough proposed that I organize a workshop at Arché at the University of St Andrews, co-funded by Arché and the CSMN, on insincerity and lying. The event took place in November 2011 with participation by Don Fallis, James Mahon, Katherine Hawley, and myself. This was another early event that greatly helped to provide momentum for my thinking about insincerity in speech. I owe a debt to Herman and Patrick for initiating this event and to the participants at the workshop who gave me valuable feedback.

Having written the two papers for these two events, "Lying and Asserting" and "Insincerity," I began to think about engaging in a larger-scale investigation of insincerity in language. Alongside other projects I began to work on papers on insincerity and testimony, and on truthfulness in communication from a Gricean perspective. At the same time I started work on two co-authored papers, "Bullshitting, Lying, and Indifference toward Truth" with Don Fallis and "What is Said?" with Anders Schoubye. The collaboration on these topics with Don and Anders, and the many discussions we have had, have been of great value to my thinking in this area. I owe a special debt to Don for innumerable exchanges, and for reading and commenting on many drafts of earlier work over the years.

In 2013 Eliot Michaelson and I began to develop the idea for a collection of essays on lying. We were fortunate in convincing an esteemed group of philosophers to contribute. As preparation for the collection we held two workshops for the contributors to interact: one at the CSMN in May 2015 and another at King's College London (co-hosted by the Institute of Philosophy) in November of the same year. Both these events were inspiring, and provided a great deal of useful feedback from, among others, Andrew Reisner, James Mahon, Jessica Pepp, Jonas Åkerman, Paul Faulkner, and Rachel Sterken.

The list of sources of valuable input for this project is endless. Some deserve explicit recognition for ideas and help in other ways, in addition to those already mentioned. In particular, Anandi Hattiangadi, Andrew Peet, Ben Caplan, Bruno Jacinto, David Konstan, Dilip Ninan, Derek Ball, Ephraim Glick, Erich Rast, François Recanati, Gunnar Björnsson, Ishani Maitra, Jed Lewinsohn, Justin Snedegar, Jennifer Lackey, Jessica Brown, Josh Dever, Kalle Grill, Larry Horn, Line Ingerslev, Matt Benton, Mikkel Gerken, Nat Hansen, Ole Hjortland, Pål Antonsen, Pär Sundström, Ralf Bader, Renaud Gagné, Salvador Mascarenhas, and Sebastian Becker.

The ideas in this book have grown out of earlier work, but it also contains much new material. The introduction and Chapter 1 are new. Chapters 2 and 3 are based on parts of "Lying and Asserting," *Journal of Philosophy 110*(1), 2013, 33–60 and "Lying, Sincerity, and Quality," forthcoming in J. Meibauer (ed.), *The Oxford Handbook of Lying*, Oxford University Press. Both chapters also contain new material. Chapters 4 and 5 are based on "Lying and Misleading in Discourse," *Philosophical Review 125*(1), 2016, 83–134, but also contain new material. Chapters 6 and 7 are based on parts of "Bullshitting, Lying, and Indifference toward Inquiry" (co-authored with Don Fallis), *Ergo 4*(10), 2017, 277–309, and on parts of "Bullshitting," forthcoming in J. Meibauer (ed.), *The Oxford Handbook of Lying*, Oxford University Press, but also contain new material. Chapter 8 is based on parts of "Insincerity," *Noûs 48*(3), 2014, 496–520. Chapters 9 and 10 are mostly new, but some parts are based on "Insincerity."

For financial support I gratefully acknowledge Riksbankens Jubileumsfond and the Swedish Collegium for Advanced Study.

Andreas Stokke, Uppsala, August 2017

Introduction

we know to tell many lies that sound like truth,
but we know to sing reality, when we will.

Hesiod, *Theogony* 27–28 (trans. M. L. West)

0.1. Sincere and Insincere Speech

Human cooperation and development are underwritten by a practice of information sharing. Given our limited lifespan and point of view, we are dependent on information acquired from others. Our limitations concern both the world and the minds of others. No one can investigate every corner of the universe, or even of their own neighborhood, and we cannot always tell what someone is thinking just by looking at their face. We depend on others to share information with us both about the world and their thoughts. By far, most of the information we acquire from others we acquire from testimony. Language is our best tool for sharing information. This system of using language to overcome our cognitive limitations relies fundamentally on sincerity. In the most ordinary case *A* tells *B* something that *A* believes, whereby *B* comes to believe it, too. There is an alignment of mind and speech in the kind of sincerity that sustains the practice of information exchange.

These truisms reveal some important features of the way we use language to inform each other. In its most general form the practice is one of inquiry, the pursuit of truth. Many of the activities we value the most are generally engaged in inquiry. Science, philosophy, history, criminal investigations, journalism, and even ordinary conversations about everyday matters all typically aim at discovering and sharing truths.

Yet it is a further truism that we sometimes disrupt the communal project of inquiry. We sometimes misinform each other, we deceive, we lie, we mislead, we misrepresent the world and ourselves, we keep secrets. We sometimes have reasons for bypassing the goals of truthful exchange. There is no one, or at least very few, who have never lied or spoken insincerely in some way.

The same limitations on knowing the world and the minds of others that force us to rely on the sincerity of our informants make it possible for others to instill false beliefs in us. Language allows us to communicate our thoughts to others. But language also allows us to speak falsely. Mirroring sincere use of language, insincere speech involves interaction of mind and language. The paradigmatic kind of insincere speech is lying. In standard cases of lying A tells B something that A believes to be false, whereby B is deceived into believing it. When we use language insincerely mind and speech are misaligned. The speaker says one thing and believes another, and the hearer is tricked into believing something that corresponds neither to the facts nor to the mind of the speaker.

Insincerity and deception are at the heart of our culture and begin at its beginnings. In Archaic Greek thought the order of Zeus is not only predicated on violence but is also established through the power of duplicity and guile. Deception allowed Zeus to overcome his father, Kronos. His triumph was sealed in part by his incorporation of his first spouse, Metis, herself the embodiment of cunning and trickery. To forestall her bearing a child that would overthrow him, Zeus tricked Metis with lies and swallowed her while she was already pregnant. Through lying and deception, Zeus thus became the sole genitor of Athena, the goddess of wisdom, to whom Metis gave birth inside him.

In the *Iliad* Achilles, the quintessential plain-spoken hero, tells Odysseus, "as I detest the doorways of Death, I detest the man, who hides one thing in the depths of his heart, and speaks forth another." (*Iliad* 9.312–13, translated by R. Lattimore) But Odysseus is the archetypal liar and deceiver. Odysseus, himself both strongly associated with Metis and favoured by Athena, often uses deception to achieve his goals. When he finally arrives home after his long journey, Odysseus deceives his wife, Penelope, and keeps his identity secret from her as he tests her and plots his revenge against her suitors. Homer tells us that, as he speaks to Penelope, Odysseus "knew how to say many false things that were like true sayings." (*Odyssey* 19.203, translated by R. Lattimore) Yet Penelope is as cunning as Odysseus and eventually tricks him into revealing his identity.

Insincere speech encompasses many other forms of discourse than simple forms of lying to deceive others. We have various ways of deceiving each other with language while avoiding outright lying. We are skilful in navigating the landscape between lying and merely misleading. We exploit the difference between outright saying what we do not believe and conveying disbelieved information in other ways. We engage in different kinds of indifferent speech including so-called bullshitting. We feign attitudes and emotions we do not have by using non-declarative language such as questions, imperatives, or exclamations. And we sometimes speak insincerely without aiming to deceive anyone.

For better or worse, insincerity is as central to our lives as sincerity. The spectrum of insincere speech ranges from trifling lies about one's feelings about a friend's new haircut to lies about the most serious matters in private and public life. Even though sincerity is demanded by our mutual dependence on information acquired from others, insincere forms of communication play a fundamental role in our interactions.

It is commonplace to think that lies are often (perhaps even always) harmful at least to some extent. Indeed, sometimes lying has catastrophic consequences. But we should recognize that arguably most lies are told in order to benefit someone. Usually, to be sure, the intended beneficiary is the liar herself, as when someone lies about themselves in order to impress their listeners. But selfish motives are not the only ones we have for insincerity. The stock example of lying to a murderer who comes to one's door and asks for the whereabouts of her intended victim is a clear example of a non-selfish, altruistic lie. Lies can prevent disasters, sometimes of enormous magnitudes.

Forms of insincere speech also serve other valuable purposes. Even the most staunch enemy of lying will sometimes feel compelled to lie to be polite or kind, or to avoid embarrassment. Sometimes things need to be conveyed indirectly for various reasons. Most people will choose to mislead while avoiding lying, in many situations. Misrepresenting the facts can serve valuable purposes. Sometimes we manage to convey things by being insincere that we could not have conveyed in the same situation by speaking truthfully. A lie can implicate something true, which could not have been asserted outright, perhaps because it would be improper to do so, or for other reasons.

This book is about the ways in which we use language to deliberately disrupt the project of inquiry, the communal project of discovering the truth. It is less concerned with examining the many and important reasons we might have for speaking insincerely than it is concerned with an examination of the nature of insincere speech itself. This means that the discussion in this book consciously avoids, among other topics, the long-standing and important philosophical debate concerning the morality of lying and insincerity.[1] The reason for this is simply a consideration concerning the length and focus of the work.

The contents of the book are divided into two parts. Part I (Chapters 1–5) is concerned with the language of insincerity, Part II (Chapters 6–10) with the attitudes involved in insincere speech. Since insincere speech lives at the intersection between language and attitudes, the two parts of the book are interrelated and themes from each interact with those of the other.[2]

0.2. Insincerity and Deception

Lies are typically a means of deception. When a child tells her parents that she has done her homework, even though she knows that she has not, she is relating disbelieved information with the aim of making her parents believe it. Many have concluded that, quite generally, to lie is to say something one believes to be false with the intention of deceiving one's audience. Chapter 1 of this book is concerned with defending the opposing view that, although lying is often aimed at deceiving its victims, lying is not always a means of deception.

The observation that lies are not in general deceptive is not just the trivial one that lies sometimes fail to deceive because they are not believed. So-called bald-faced lies are lies that are told without any intentions of deceiving someone else. This can happen in situations where a lie is told that everyone already knows to be false. An unfaithful spouse might

[1] For a small sample of the literature on this post 1900, see, e.g. Ross (2002 [1930]), Paton (1954), Isenberg (1964), Bok (1978), Kupfer (1982), Korsgaard (1986), MacIntyre (1995), Williams (2002), Mahon (2006), (2009), Faulkner (2007), Wood (2008), Carson (2010), (in press), Saul (2012), Shiffrin (2014), Stokke (2017b). See also Michaelson and Stokke (in press) for a historical overview.
[2] References to, and discussion of, work on the topics mentioned in the Introduction are given in the subsequent chapters of the book.

tell her partner that she is not having an affair, even though she knows that her partner knows that she is. And, as we will see in Part I, there are many situations in which we lie even though we cannot be described as intending to deceive anyone.

One suggestion in defense of the traditional view of lying is that bald-faced lies do involve deception albeit not of the standard kind whereby the liar aims to cause her listener to come to believe something false. However, as I argue in Chapter 1, even though there are many ways of deceiving someone beyond causing them to have false beliefs, one can lie without engaging in any of these forms of deception.

The recognition that lying cannot be understood generally as a species of deception prompts the quest for an alternative way of understanding insincere speech. Indeed, as I argue in Chapter 3, not only lying but other forms of insincere speech are not always aimed at deception. One can say something true and thereby implicate something one believes to be false without aiming to deceive anyone by doing so. Once it is understood that insincere speech is not simply a means of deception, we need to look closer at insincere use of language, first, in terms of the ways of communicating it involves, and second, in terms of the attitudes behind it. These two aspects of insincere speech are reflected in the two parts of this book.

The landscape of insincere speech is wider than the paradigmatic case of lying in which the liar asserts something she believes to be false. On the one hand, we speak insincerely in many ways other than outright assertion. On the other hand, we can be insincere in other ways than by communicating what we believe to be false. Part I explores the breadth of insincerity as a linguistic phenomenon. Part II is devoted to examining the ways in which insincere speech is broader than standard lying in terms of the attitudes of the insincere speaker.

0.3. Assertion and What is Said

Part I offers an account of lying in terms of assertion that does not make intentions to deceive a necessary condition on lying. Instead, on the view I defend, a lie is an insincere assertion. You lie when you assert something you believe to be false. One consequence of this view is that there can be true lies. That is, if one asserts something one believes to be false, one is not exonerated from lying if it turns out that what one asserted was in fact true. A lie need not be false, although it needs to be disbelieved.

The main challenge for a view of lying as insincere assertion is to spell out what it is to assert something in a way that is broad enough to capture the nature of lying and narrow enough so as not to obscure the distinction between lying and other kinds of insincere speech. The bulk of Part I is dedicated to providing such a detailed way of understanding lying in terms of assertion.

I argue that the notion of assertion involved in this characterization of lying should be understood as saying something and thereby proposing that it become part of the background information that is taken for granted for the purpose of the conversation. Conversational background information of the kind at issue here is standardly called "common ground" information. This means that my account of lying, and of insincere speech more generally, turns on two central components. One is the notion of the common ground of a discourse. The other is the notion of saying something, or what is said by an utterance in a given context.

After considering, and rejecting, an alternative understanding of lying in terms of Gricean maxims in Chapter 2, a detailed picture of the notion of common ground information, and of its function in discourse, is presented in Chapter 3. Something is common ground among a group of discourse participants when it is commonly believed to be accepted for the purpose of the conversation. Since something can be common ground even though it is known, or believed, to be false, one can assert something even though everyone knows or believes it to be false, and hence one can lie without intending to deceive. Assertions do not necessarily aim at being believed.

Chapters 4 and 5 are dedicated to providing an account of what is said and assertion. This way of understanding these notions is founded on an understanding of discourse as oriented toward inquiry. The fundamental aim of a discourse is to incrementally accumulate true information with the ultimate goal of reaching a state of information that adequately and fully characterizes what the world is like, or how things are.

Yet our aims in conversation are usually much more modest. We are typically engaged in piecemeal steps toward reaching the truth about a particular topic of conversation. Such a topic of conversation, or subinquiry, can be represented as a so-called question under discussion. We might be interested in questions such as *What is the weather like?*,

Did you like the movie?, *Where were you last night?*, or *Is Smith guilty of embezzling funds from his firm?*

One central aim of Part I is to argue for a notion of what is said that is sensitive to questions under discussion, while being constrained by linguistic meaning in a particular way. Roughly, what is said by a declarative sentence relative to a question is the answer to the question that is either entailed by or entails the linguistic meaning of the sentence. This understanding of what is said has the consequence that one and the same declarative sentence can be used to say and assert different things depending on which question it is addressing. If asked, "What did you do yesterday after you had left your mother's apartment?" responding with "I went to the movies," is a way of asserting that you went to the movies yesterday after you had left your mother's apartment. Yet the same utterance can be used to assert something different when responding to another question, such as *Why didn't you come straight home from work last night?*

Since saying something is required for making an assertion, and making an assertion is required for lying, assertion and lying are likewise sensitive to how the discourse is structured in terms of which question is under discussion. Uttering one and the same declarative sentence might be a lie relative to one question under discussion and not a lie relative to another. Indeed uttering one and the same declarative sentence might be a lie relative to one question under discussion while being merely misleading relative to another.

0.4. Lying and Misleading

A chief reason for characterizing lying in terms of assertion is to set off lying from non-linguistic forms of deception and insincerity. Wearing disguises, faking emotions, pointing in the wrong direction, feigning laughter, shedding crocodile tears—these are all ways of leading others away from the facts. These kinds of behavior are commonplace and yet complex. But such deceptive maneuvers are not lies, although they may be accompanied by lies if they involve putting into words something one believes to be false. If you put on a fake moustache, you may deceive someone into thinking you have a moustache, but you have not lied to them unless you tell them that you have a moustache. For this reason, at least, all reasonable theories of lying agree that you have not lied unless you have made what is variously called a statement, saying something, or an assertion.

There is another, perhaps more significant, reason for emphasizing that lying necessarily involves linguistic communication, and in particular, involves the kind of direct or explicit form of communication associated with assertion. We want to distinguish utterances that are outright lies from utterances that are deceptive or misleading but not lies. The distinction between lying and merely misleading is important to us. It is reflected in our law codes, in much moral thinking, and in many systems of religious beliefs and practices. You can be convicted of perjury if you lie, but you may not be if you say something true that is nevertheless misleading. Vast amounts of effort, time, and resources have been put into deciding whether certain statements by politicians, religious authorities, and courtroom witnesses were *bona fide* lies or merely misleading. Even outside official or formal discourse, most of us prefer misleading someone while avoiding lying outright in many situations.

The classic contrast between lying and merely misleading is the contrast between asserting disbelieved information and conversationally implicating such information by asserting something believed to be true. If you are asked, "Are you going to the party?" you are lying if you answer, "No," while you are planning to go. Yet if you answer, "I have to work," you are not lying if you do have to work, even if you are still planning to go to the party. Yet, in the latter case, you are clearly being misleading.

Since assertion and lying are relativized to questions under discussion, on my account, so too is the distinction between lying and merely misleading. This sensitivity to discourse structure, or the topic of conversation, opens up a vast space for misleading beyond the classic contrast between assertion and conversational implicature. We will see that there are multiple ways of misleading relative to questions under discussion by exploiting different kinds of linguistic phenomena including context-sensitivity, incompleteness, presuppositions, and prosodic focus.

Defining a formal notion of contextual question-entailment allows us to be precise about when it is possible to mislead with respect to a question under discussion while avoiding outright lying. In a context where a complete answer to one question implies a partial answer to another question, one may contribute an answer to one question that one believes to be true and thereby imply an answer that one believes to be false to another question.

0.5. Indifferent Speech

In Part II of the book I turn to considering the attitudes that may lie behind insincere speech. Insincerity can take the form of many other attitudes in and toward speech than the communication of disbelieved information. One of these ways involves indifference toward what one says. When lying, people say things they believe to be false. But people also sometimes say things without really caring about them. Chapter 6 opens Part II by discussing the ways in which we sometimes speak while being indifferent toward what we say.

A well-known form of careless speech is the kind exhibited by speakers who say things without caring whether what they say is true or false. This kind of speech has been called "bullshitting." Chapter 6 argues that indifference toward truth in speech is a more differentiated phenomenon than this kind of indifference toward the truth-value of what one says. Sometimes people say things they care very much about, but they nevertheless speak with indifference in another sense.

Indifference toward one's speech sometimes take the form of indifference not toward the particular things one says but indifference toward the project of inquiry, as manifested in specific subinquiries, or questions under discussion. In some situations, people are required to say things they believe to be true, but they may do so not with the aim of contributing to the resolution of a question under discussion. In other situations people evade one question under discussion by addressing, or introducing, another one. In doing so they may be disregarding the truth about the first question while being concerned with being truthful about the second question.

Since one can make statements that one believes to be false while at the same time not caring about making contributions to questions under discussion, one can speak with indifference while lying. Bullshitting and lying are compatible categories. Yet we will see that most lying is distinct from bullshitting. Most liars are not indifferent toward what they say. Chapter 7 distinguishes different kinds of lying and shows that liars usually care about contributing to questions under discussion.

0.6. Opacity and Shallowness

A further complexity of insincere speech stems from the commonly accepted idea that our own attitudes are not always transparent to ourselves. One may be in a particular state of mind and not be aware of it, and one can be mistaken about which state of mind one is in. The self is opaque. Since insincere use of language involves an interaction between mind and speech, the phenomenon is complicated by the recognition of the opacity of the self.

Chapters 8 and 9 are concerned with this dimension of insincere speech. Broadly two approaches to insincere speech can be taken in light of the recognition that our attitudes are not always transparent to ourselves. On a deep conception of insincerity, whether one speaks insincerely or not may depend on attitudes that one is unaware of or mistaken about. On a shallow conception, by contrast, insincerity in speech depends on the speaker's conscious attitudes.

This book defends a shallow conception of insincerity in this sense. Someone who asserts something they consciously believe to be false is insincere, on this view, even if they harbor an unconscious belief, hope, or desire that their assertion is true. For example, if someone is self-deceived, they may have false beliefs about what they believe. You might believe that you believe that women are just as good candidates for a job, while you do not in fact believe that they are. On a shallow view of insincerity, whether or not you speak insincerely depends on your conscious state of mind. Hence, you would not be insincere, on this view, if you were to assert that women are just as good candidates as men. You may be lacking in other qualities, and you might be blameworthy for various reasons, but your utterance is not insincere if it corresponds to what you consciously take yourself to believe. Similarly, someone may consciously intend to deceive another by lying, even if her underlying, unconscious motivations are praiseworthy and truthful. On a shallow conception, such an utterance is insincere in virtue of the speaker's conscious intention to lie and deceive.

Yet even people's beliefs about what they believe may not be what makes their speech insincere or not. Instead, on the view I defend in Part II, what is relevant for insincerity in speech is what a speaker mentally assents to. Mental assent is a conscious attitude of affirming a proposition that has been taken under consideration. This attitude of mental assent is distinct from what one believes about one's beliefs. One might mentally assent to a proposition even if one believes one does not believe it, or if one does not believe one believes it. If one believes the diagnosis of an incompetent therapist that one does not believe that one has had a good childhood, one might nevertheless be inclined to mentally assent to having had a good childhood, since that is what one finds oneself judging about the matter when consciously considering the question. Asserting that one has a good childhood, in such a state, is not insincere even though what one says conflicts with what one takes oneself to believe.

At the same time people do not always actively go through a process of assenting to what they intend to say before they say it. We sometimes think while we speak. Such spontaneous ways of speaking need not be insincere. We often speak simultaneously with assenting to what we say. Conversely, our spontaneity sometimes leads us to speak against our own intentions. I might resolve to tell the truth about a particular matter and yet find myself embellishing on my story, even lying, when confronted with my audience.

The broadest characterization of insincere speech is a negative one. To speak insincerely, in the most general terms, is to lack certain conscious attitudes toward what one is communicating. In particular, one general trait of different kinds of insincere speech is the absence of conscious intentions to contribute an answer to a question under discussion that one assents to while at the same time avoiding contributing information one does not assent to. This general characterization, offered in Chapter 9, is broad enough to capture various ways of lying, misleading while avoiding lying, bullshitting, as well as insincere exploitation of presuppositions and other linguistic phenomena. We should not be surprised by the generality resulting from such a bird's-eye view of the expansive landscape of insincere speech. As we will see throughout both Parts I and II, more particular phenomena lend themselves to more narrow characterizations.

0.7. Communicating Attitudes

The final chapter of the book explores the way in which we use various linguistic forms other than simple utterances of declarative sentences to communicate our attitudes in language. Beyond the declarative sentence form, natural languages incorporate exclamative ("How nice he is!"), imperative ("Be nice!"), and interrogative ("Is he nice?") sentence forms, as well as non-sentential exclamations like "Thanks!" or "Sh!" All these forms are used, among many other things, to communicate attitudes. In normal circumstances utterances of such non-declarative forms result in it becoming common ground that the speaker has a certain attitude. For example, uttering "Is Joe nice?" usually results in it becoming common ground that the speaker wants to know whether Joe is nice. Similarly, an utterance of "Thanks for doing the dishes!" usually results in it becoming common ground, roughly, that the speaker is grateful to the addressee for doing the dishes.

As in the declarative realm, insincerity in the non-declarative realm is seen to depend on the speaker's conscious attitudes. A simple view is that a non-declarative utterance is insincere when the speaker lacks the attitude it communicates. Analogously to the complications arising for declarative utterances, recognition of the opacity of our attitudes likewise renders this simple view of non-declarative utterances inadequate. Someone who asks a question thereby communicates that she wants to know the answer. She might at the same time consciously think she does not care about the answer, while unconsciously she really wants to know the answer. In this situation deep views of insincerity will tend to deem the utterance as not insincere. By contrast, on the shallow conception of insincerity I favor, such an utterance is insincere because of its conflict with the speaker's conscious state of mind. Correspondingly, if someone uses an imperative utterance to order someone to do something they consciously want them to do while unconsciously not wanting them to do it, the utterance will not be seen as insincere on a shallow view of the kind I defend.

The same dialectics applies to non-sentential utterances of exclamations. An utterance of "Thanks!" is insincere when the speaker lacks a conscious attitude of gratitude, even if she harbors unconscious feelings of gratitude toward the same thing. An utterance of "Sh!" is insincere if the speaker does not consciously want the addressee to be quiet, even if she unconsciously does not want the addressee to be quiet.

Accounting for non-sentential exclamations provides a useful way of approaching the issue of when an act is a communicative act. In particular, the mere production of an otherwise meaningless sound, as when screaming upon being hurt, may be a communicative act, as when one deliberately cries out to attract help. One may also utter a sound that one knows to be meaningful even though one does not know which meaning it has but still thereby perform a communicative act.

For example, someone using a phrase in a foreign language without knowing its meaning might thereby try to communicate to someone that they speak that language. And one can produce sounds of which one knows the meaning but without communicating anything, as when uttering a sentence to test a microphone.

By paying attention to these differences it can be seen that only communicative acts can be evaluated as insincere or not. If one utters a sentence in one's sleep, even in a language that one fully understands, one is not insincere if what it would otherwise communicate does not correspond to one's waking attitudes.

Even though non-declarative utterances can be insincere, they cannot be used to tell lies. Non-declarative forms cannot be used to make assertions, although they may be used to implicate or communicate things in other ways. Chapter 10 sketches a view of non-declarative linguistic forms according to which their compositional meanings are not of the kind that can be used to say things in the strict sense of Part I by which what is said by an utterance is the answer to a relevant question under discussion that stands in an entailment relation to its compositional content.

PART I

Language

1

Lying, Deception, and Deceit

You invite me to dinner at your house. I have nothing planned for the evening. But since I would rather stay at home and watch TV, I make up the story that I am having dinner with my mother that night, and I tell you that in order to make you think that I am unable to accept your invitation. This kind of lying is familiar and is arguably the most common kind. Perhaps for this reason, a long tradition in philosophy, going back at least as far as Augustine's two treatises, *Lying* (*De mendacio*) (1952 [395]b) and *Against Lying* (*Contra mendacium*) (1952 [395]a), has understood lying as a species of deception. But, as we will see in this chapter, many lies are in fact told without intentions to deceive. This means that the view of lying as a species of deception must be abandoned.

1.1. The Augustinian Definition of Lying

According to the traditional view, to lie is to say something one believes to be false with the intent to deceive one's listener.[1] This view deserves to be called the *Augustinian Definition of Lying*, which we may spell out as follows:[2]

---

[1] For modern endorsements, see, e.g. Isenberg (1964), Chisholm and Feehan (1977), Bok (1978), Kupfer (1982), Davidson (1985), Simpson (1992), Adler (1997), Williams (2002), Frankfurt (2005 [1986]), Faulkner (2007), (2013), Dynel (2011). An interesting historical exception is Aquinas (1922 [1265–74]); on this, see Williams (2002, 292, n. 26). It should be noted that not all these authors would endorse the Augustinian Definition of Lying, as stated here, even if they all hold views on which lying necessarily involves deceptive intentions. Simpson (1992) and Faulkner (2007), for example, take lying to necessarily involve a breach of trust, and it can be questioned whether (LD3) captures this view sufficiently.

[2] There is some controversy about to what extent, and precisely in what form, Augustine espoused an account of lying in terms of deception. For discussion, see e.g. Griffiths (2001). In this book I use this label for two main reasons. First, it is undeniable that the traditional conception of lying in philosophy is one according to which lying is a species of deception.

The Augustinian Definition of Lying

A lies to *B* if and only if there is a proposition *p* such that:

(LD1)   *A* says that *p* to *B*, and

(LD2)   *A* believes that *p* is false, and

(LD3)   By saying that *p* to *B*, *A* intends to deceive *B* into believing that *p*.

The Augustinian Definition of Lying correctly classifies my story about my dinner plans as a lie. I say that I am having dinner with my mother (LD1), but I believe that I am not (LD2), and I say what I do in order to deceive you into believing that I am having dinner with my mother (LD3).[3]

Even though this conception of lying captures the most common kind of lying, a number of philosophers have argued that lying does not necessarily involve intentions to deceive.[4] That is, even if you do not aim at deceiving your listener, you might still be lying. One central type of counterexample to the traditional view involves what Roy Sorensen (2007) has called *bald-faced lies*. To a first approximation, a bald-faced lie is a consciously undisguised lie, i.e. a lie that is told despite the recognition that the relevant participants realize that it is a lie.

Here is an example that Thomas Carson (2006, 290), (2010, 21) gives:[5]

The Cheating Student

A student accused of cheating on an exam is called to the Dean's office. The student knows that the Dean knows that she did in fact cheat. But as it is also well known that the Dean will not punish someone unless they explicitly admit their guilt, the student says,

(1)   I didn't cheat.

Second, it is fair to say that most philosophers think that Augustine's treatises provide the *locus classicus* for this view.

[3] The definition is arguably too narrow in that lying is compatible with merely intending to deceive about one's own beliefs, rather than intending to deceive about what one says. See Chisholm and Feehan (1977, 151–152), Fallis (2010, 8–9). See Fallis (2010) for discussion of a number of alternative candidate definitions of deceptive lying. Since I endorse the view that lying does not necessarily involve intentions to deceive, I will not engage in the project of finding a suitable definition of deceptive lying. The difficulties with this project are just more arguments in favor of the alternative view.

[4] E.g. Carson (2006), Sorensen (2007), Fallis (2009), Stokke (2013).

[5] This description of the case differs in some respects from Carson's. See below for discussion.

Although the student says something she believes to be false, she does not intend to deceive the Dean. Even so, the student is lying. Hence this is a bald-faced lie.

The suggestion that, as opposed to the Augustinian view, lying does not necessarily involve intentions to deceive has met with criticism.[6] In particular, there are broadly two ways one can try to uphold the Augustinian Definition of Lying, or something like it, in the face of examples like that of the cheating student. First, one can deny that bald-faced lies are lies.[7] Second, one can accept that bald-faced lies are lies, but insist that they do involve deception, even though not of the kind captured by (LD3). We will discuss each in turn. I will argue that none of them is successful, and hence that the Augustinian Definition of Lying is in need of revision.[8]

1.2. Are Bald-Faced Lies Lies?

The first of the strategies for upholding the traditional view mentioned above should strike us as unpromising. It is highly counterintuitive to insist that the student in Carson's example did not lie to the Dean. Suppose, for example, that subsequent to the interview, the student's parents hear about what happened. Imagine that they confront the student with, "What were you thinking? You lied to the Dean!" If the defenders of the traditional view of this first stripe are right, it should be perfectly fine for the student to respond with something like, "No, I didn't lie to the Dean. She knew I wasn't telling the truth." Yet, this reply is clearly infelicitous— we might even think it is barely intelligible. Indeed, so is a reply along the lines of, "OK, I admit what I did was wrong. But I didn't lie. She knew I wasn't telling the truth."

By contrast, Jörg Meibauer (2014) argues that bald-faced lies are not lies because they are not *assertions*. (A similar argument is made by Keiser, 2015. See Chapter 3.) As we will see in the next chapter, I agree—along with many others—that you lie only if you make an assertion. But I do not think that there are convincing reasons to think

---

[6] One worry is that the claim that lying is not a species of deception makes it hard to explain what is morally wrong with lying. See, e.g. Mahon (2011), Lackey (2013).

[7] See e.g. Mahon (2011), Meibauer (2011), (2014), Faulkner (2013).

[8] See also Rutschmann and Wiegmann (2017) for experimental support for the claim that an intention to deceive is not a necessary condition on lying.

that utterances such as the student's statement to the Dean are not assertions.

Meibauer defines assertion so that intending to make the listener believe what you say is a necessary condition on assertion. More particularly, Meibauer's motivation for denying that bald-faced lies are lies is that the bald-faced liar:

> does not really present p as true in the context since he *lets shine through* that p is false. He would not feel committed to the truth of p, and he would not be ready to provide further evidence. (Meibauer, 2014, 140)

However, this arguably runs contrary to the way most theorists and non-theorists will be inclined to think of the case of the cheating student.[9]

First, there is no reason to think that the student "lets shine through" that her statement is false. Of course, the student knows that the Dean knows that what she is saying is false. But she is not indicating this in any way. For example, if one says something one believes to be false while winking at the speaker, this is naturally understood to be a way of "letting it shine through" that what one says is false, and many would take this kind of case as one in which no assertion has been made. But nothing of the sort is going on in Carson's example. Undoubtedly there are also more subtle ways of "letting it shine through" that what one says is false. Yet there is no reason to think that something like this characterizes bald-faced lying in general.

Second, the student is clearly committed to her statement. There is no way for the student to defend herself later by claiming that she was not in earnest, or the like, as you can do if you were winking or made a joke. (I return to these kinds of non-committing ways of speaking in Chapter 3.)

Third, the student might not be ready to provide further evidence, simply because there is no further evidence, but that does not show that she is not committed to the statement. Indeed, if the student *could* produce evidence that would make it doubtful that she cheated, she would.

---

[9] Meibauer (2014) discusses a different example concerning a husband who denies being unfaithful even though both he and his wife know that he is being unfaithful, and both know that they know this. There may be cases in which the notion of letting one's untruthfulness "shine through" is applicable, and this may be one of them. (Indeed, it seems undeniable that something like this sometimes happens, whether in cases of bald-faced lying or not.) However, insofar as the suggestion is supposed to be illuminating of bald-faced lying in general, it should equally apply to the case of the cheating student.

We should conclude that one cannot argue that the student's utterance is not a lie by arguing that it does not have the common characteristics of an assertion.

Another way of denying that bald-faced lies are lies is to simply restrict the notion of lying. Marta Dynel (2011) suggests:

> The folk term "bald-faced lie" should not be mistakenly equated with the concept of a lie approached theoretically.   (Dynel, 2011, 151)

However, no sensible theories of lying propose to *equate* the terms "bald-faced lie" and "lie." Any sensible theory must acknowledge the datum that many lies are deceptive lies. Furthermore, it is implausible to claim that the student merely lied in some loose sense of *to lie*. Rather, it is the insistence that the student did not lie that relies on a non-standard sense of the word. If one wants to deny that bald-faced lies are lies, one will be forced to admit that one is confining one's notion of lying to a subclass of what we ordinarily take to be lies.

So it seems implausible that the traditional view according to which lying necessarily involves deception can be upheld by denying that bald-faced lies are lies. We now turn to the other way of defending the traditional view, that is, the idea that bald-faced lies, despite first appearances, do involve deception of some kind.

1.3. Eight Ways of Deceiving Someone Else

The second strategy for defending the traditional conception of lying as a species of deception is, at least at first sight, more promising. It is undeniable that there are other ways of deceiving people than the one encapsulated by (LD3), that is, getting them to believe something false. Perhaps we should think that the cheating student intends to deceive the Dean in some other way.

What are the ways in which someone can deceive someone else? In their authoritative study of lying and deceptive intentions, Roderick Chisholm and Thomas Feehan (1977) provided an eightfold taxonomy of ways in which a person L can deceive another person D with respect to a proposition p. These are summarized below:

1. Commissive
   a. Positive
      i. *Simpliciter*: L contributes causally toward D's acquiring the belief in p.

     ii. *Secundum quid*: L contributes causally toward D's continuing in the belief in p.

  b. Negative

     i. *Simpliciter*: L contributes causally toward D's ceasing to believe in not-p.

     ii. *Secundum quid*: L contributes causally toward preventing D from acquiring the belief in not-p.

2. Omissive

  a. Positive

     i. *Simpliciter*: L allows D to acquire the belief in p.

     ii. *Secundum quid*: L allows D to continue in the belief in p.

  b. Negative

     i. *Simpliciter*: L allows D to cease to have the belief in not-p.

     ii. *Secundum quid*: L allows D to continue without the belief in not-p.

Applied to the example of the cheating student, L represents the student, D the Dean, and p the proposition that the student did not cheat.

We can now ask whether the student's lie falls under any of these categories. There are two important features of the case that bear on this question:

D1   The Dean does not believe p (= that the student did not cheat.)

D2   The Dean knows, and hence believes, not-p (= that the student cheated.)

In the description of the case I gave above, it was made explicit that the student knows that the Dean knows she did cheat. This entails D2 (given that knowledge entails belief.) Further, supposing that the Dean does not hold contradictory beliefs, D1 is a safe assumption about the case.

It is immediately clear that D1 and D2 together imply that all of Chisholm and Feehan's cases of deception *secundum quid* are ruled out. Given D1, it is ruled out that the student's lie contributes causally to the Dean's continuing to believe p (1aii), and given D2, it is ruled out that the lie contributes causally to preventing the Dean from acquiring the belief that not-p (1bii). Likewise, D1 rules out that the lie allows the Dean to continue in the belief that p (2aii), and D2 that it allows the Dean to continue without the belief that not-p (2bii).

Deception *secundum quid*, in Chisholm and Feehan's sense, is closely related to what is often called *keeping someone in the dark*. Here is how Carson (2010) characterizes the latter notion:

A person S keeps another person S1 in the dark about X (where X is something that S knows and S1 doesn't know) if, and only if, either: 1. S actively and intentionally prevents S1 from learning about X, or 2. S fails to inform S1 about X when either: (i) S knows that S1 wants the information in question and S can easily give it to S1, or (ii) S occupies a role or position in which he is expected to provide S1 with the sort of information in question. (Carson, 2010, 54)

On this definition, the requirement that X be something S knows and S1 does not know already implies that the student's lie does not keep the Dean in the dark. Bluntly, the lie does not *keep* the Dean in the dark because the Dean is not in the dark to begin with. This is what D1 and D2 reflect. Deception *secundum quid* is ruled out because the student's lie does not prevent the Dean from learning the truth or from ceasing to believe a falsehood.

If the student's lie is not deceptive *secundum quid*, can it be said to be deceptive *simpliciter* instead? One way in which the lie would be a case of commissive, positive deception *simpliciter* (1ai) is if the lie succeeded in changing the Dean's mind concerning the student's innocence. Clearly, there might be some situations in which that happens—perhaps the evidence for cheating is not too strong to begin with, or perhaps the Dean wants to be persuaded, etc. But what matters is that we can easily imagine versions of the case where it does not, i.e. where the student's statement does not affect the Dean's beliefs. And furthermore, in such situations, the student's statement is intuitively a lie. The same holds for the suggestion that the lie causes the Dean to lose the belief that the student did cheat, and hence commissive, negative deception *simpliciter* (1bi) is likewise ruled out. Moreover, these observations apply, *mutatis mutandis*, to the omissive versions of deception *simpliciter*.

Yet, it might be said that, even if the lie does not succeed in *completely* changing the Dean's mind or in making her *completely* cease to believe the truth, the lie may very well decrease the Dean's confidence in the truth or make her less certain. That is, the lie might affect the Dean's credences with respect to the student's innocence. Indeed, Chisholm and Feehan are explicit that their taxonomy does not take into account degrees of belief, although arguably a lot of deception is aimed at lowering credences in the truth or increasing credences in falsehoods, or have other related goals.

However, the considerations above concerning non-graded belief apply here as well. Undeniably, there are plausible versions of the case in which the student's statement does make the Dean less certain about her guilt, or makes the Dean more certain about her innocence, or something similar. But it is equally clear that there are versions of the case where it does not, and in which the student's statement is a lie.

1.4. Intending to Deceive

There are instances of the example, then, where the student's lie is not deceptive in any of Chisholm and Feehan's eight senses, nor in terms of affecting the Dean's credences. However, at this point defenders of deceptive accounts of lying should object that what needs to be shown is not that the student's lie does not *succeed* in being deceptive in any of these ways, but rather that the student's lie is not *intended* to be deceptive in some plausible way.

There are clearly versions of the example that can be put forward in which the student does intend to deceive the Dean, even if the lie does not succeed in doing so. Most obviously, if the student were unaware that the Dean knows that she cheated, her lie might very well be intended to be deceptive in the most straightforward sense—that is, as in (1ai), it might be aimed at making the Dean believe what it falsely asserts. Situations in which a liar tries to deceive someone else into believing something false, but fails because the other party already knows the truth of the matter, are familiar.

However, the issue is whether there are versions of the example where the student cannot plausibly be described as intending to deceive in any of these ways. How can it be argued there are situations of this kind?

One route is to appeal to a general constraint on intention formation. In particular, it is common to think that intentions are constrained by what one believes one can or will do.[10] I cannot intend to fly by flapping my arms, to set fire to my desk by looking at it, or to count all the electrons

---

[10] See e.g. Audi (1973), Grice (1973), (1989, 98), Davidson (1989 [1978]), Velleman (1989), Neale (2005), Mele (2010), Stokke (2010), Kissine (2013, ch. 2), Fallis (2014a). See also Velleman (1989, 113–115) for discussion and more references.

in the universe, since I do not believe I can do any of these things. It is hard to specify a precise principle that captures this idea, but we can try working with the following relatively weak formulation:

Belief-Intention Constraint

A intends to ϕ only if A believes that she can ϕ.

According to the Belief-Intention Constraint, even if one can intend to ϕ when one believes it is *unlikely* that one will succeed in ϕ'ing, one cannot reasonably be described as intending to ϕ if one believes that one is sure to fail in ϕ'ing. So, given this principle, if there are versions of the example in which the student believes that she cannot change the Dean's mind or cannot succeed in deceiving the Dean in any sense, these will be cases in which the student cannot plausibly be described as intending to deceive the Dean.

It seems clear that there are cases of this kind. Indeed, it is easy to imagine such situations. The version of the example described earlier, in which the student knows that the Dean knows that she cheated is naturally interpreted as a situation in which the student does not believe that she can deceive the Dean, in any of the ways we considered above. That is, the student does not believe that she can change the Dean's mind, or that she can alter the Dean's credences, or the like. Yet, intuitively, the student is lying on such occasions.

To be sure, there may be versions of the case in which the student has convinced herself that if she but tells the Dean that she is innocent, the Dean will believe her, despite the overwhelming evidence against her. Or, perhaps more plausibly, there might be situations in which the student believes that she can make the Dean less certain just by proclaiming her innocence. But why should we suppose that there are no versions of the case in which the student does not have such beliefs? As noted above, the most reasonable interpretation of the student is one that sees her as not believing that she can alter the Dean's beliefs or credences just by making her statement.

But moreover, cases in which the student is not correctly described as intending to deceive the Dean can also arise even if the student *does* believe that she *could* change the Dean's mind. As Carson says, "The student may not care whether or not others know that he cheated, but simply want to have his grade changed." (Carson, 2010, 21) In such a case, a goal of deceiving the Dean might simply not be part of the student's intentions in making his statement.

The conclusion to take from this is that there are lies that are not intended to, and do not succeed in, deceiving the listener in any of the senses we have considered so far. But perhaps there are ways that lies can be deceptive that we have overlooked. Next, I turn to considering an alternative construal of deception.

1.5. Deception and Concealment

Jennifer Lackey (2013) has argued that we should distinguish between *deceit* and *deception*. She describes this distinction as follows:

Deceit: A deceives B with respect to whether *p* if and only if A aims to bring about a false belief in B regarding whether *p*.

Deception: A is deceptive to B with respect to whether *p* if A aims to conceal information from B regarding whether *p*. (Lackey, 2013, 241)

Since it is reasonable to interpret "bring about" along the lines of "contribute causally to," Lackey's notion of deceit is just Chisholm's and Feehan's notion of commissive, positive deception *simpliciter* (1ai), i.e. the notion of deception involved in the Augustinian Definition of Lying. Yet, Lackey agrees that bald-faced lies are lies, and she therefore rejects (LD3). Instead, she proposes that lying should be characterized in terms of her alternative notion of deception.

Here is Lackey's (2013, 237) definition of lying:

Lackey's Definition of Lying
A lies to *B* if and only if

(LL1)   *A* states that *p* to *B*, and
(LL2)   *A* believes that *p* is false, and
(LL3)   *A* intends to be deceptive to *B* in stating that *p*.

Lackey's condition (LL3) contrasts with the traditional condition on lying (LD3), on which lying necessarily involves the intention to induce false beliefs in the audience. Yet, Lackey explicitly holds that (LL3) is implied by (LD3):

concealing information is sufficient, though not necessary, for being deceptive; thus, it is merely one instance of a more general phenomenon. Obviously, another way of being deceptive is to be deceitful, where one's aim is to bring about a false belief in one's hearer. (Lackey, 2013, 237)

Further, since Lackey agrees that the bald-faced liar is lying, she must construe (LL3) in a way that does not rule out cases such as the student's lie to the Dean. She specifies that:

Concealing information regarding whether p can be understood broadly here, so that it subsumes, among other phenomena, concealing *evidence* regarding whether p.   (Lackey, 2013, 241)

Accordingly, Lackey claims that the cheating student is being deceptive to the Dean, in this sense:

In the case of the student's bald-faced lie to the Dean, while he does not intend to deceive the Dean into falsely believing that he did not cheat, he does intend to conceal crucial evidence from the Dean that is needed for punishment from the university—namely, an admission of wrongdoing.   (Lackey, 2013, 241–2)

Against this, Don Fallis (2014a) has objected that:

the student does not aim to *conceal* his confession. There is no confession to be concealed since he has not confessed. It is not like when a criminal conceals or destroys existing evidence of his crime.   (Fallis, 2014, 10)

I take this to accord with the way we think of concealment more generally. If I do not have a recipe for bouillabaisse, I cannot conceal my recipe for bouillabaisse from anyone, nor can I intend to do so. No one can conceal, or intend to conceal, the king of France, and so on.[11]

However, perhaps the student can instead be said to intend to conceal *information* from the Dean. What information? There are two salient candidates, p_1 and p_2.

p_1 That the student cheated.

p_2 That the student believes she cheated.

If it can be argued that the student is correctly described as intending to conceal either p_1 or p_2, the student counts as lying on Lackey's definition, and we would have a case for taking the student's lie to be deceptive after all.

---

[11] As these examples suggest, it is plausible to think that "The student is concealing her confession" suffers from presupposition failure, and as such, on some views, the claim is not false, but undefined, or neither true nor false. But even if it is neither true nor false that the student is concealing her confession, this is enough to contradict Lackey's claim that the student is concealing her confession.

In considering the suggestion that the student intends to conceal p_1, Fallis writes:

> You can certainly aim to conceal information from someone if you do not know that she already knows it. But since the student knows that the Dean already knows that he is guilty, aiming to conceal this information would seem to require his aiming to change the past. And it is not at all clear that you can aim or intend to do things that you take to be impossible [...]. (Fallis, 2014a, 8)

In other words, in line with what we have been assuming above, Fallis takes it that the student knows that the Dean knows she cheated. Given this, Fallis appeals to (a version of) the Belief-Intention Constraint in order to conclude that the student does not intend to (or "aim to") conceal from the Dean that she cheated.

More generally, it is hard to deny that there are many plausible versions of the example in which the student knows that the Dean knows both p_1 and p_2. In many of these cases, it is reasonable to think that the student does not believe that she can succeed in concealing either p_1 or p_2 from the Dean simply by making her statement of innocence. Yet, in such cases, this statement is still intuitively a lie. But, given the Belief-Intention Constraint, the student does not intend to conceal either p_1 or p_2 from the Dean, in such cases.

Lackey explicitly rejects this line of reasoning:

> one can be deceptive in the relevant sense, even if the information that one is aiming to conceal is common knowledge. In other words, ignorance of that which is being concealed is not necessary to be the victim of deception. To see this, notice that deception requires that A aims to conceal information from B, and A can certainly aim to do this even if A is ultimately, perhaps even inevitably, unsuccessful in achieving this. I can aim to win a marathon even if I know that I will ultimately fail to achieve this goal. (Lackey, 2013, 242)

There is a shift in this passage from the claim that someone can aim to conceal information even if they are ultimately, or inevitably, unsuccessful to the claim that someone can aim to do something even if they know that they will ultimately fail. The latter claim is what is needed, and amounts to a rejection of the Belief-Intention Constraint. Many will find this an implausible move. It has the consequence that I can intend to fly by flapping my arms, I can intend to swim from Stockholm to London, I can intend to survive without food or drink for a year, I can intend to stop the Earth from moving by scratching my head, and so on. To me, these are all implausible ideas. Similarly, Alfred Mele writes:

Few philosophers of action would maintain that people who believe their chances of winning today's lottery is about one in a million intend to win the lottery, no matter how strongly they desire to win. (Mele, 2010, 108)

Accordingly, Mele describes the standard view as follows:

A relatively popular claim is that having an intention to A requires believing that one (probably) will A. (Mele, 2010, 108)

The Belief-Intention Constraint we formulated above is weaker than this principle in that one might believe that one can do something even if one does not believe that one (probably) will do it. But since we can imagine versions of the Cheating Student example in which the student has neither of these beliefs, on either principle, these will be cases in which the student does not intend to deceive the Dean.

Does this mean that the question of whether lying necessarily involves deceptive intentions (in Lackey's sense) stands and falls with the Belief-Intention Constraint? It does not. Rather, the question depends on whether there are cases in which someone lies while not having deceptive intentions of any kind. There is no reason to think there are no such cases.

We do not have to imagine that the student is making a desperate bid to hide her guilt, or that she has the implausible idea that she can do so just by proclaiming her innocence. Avoiding such assumptions about the student is more charitable, and arguably squares better with our intuitive sense of the case. Supposing that the student does not intend to conceal either her guilt or her awareness of it from the Dean is a natural way of understanding the example, especially given the assumption that the student knows that the Dean knows she knows she cheated. Even so, the student's utterance is still clearly a lie.

1.6. Withholding Information

Lackey explicitly takes concealing information to be distinct from *withholding* information:

concealing information is importantly different from *withholding* information. To withhold information is to fail to provide it, rather than to hide or keep it secret.
(Lackey, 2013, 241)

Yet, arguably, the student can be seen as withholding information from the Dean.

Fallis observes:

> While the student is not aiming to conceal his confession, it does make sense to say that he is aiming to *withhold* his confession. (Fallis, 2014a, 10)

But Fallis further argues that, even so, the student cannot be said to withhold *information* from the Dean:

> But the student does not aim to conceal, or withhold, any information that is relevant to his guilt. If an object (or an event) might convey some information about some topic, but you already have that information, I cannot withhold the information from you by withholding the object (or the event).
>
> (Fallis, 2014a, 10)

However, this is right only to the extent that we are considering withholding information to necessarily involve preventing someone from obtaining it. Yet, as we have seen, as Lackey construes this notion, to withhold information is "to fail to provide it" (Lackey, 2013, 214). Clearly, in this sense, I can withhold both evidence and information. Suppose, for example, that I have the dagger that I know is the murder weapon in my house. Furthermore, I know that you know that I know that you know (and so on.) Yet, I refuse to give up the dagger, or I simply refuse to even answer any questions about it. Thereby I am undeniably withholding evidence.

Am I also withholding information? I think I am. Of course, I am not preventing you from *acquiring* information, such as the information that the dagger is the murder weapon, or the like. But I am blocking your access to make use of that information for various purposes. In the same sense, the student is clearly blocking the Dean's access to make use of the information that they both have, i.e. that the student cheated. It is not unreasonable to describe such acts as acts of withholding information.

Nevertheless, we should not conclude that doing so is a way of being deceptive. There is no attempt to deceive in such cases, even though there is a clear attempt to obstruct the goals of another or of blocking their plans.

1.7. My Definition of Lying

There are lies that are not intended to deceive. This means that the Augustinian Definition of Lying must be replaced. Arguing for such a replacement is one of the main tasks of Part I of this book.

My account of lying is an instance of the following general view that to lie is to *assert* disbelieved information:[12]

The Assertion-Based Definition of Lying
A lies to *B* if and only if there is a proposition *p* such that

(LA1)   *A* asserts that *p* to *B*, and

(LA2)   *A* believes that *p* is false.

This general conception of what it is to lie has been endorsed by many writers on lying.[13] Yet these proposals differ from each other in relying on different accounts of assertion.

I will argue that the account of assertion needed to define lying is (a version of) the one contained in the influential theory of communication developed in the work of Robert Stalnaker (1999 [1970]), (1999 [1974]), (1984), (1999 [1978]), (1999 [1998]), (2002), (2014). According to this view, to assert that *p* is to make a bid for *p* to become *common ground*. Furthermore, I will argue that assertion requires *saying* something, as opposed to, for example, merely implicating it. Hence, I will endorse the following necessary conditions on assertion:

In uttering a sentence *S*, *A* asserts that *p* only if

(A1)   *S* says that *p*, and

(A2)   by uttering *S*, *A* proposes to make it common ground that *p*.

So, in asserting that *p*, a speaker makes an utterance that says that *p* and thereby proposes to make it common ground that *p*.

Consequently, my definition of lying is that you lie when you say something you believe to be false and thereby propose that it become common ground:

The Common Ground Definition of Lying
A lies to *B* if and only if there is a proposition *p* such that

(L1)   *A* says that *p* to *B*, and

(L2)   *A* proposes to make it common ground that *p*, and

(L3)   *A* believes that *p* is false.

---

[12] Throughout this book, I use *disbelieve*, and cognates, such that "*A* disbelieves that *p*" means that *A* believes that not-*p*.

[13] E.g. Chisholm and Feehan (1977), Adler (1997), Carson (2006), (2010), Sorensen (2007), Fallis (2009), Stokke (2013), Saul (2012).

This is the account of lying I will defend in the rest of Part I. My main focus will be on (L1) and (L2), that is, on providing a satisfactory theory of what is said, and hence of the lying–misleading distinction. Before turning to this, I want to end this chapter by saying a few words about (L3).

1.8. True Lies and Disbelief

The first thing to note about (L3) is that it identifies a propositional attitude, belief, and then imposes the constraint that you lie only if you have that attitude toward the negation of what you say. The idea that belief, as opposed to some other attitude, is the right attitude to fix on here is not an obvious one. Chapters 8 and 9 of this book are devoted to this particular question, that is, the question of which mental attitudes are involved in lying, and in insincerity more generally. However, until then, I will simply assume that belief is the attitude we should be focused on when trying to characterize lying and other forms of insincere speech. Indeed, the assumption is arguably right for a very large range of cases.

Having set aside this issue of belief vs. other attitudes, there are two important implications of (L3) I want to focus on here. First, according to this view, lying does not require saying something that is in fact false, but merely requires saying something one believes to be false. Second, it is not enough for lying that one says something one fails to believe. Rather, in order to lie, one must say something that one disbelieves, that is, that one believes to be false. I will comment on each in turn.

The first point means that one can lie even if what one says turns out to be true. There are true lies. This claim has been the orthodox view. For example, Augustine wrote:

it happens that a person who is actually lying may say what is true, if he believes that what he says is false, yet offers it as true, even if the actual truth be just what he says. (Augustine, 1952 [395]b, 55)

Against this tradition, Thomas Carson (2006), (2010) holds a view according to which

In order to tell a lie, one must make a false statement. Showing that a statement is true is always sufficient to counter the accusation that one has told a lie.
(Carson, 2010, 15)[14]

---

[14] For another defense of this view, see Eriksson (2011a).

Carson (2010, 16) admits, though, that this claim "rests on disputed intuitions." And it is safe to say that most who have theorized about lying have had different reactions than Carson's.[15]

Consider one of Carson's central examples:

Crossed Lines
I go fishing on a boat with a friend, John. He and I both catch a fish at the same time. Although we don't realize it, our lines are crossed. I have caught a very big fish and John has caught a little one, but we mistakenly believe that I caught the small fish and John caught the big one. We throw the two fish back into the water. I go home thinking that I caught a small fish. When I return, my father, an avid fisherman, asks me how I did. I say that I caught a very large fish and threw it back into the water, thereby intending to deceive him about [the] size of the fish that I caught. (Carson, 2010, 16)

Carson reports:

My linguistic intuitions tell me that a lie must be a false statement, and that, therefore, what I say in this case is not a lie. I intend to lie in this case but I do not. (Carson, 2010, 16)

Many will be attracted to the opposite verdict on this case. I am among those who think that the mere fact that the fisherman's story is true—even though no one is aware of this—is not sufficient to show that no lie has been told.

Indeed, there are many cases in which intuitions appear to be clearly in conflict with Carson's view. Here is an example.

Rats
In a foregone age in which people believed in spontaneous generation, Robert is asking his friend Thomas for advice before taking an exam. Robert asks, "Where do rats come from?" Thomas believes that rats are generated spontaneously by wet dirt, and he knows that this is the answer that will be taken as correct on the exam. But he wants Robert to

---

[15] Lycan (2006) (also cited in Carson, 2010, 17) reports that 40 percent of his students disagree with the claim that saying something false is necessary for lying. Turri and Turri (2015) have reported similar empirical data. As these results suggest, in everyday situations, we sometimes do accept as a defense against having lied that what one said turned out to be true. I would venture that, most people, upon reflection, agree that the mere fact that what was said is true does not imply that no lie was told.

fail the exam and so he tells him, "They are born by other rats." Robert trusts Thomas's response and gives it as his answer on the exam, which he thereby fails.

I think Thomas lied to Robert, and I suspect most will agree. However, on a view like Carson's, he is exonerated from lying by the fact—unsuspected until hundreds of years later—that what he said was true.

Here is another example:[16]

Weapons of Mass Destruction
A politician, Tony, wants to make the public believe that there are weapons of mass destruction in Iraq in order to justify a war. Yet Tony has been presented with convincing evidence that there are no weapons of mass destruction in Iraq, and he believes there are none. During an interview, he says:

(2)   There are weapons of mass destruction in Iraq.

A war ensues. But later it is discovered that, even though Tony believed that the Iraqis did not have weapons of mass destruction, and he knowingly said something he believed to be false, in fact the intelligence was mistaken and there were such weapons in Iraq at the time.

I think it is clear that Tony lied to the public in this case.

Another reason for rejecting the view that lies must be false comes from the observation that those lied to are typically not appeased by a subsequent revelation that what they were told was in fact true, even though their informant believed it was false.

Suppose, for example, that the father in Carson's story somehow subsequently discovers the truth about the crossed lines. Further, imagine that he can see clearly that neither of the two fishermen knew at the time, or has later found out. So, while the father has hitherto believed that the son was sincerely telling him what happened on the fishing trip, what the father now discovers is that his son told him something he believed to be false, even though it was in fact true, unbeknownst to him. On Carson's view, this discovery is a discovery not that the son has lied, but that the son tried to lie, but failed. Yet, the father is likely to feel just as indignant as he would feel had he not also found out the truth about the crossed lines.

---

[16] Adapted from Saul (2012, 4).

The same clearly applies to the case of Tony. The public is not consoled by the subsequent revelation that what Tony said was in fact true, even though he believed otherwise. What matters to their feeling of resentment, it seems, is that Tony related disbelieved information to the public.

This puts pressure on the view that lies must not only be believed to be false, but must also in fact be false. To be sure, Carson might now claim that trying, unsuccessfully, to lie by saying something one incorrectly believes to be false is just as bad morally as trying to lie and succeeding. This, however, looks like a cost for the view, and it is not clear why, at this point, we should not simply concede the majority opinion that what matters for whether a lie has been told is what the speaker believes, not the actual truth-value of what she says.

Given this, and since the view that one lies only if one says something false is clearly the minority view, I will assume in this book that lying is compatible with saying something true.

The second point to consider in connection with (L3) is the claim that lying requires saying something one believes to be false. One aspect of this idea is more or less uncontroversial. Namely, that if you say something you believe to be true, you are not lying. In a 2013 piece on the fragile reliability of memory, the neurologist and popular science writer, Oliver Sacks, wrote:

For the most part the people who claim to be abducted by aliens are not lying when they speak of how they were taken into alien spaceships, any more than they are conscious of having invented a story—some truly believe that this is what happened. (Sacks, 2013)

What is more controversial is the claim, built into (L3), that lying involves saying something one believes to be false, as opposed to merely saying something one does not believe. The former condition entails the latter, but not *vice versa*. Hence, a view that accepts that lying merely requires saying something one fails to believe will be broader than the stronger view I favor. In particular, the weaker view will accept that cases in which the speaker is *agnostic* about the truth-value of what she says can be cases of lying.[17] Here is an example:[18]

---

[17] For a view of this kind, see Shiffrin (2014).
[18] From Stokke and Fallis (2017). See also Fallis (in press).

Umbrella

Thelma wants to sell Tom an umbrella. She knows that Tom is going to Chicago. Even though Thelma has no idea whether this is true or not, she invents the story that it is always raining in Chicago at that time of year, and she tells this to Tom in order to make him buy the umbrella.

Given the view that you lie only if you say something you believe to be false, Thelma is not lying. I think this is the right verdict on this case. However, I also think that Thelma is guilty of another kind of insincere speech. Namely, as I will argue in Chapter 7, I think Thelma is *bullshitting*.

One key motivation for the view that lying requires asserting disbelieved information, rather than just asserting information one fails to believe, is the suggestion that, as opposed to bullshitting, lying is a speech act with a specific kind of purpose. In his seminal work on bullshitting, Harry Frankfurt (2005 [1986]) writes:

Telling a lie is an act with a sharp focus. It is designed to insert a particular falsehood at a specific point in a set or system of beliefs, in order to avoid the consequences of having that point occupied by the truth.

(Frankfurt, 2005 [1986], 51)

For reasons that will become clear, we cannot accept this idea as it is explicitly formulated here. First, as already noted, on my view a lie is designed to convey a *believed* falsehood. Second, since lies are not necessarily intended to deceive, they do not always have the goal of making the speaker believe what is said. Yet, the spirit of Frankfurt's suggestion is right. A lie, on the view I will defend, is designed to make disbelieved information common ground, in order to avoid the consequences of having the common ground contain something one believes to be true. For this reason, cases in which the speaker is agnostic about what she says are not lies.

Having offered these remarks on (L3), I will devote the rest of Part I of this book to (L1) and (L2), that is, to the claim that lying involves saying something one believes to be false, and thereby proposing that it become common ground.

2

Lying and Gricean Quality

As we have seen, my account of lying is an instance of the general idea that lying is a matter of asserting disbelieved information, or, as it is sometimes put, that a lie is an insincere assertion. This view is therefore one on which lying characteristically involves the speaker's communicative goals. As advertised, I think that the right way to understand insincere speech is in terms of the theory of communication found in the work of Robert Stalnaker (1999 [1970]), (1999 [1974]), (1984), (1999 [1978]), (1999 [1998]), (2002), (2014). In this chapter I will be concerned with arguing against an alternative way of thinking of lying in terms of the liar's communicative goals. In particular, I will be concerned with arguing against conceptions of lying based on the Gricean maxims of Quality.

2.1. The Gricean Category of Quality

Paul Grice (1989) established an understanding of conversations as cooperative enterprises aimed at information sharing. Grice suggested that this kind of activity is governed by his Cooperative Principle and the maxims of conversation, which were to be thought of, roughly, as principles that rational creatures would (or should) follow given an interest in exchanging information in this way.[1]

The Cooperative Principle is stated as follows (Grice, 1989, 26):

Cooperative Principle
Make your contribution such as is required, at the stage at which it occurs, by the accepted purpose or direction of the talk exchange in which you are engaged.

---

[1] See in particular Grice (1989, 29–30).

In turn, the maxims were divided into four categories, Quantity, Quality, Relation, and Manner. Among these the category of Quality included a supermaxim and two specific maxims:

> **Supermaxim of Quality:**   Try to make your contribution one that is true.
>
> **First Maxim of Quality:**   Do not say what you believe to be false.
>
> **Second Maxim of Quality:**   Do not say that for which you lack adequate evidence.

It has been suggested (see e.g. Wilson, 1995, Meibauer, 2005, Dynel, 2011, Fallis, 2009, 2012) that lying can be characterized in terms of one or more of these maxims. By contrast, I will argue that there is no satisfactory way of doing so. In making this case, I focus on the Supermaxim of Quality and the First Maxim of Quality. I take it that the arguments I give also rule out putative conceptions of lying in terms of the Second Maxim of Quality. We will see that, in general, these Gricean proposals are bound to fall foul of particular facts concerning bald-faced lies, and concerning the way such a definition must locate lying in relation to the saying–meaning distinction. In particular, I consider two kinds of cases that have been discussed in the literature, namely cases involving *irony* and cases involving *false implicature*.

2.2. Lying and the First Maxim of Quality

Given that lying involves saying something one believes to be false, lies are violations of the First Maxim of Quality. But moreover, a great many ordinary examples of lies are cases in which a speaker violates the First Maxim of Quality *covertly*. Arguably the most common type of lying is that in which the liar says something she believes to be false while hoping that the hearer will not detect that she is doing so. In particular, the typical purpose of lies is to deceive in the sense of making the hearer acquire a false belief. The success of this ordinarily depends on the hearer being unaware that the speaker is relating disbelieved information.

Grice himself observed that covert violations of maxims often have deceptive effects. In distinguishing different ways in which a speaker can fail to fulfill the maxims, Grice wrote:

He may quietly and unostentatiously *violate* a maxim; if so, in some cases he will be liable to mislead. (Grice, 1989, 30)

Hence, it is not unnatural to think that lying, in general, might be characterized in terms of such covert violations. For example, Deirdre Wilson and Dan Sperber (2002), who call the First Maxim of Quality the *maxim of truthfulness*, suggest:

Lies are examples of *covert violation*, where the hearer is meant to assume that the maxim of truthfulness is still in force and that the speaker believes what she has said. (Wilson and Sperber, 2002, 586)

So, according to Wilson and Sperber, to lie by covertly violating the First Maxim of Quality is to say something one believes to be false while intending that the hearer believe that one believes what one says.[2]

An immediate question that arises is how to understand the notion of *saying* something that this proposal involves. Importantly, Grice himself held a particular, strong conception of what it is to say something. As Stephen Neale (1992) points out:

it is Grice's view that a statement of the form 'by uttering x, U said that p' entails the corresponding statement of the form 'by uttering x, U meant that p'.

(Neale, 1992, 523)

Famously, Grice analyzed the notion of what a speaker meant in terms of his concept of audience-directed, communicative intentions. On this understanding, a speaker S meant that p if and only if, roughly, S intended her audience to believe that p as a result of their recognizing this intention (cf. Neale, 1992, 515.) In other words, that S said that p entails that S meant that p, and that S meant that p entails that S intended her audience to believe that p as a result of their recognizing this intention. Hence, on this notion of saying, that a speaker said that p entails that she intended her audience to come to believe that p (by recognizing this intention.)

Given this notion of saying something, the proposal that lies are covert violations of the First Maxim of Quality amounts to the suggestion that you lie when you say something you believe to be false and you thereby intend both that the hearer believe what you say and that the hearer

---

[2] See also Dynel (2011, 141). Wilson and Sperber's (2002) purpose is to argue against the Gricean view that conversations are governed by Quality maxims. See also Wilson (1995).

believe that you believe what you say. In other words, given this Gricean construal of the notion of saying something, the suggestion that lies are covert violations of the First Maxim of Quality entails the Augustinian Definition of lying, that is, the view that in lying the speaker says something she does not believe and thereby intends to deceive the hearer into believing it.

However, as we have seen, this traditional conception of lying is too narrow. In particular, bald-faced lies are not cases in which the liar intends that the hearer believe what she says. For example, the cheating student does not intend that the Dean believe that she is not guilty, when she tells him that.

We can extract a general conclusion from this. If lying is to be defined in terms of saying, then in order to rule in bald-faced lies, it must be formulated in terms of a notion of saying such that a speaker can say that p without this entailing neither that she intends her audience to believe the proposition put forward nor that she intends her audience to believe that she herself believes that proposition. Indeed, both speaker and audience may know the proposition to be false, as in the case of the cheating student.

If we abandon the strong Gricean notion of saying something, can the proposal that lies are covert violations of the First Maxim of Quality be defended? Supposing that saying something does not necessarily involve intending that one's hearer come to believe what one says, Wilson and Sperber's suggestion amounts to the claim that you lie when you say something you believe to be false while intending that the hearer believe that you believe what you say.

This, however, is likewise too strong. Even if one grants that saying something does not require trying to make one's hearer believe what one says, bald-faced lies still cannot be seen as covert violations of the First Maxim of Quality. That is, they are not cases in which the speaker violates the First Maxim of Quality while "the hearer is meant to assume that the maxim of truthfulness is still operative and that the speaker believes what she has said." (Wilson and Sperber, 2002, 586) For example, the cheating student does not think the Dean will think she believes what she says when she denies her guilt. We cannot characterize lying, in general, as covert violations of the First Maxim of Quality, since bald-faced lies are not cases in which the speaker intends the hearer to think that she believes what she says.

In light of this, an alternative suggestion is to characterize lying simply in terms of violations of the First Maxim of Quality, covert or overt. In an important paper Don Fallis (2009) suggested a definition of this kind:[3]

The Quality Definition of Lying
S lies to X if and only if

(LQ1)   S states that p to X,

(LQ2)   S believes that the First Maxim of Quality is in effect, and

(LQ3)   S believes that p is false.

According to this definition, lying is not a matter of covertly violating the First Maxim of Quality. Rather, on this view, a lie is simply a statement that violates the First Maxim of Quality, whether covertly or overtly. Bald-faced lies satisfy these conditions, i.e. they are statements of disbelieved information made while the speaker believes that First Maxim of Quality is in effect.

However, as we will see next, there are many ways of violating the First Maxim of Quality without lying. In particular, standard cases of *irony* are counterexamples to the Quality Definition.[4]

2.3. Irony and the First Maxim of Quality

Irony is the classic case in which what is said and what is meant diverge. For instance, in giving examples of "phenomena which are obviously part of what is meant by the speaker but not part of what her linguistic string means," Robyn Carston (2002) says:

The textbook case is irony and its standard characterization is that of saying one thing while meaning the opposite.   (Carson, 2002, 15)

Suppose we are discussing movies. You tell me you think *Titanic* is a great movie. Appalled, I exclaim in a sarcastic voice:

(1)   [Ironically] Oh yeah, *Titanic* is a great movie!

---

[3] In another paper Fallis (2010) discusses various proposals for how to define the specific case of deceptive lying, i.e. the type of lying of which bald-faced lying is not an instance. Here I am only interested in the proposal of Fallis (2009) explicitly designed to cover the broad phenomenon of lying, including lying without the intent to deceive. Fallis (2013) proposes another account of lying.

[4] Cf. Stokke (2013). For similar arguments, see Pruss (2012), Faulkner (2013).

This is a straightforward example of the classic kind of irony in which what the speaker means is the negation of what she says. What I wanted to convey is that *Titanic* is a *bad* movie.

Although I did not lie, I said something I believe to be false, namely that *Titanic* is a great movie. Fallis acknowledges that an ironic speaker of this kind "is certainly *saying* something that he believes to be false." (Fallis, 2009, 53) In other words, (LV1) and (LV3) are both satisfied in this case. If (LV2) is also satisfied in cases of irony, then such cases are counterexamples to the suggestion that to lie is to violate the First Maxim of Quality. That is, they will be cases in which someone states disbelieved information while believing that the First Maxim of Quality is in effect. But since someone who is being ironic in the manner of (1) is not lying, the Quality Definition will thereby be seen to be too broad.

It has been suggested that the First Maxim of Quality is not in effect in these cases. For example, Wilson and Sperber (2002) write:

Metaphor, irony and other tropes [. . .] are *overt violations (floutings)* of the maxim of truthfulness, in which the hearer is meant to assume that the maxim of truthfulness is no longer operative, but that the supermaxim of Quality remains in force, so that some true proposition is still conveyed.

(Wilson and Sperber, 2002, 586)

Similarly, Fallis argues that the First Maxim of Quality "is not in effect" in these cases and that "by flouting this norm of conversation, [the ironic speaker] turns it off." (Fallis, 2009, 53)

But although understanding irony as involving *flouting* the First Maxim of Quality is in line with the Gricean analysis of this kind of speech act, the claim that when a speaker flouts a maxim, she does not believe it is in effect is in direct opposition to it.

According to the orthodox Gricean conception, irony is an example of (particularized) conversational implicature.[5] That is, it is a speech act in which the speaker flouts a maxim of conversation, in this case the First Maxim of Quality, in order to trigger the kind of reasoning on the part of the audiences that Grice held was the source of such implicatures. Familiarly, the Gricean view is that an implicature of this kind arises when it is required in order to square the fact that the speaker said what she did with the presumption that she is observing the maxims and the Cooperative Principle.

---

[5] Cf. Grice (1989, 34).

For this reason, to flout a maxim, in the sense that is intended to trigger implicature, is to "blatantly fail to fulfill it." (Grice, 1989, 30) For Grice, "when a conversational implicature is generated in this way, [...] a maxim is being *exploited*." (Grice, 1989, 30) That is, the speaker violates a maxim in a way that is obvious to everyone involved in order to get them thinking about what her intentions could be in doing so.

One cannot flout a rule, in this sense, if one does not believe that it is in effect. Suppose that it is a rule in our town that you cannot cross at a red light, except on Sundays where it is allowed to do so, because there is little or no traffic on those days. On days other than Sunday, I can flout this rule. That is, I can violate it in a way that calls attention to itself, and will most likely get people thinking about what my intentions could be in doing so. But I cannot do so on Sundays. Even if I cross at a red light in a way that calls attention to itself on a Sunday, I do not thereby flout the rule against crossing at a red light. No one will attempt to interpret my actions by trying to square my behavior with a presumption that I am obeying the rule against crossing at a red light. The reason is clear—the rule is not in effect on Sundays.

In order to flout a rule, I must assume the rule is in effect. And moreover, when flouting a rule, I do not intend for my audience to think the rule is "no longer in force" (Wilson and Sperber, 2002, 586). Rather, my purpose is to trade on the fact that the rule is operative, and believed to be operative by everyone involved, so that my overtly violating it will trigger the intended inference.

Similarly, when someone is being ironic, on the Gricean view, their strategy is to violate the First Maxim of Quality in a conspicuous way. This strategy depends on the belief that the First Maxim of Quality is in effect. Consequently, when someone is being ironic in this way, they satisfy (LQ2), in addition to (LQ1) and (LQ3). For example, when uttering (1), I believe that the First Maxim of Quality is in effect. This is the reason I think I can succeed in communicating that *Titanic* is a bad movie by saying that it is a great movie, given that it is obvious from my tone of voice that I believe the former, and not the latter. However, given this, I am incorrectly classified as lying, according to the Quality Definition.

So, since lying, in general, cannot be characterized as either covert or overt violations of the First Maxim of Quality Lying, someone who wants to pursue an account of lying in terms of Quality should look elsewhere.

2.4. Falsely Implicating and the Supermaxim of Quality

At this point some might be attracted to a suggestion to define lying in terms of *what is meant* rather than what is said. That is, one would claim that the right definition of lying is that you lie if you convey, or mean, something you believe to be false. One way of spelling out such a view would be as the claim that to lie is to violate the Supermaxim of Quality, "Try to make your contribution one that is true."[6] Assuming that this kind of theory could be worked out satisfactorily, it would meet the challenge. It would predict that my utterance in (1) is not a lie. That is, the view would be that, even though I said something I believe to be false, I did not violate the Supermaxim of Quality because what I wanted to contribute to the conversation was something I believed to be true.

This suggestion amounts to the claim that, in suitable conditions, falsely implicating is a form of lying. Such a view has been endorsed by a few writers on lying (e.g. Meibauer, 2005, Dynel, 2011.) Yet this view is almost universally rejected. Fallis summarizes the majority view when he writes:

you are not lying if you make a statement that you believe to be true. In fact, you are not lying even if you intend to deceive someone by making this statement.

(Fallis, 2009, 38)

Similarly, Bernard Williams (2002) gives the following example:[7]

"Someone has been opening your mail," she helpfully says, and you, trusting her, take it that it was not the speaker herself. If you discover that it was the speaker, you will have to agree (if through clenched teeth) that what she said was true. So, you must also agree, she did not tell you a lie. (Williams, 2002, 96)

The claim that saying something one believes to be true in order to implicate something one believes to be false is a way of lying thus rejects one of the most fundamental distinctions we make about verbal insincerity. This is the distinction between lying *per se* and other forms of linguistic deception and misleading. (This will be the main topic of Chapter 5 of this book.)

---

[6] We assume that the effort that is required is met by trying to make the contribution such that one believes to be true, and does not require, for example, that one try to make the contribution such that one knows to be true.

[7] Despite what might be inferred from this passage, Williams does not endorse the view that you lie only if you say something false, but rather agrees with the more common view that you lie only if you say something you believe to be false. See Williams (2002, 96).

Familiarly, this distinction is central to many systems of law and to a number of religious traditions. The enormous amount of attention paid to the difference between lying and misleading while not lying in legal practices (see e.g. Solan and Tiersma, 2005, Saul, 2012) and in religious contexts such as that of the medieval casuists (see e.g. Williams, 2002) will be left unexplained by a view that insists on conflating lying and false implicature.

Moreover, even philosophers such as Adler (1997), Williams (2002), and Saul (2012), who think that, in certain circumstances, lying and falsely implicating may be equally morally problematic, still take great care to distinguish the two phenomena. For example, Jonathan Adler argues that while falsely implicating is not lying, it is a form of deception that in some circumstances can be just as morally and epistemically wrong as lying. Adler's motivations arise directly from an assertion-based conception of lying. According to Adler, in the standard case:

lying is a significantly worse choice than other forms of deception. Both choices aim for the victim to believe falsely, but only lying does so through asserting what one believes false.   (Adler, 1997, 435)

Whether or not one ultimately wants to claim, as Adler does, that the impropriety of deception by means of false implicature and of lying is, at least sometimes, equal, few would disagree that the two are to be distinguished.

Adler discusses the following biblical example:

Abraham, venturing into a dangerous land and fearing for his life if Sarah is taken as his wife, tells Abimelech the king that she is his sister. God appears to Abimelech to warn him away from taking Sarah because "She is a married woman." Frightened, Abimelech confronts Abraham, who defends his obvious deception by denying that he lied:
... they will kill me for the sake of my wife. She is in fact my sister, she is my father's daughter though not by the same mother; and she became my wife...
(Adler, 1997, 435)

Most commentators, going back at least as far as Augustine (1952 [395]a), have defended Abraham as not having lied, although he is guilty of deception. Augustine wrote of Abraham:

Thus, he concealed something of the truth, but did not say anything false in concealing the fact that she was his wife and in saying that she was his sister.
(Augustine, 1952 [395]a, 152)

The kind of deception Abraham perpetrates is that of implicating something he believes to be false.[8] According to the Book of Genesis, Abraham's original utterance was:[9]

(2)   She is my sister.

The obvious, Gricean way to explain this case is as exploiting Grice's (1975, 26) First Maxim of Quantity:

First Maxim of Quantity: Make your contribution as informative as is required (for the current purpose of the exchange).

The king will take Abraham as having implicated that Sarah is not his wife because that assumption is needed to make his uttering (2) consistent with the presumption that he is obeying the First Maxim of Quantity.

But if lying is defined as violating the Supermaxim of Quality, Abraham counts as having lied, contrary to the judgments of most who have thought about this case. Abraham makes a statement that he believes to be true, namely that Sarah is his sister, while intending to deceive the king by implicating that she is not his wife. But intuitively, he is not lying.

Lying cannot be defined in terms of what is meant, or conveyed, but must be defined in terms of what is said. And moreover, as we have seen, the notion of saying something used to characterize lying must be weak enough so as to allow that bald-faced liars say things without intending their audience to believe them.

---

[8] Adler (1997, 438) indicates that he does not consider Abraham's utterance as a case of conversational implicature, but rather as of another type of pragmatic inference. By contrast, I think it is plausible to treat the case as conversational implicature, in the way I suggest in the text. For those who do not agree with this line on the example, I refer to the other cases of false (conversational) implicature that Adler discusses. The point I am interested in making concerns this phenomenon, and is independent of what the right analysis of this particular case turns out to be.

[9] See *Genesis* 20.2.

3

Common Ground

The Gricean proposals for characterizing lying we considered in the last chapter share the assumption that lying is to be characterized in terms of communicative goals. As I have said, I agree with this general thought. However, instead of characterizing lying in terms of Gricean maxims, I propose to define lying in terms of the framework for understanding communication stemming from the work of Robert Stalnaker (1999 [1970]), (1999 [1974]), (1984), (1999 [1978]), (1999 [1998]), (2002), (2014).[1]

Here is my definition of lying again:

The Common Ground Definition of Lying
A lies to B if and only if there is a proposition p such that

(L1)   A says that p to B, and

(L2)   A proposes to make it common ground that p, and

(L3)   A believes that p is false.

As noted, there are two crucial notions involved in this definition, namely the notion of saying in (L1) and the notion of common ground in (L2). In order to capture the phenomenon of lying, both these notions need to be understood in particular ways. I devote this chapter to the notion of common ground, and Chapter 4 to spelling out my account of what is said. We will see that, once these pieces are in place, this account of lying has the right results for all the cases we have looked at so far as well as a number of other cases. In Chapter 5 we will see that, moreover, my account captures the distinction between lying and merely misleading correctly.

---

[1] In doing so we are not committing ourselves to a view of the final analysis of the phenomenon of assertion. For recent discussion of this view of assertion, see e.g. Egan (2007), Hawthorne and Magidor (2009), Stalnaker (2009), MacFarlane (2010). What we are after is just to capture the aspects of assertion that are relevant for defining lying.

3.1. Two Roles for Common Ground Information

According to the Stalnakerian framework for theorizing about communication, conversations evolve against a background of mutually shared information called the *common ground*. The common ground of a conversation plays two main roles. On the one hand, our utterances have the goal of adding to, or updating, the shared background information. On the other hand, according to Stalnaker, we rely on what is common ground, in this sense, to support various context-sensitive elements of our languages.

Here is a simple example to illustrate this. Consider an utterance of (1).

(1)   I bought the car.

Suppose Joan uses (1) to let Alice know that she bought a particular Saab that they have been looking at or talking about earlier. For her to do so, Alice need to know at least two things: who the speaker is and which car is being talked about. Typically, the common ground will contain information sufficient for settling both these things, when such an utterance is made, and so it will be easy for Alice to understand that the information conveyed by the utterance is that Joan bought that particular Saab. Given this, Joan's utterance has the effect that it now becomes common ground that she bought the Saab.

As this example illustrates, on the one hand, an assertion is a proposal to add to, or update, the common ground with new information. As Stalnaker says:

First, speech is action, and speech acts should be understood in terms of the way they are intended to affect the situation in which they are performed.
(1999 [1998], 98)

On the other hand, common ground information is used to support various context-sensitive aspects of utterances. Stalnaker writes:

Second, speech acts are context-dependent: their contents (and so the way they are intended to affect the situation) depend not only on the syntactic and semantic properties of the types of expressions used, but also on facts about the situation in which the expressions are used.   (Stalnaker, 1999 [1998], 98)

In this second capacity, the common ground is used for many purposes. As illustrated by (1), one of the more conspicuous is keeping track of presuppositions. Briefly, on this view, using a presuppositional expression like *the car* is felicitous only if what it presupposes is already common ground. We will see in much more detail throughout this chapter and the rest of Part I what this idea amounts to, and what it implies for the spectrum of insincere modes of speech.

As emphasized above, Stalnaker also suggests, at least in some places, that common ground information is used to determine the referents of indexicals like I.[2] This point is more contentious than the core Stalnakerian idea that common ground is used for retaining information that has previously been communicated. However, for convenience, I will continue to speak in terms of this idea in this chapter. In Chapter 4, I will offer more detailed discussion of the role of context-sensitive expressions in determining what is said.

How does information enter the common ground? There are many ways in which a piece of information may become common ground. For example, it may be common ground that there is a president before an utterance of (2), just because this is something that people know or are expected to know.

(2)   The President is in Washington.

But an utterance of (2) may also have the effect of making it common ground that there is a president through the familiar mechanism that David Lewis (1979) called *accommodation*, that is, the participants might adjust the common ground to include the new information. Moreover, Stalnaker (1999 [1998], 101) points out that a use of I does not require that it be common ground who the speaker is before the utterance is made; that information may become common ground simply because it is obvious who is making the utterance.[3] Similarly, a piece of information may become common ground simply by perceptual salience. As Stalnaker (1999 [1978], 86) says, if a goat walks into the room, it may become

---

[2] It is controversial whether Stalnaker is to be interpreted as holding this view. Stalnaker (1999 [1998], 98) seems to be a clear statement of it. Glanzberg (2002) clearly assumes that Stalnaker holds that the referents of expressions like I are determined by common ground information. Yet Stalnaker (2014, Ch. 1) can be seen as suggesting that other notions of contexts are more apt for playing the role of settling content. For relevant discussion, see Huvenes and Stokke (2016).

[3] On this, see also von Fintel (2008).

common ground that a goat is in the room, as witnessed by the fact that one can felicitously ask a question like, "How did that thing get in here?"

This basic picture of how communication works will be refined through this and the following two chapters. The first thing I want to turn to is the question of what more precisely it means to say that a piece of information is common ground.

3.2. Belief and Acceptance

According to one version of this framework, the common ground of a conversation is the set of propositions that are *common belief*:

It is common ground that *p* in a group if all members believe that *p*, and all believe that all believe that *p*, and all believe that all believe that all believe that *p*, etc.

Adopting this view of the common ground means that asserting that *p* is a proposal for the participants (including the speaker) to believe that *p*. Most commonly, therefore, the speaker herself will already believe that *p* when she asserts it. By asserting that *p* the speaker is inviting the other participants to share her belief that *p*.[4]

This version of the common ground view of assertion will not do for our purposes. The reason is that the phenomenon of bald-faced lies shows that asserting that *p* is not necessarily aimed at making one's audience believe that *p*. If to assert that *p* is to say that *p* and thereby propose that *p* become common ground, and the common ground is defined in terms of belief, then bald-faced lies cannot be assertions. For example, the cheating student we discussed in Chapter 1 is not proposing that both the Dean and herself believe that she did not cheat.

Fortunately, as I explain below, this version of the common ground view of assertion is not only inadequate for our purposes, but also does not do justice to the way common ground information is understood by Stalnaker. Instead, as we will see, the correct version is just what we need to define lying in terms of assertion.

Stalnaker is adamant that common ground information is to be characterized in terms of an attitude weaker than belief. The main reason is

---

[4] For a version of this conception of the common ground view of assertion, see Egan (2007).

that, as he frequently emphasizes, common ground information that is known (or believed) to be false is no obstacle to communicative success.[5]

> Successful communication is compatible with presuppositions that are recognized to be false, but the information that they are being presupposed must be actually available, and not just assumed or pretended to be available.
>
> (Stalnaker, 2002, 716)

For this reason, instead of belief, Stalnaker proposes to define common ground information in terms of *acceptance*. Acceptance is a non-factive propositional attitude weaker than belief.[6] That is, that a subject S accepts that p does not entail that p is true, nor that S believes that p.

However, it would be inadequate to simply define the common ground as a set of propositions that the participants mutually accept. Interestingly, Stalnaker uses the example of lying in order to motivate this point:

> Even the liar, if he really intends to communicate, has to believe that the infor-mation needed to interpret his lies will really be common ground. So we might identify the common ground with common *belief* about what is accepted.
>
> (2002, 716)

Although this remark is not developed further by Stalnaker, I take it to be clear that what is meant by it is the following. Suppose that someone wanted to lie by uttering (2). For example, suppose the President is not in Washington and the speaker knows this, but wants to deceive his hearers into believing that she is. Then Stalnaker's point is that, just as in the normal situation, the speaker has to rely on its being common ground that there is a (unique) President. In this way lies exploit the common ground in the same way as sincere assertions.

In light of the fact that common ground information does not have to be the object of belief, although it must be believed to be available, Stalnaker (2002, 716) proposes the following definition of the common ground:

> It is common ground that p in a group if all members accept (for the purpose of the conversation) that p, and all believe that all accept that p, and all believe that all believe that all accept that p, etc.

---

[5] See also Stalnaker (1999 [1970], 39), Stalnaker (1999, 11).

[6] This notion of acceptance is to be distinguished from mental assent which I discuss in Chapter 7. For relevant discussion, see e.g. Cohen (1989) and Stokke (2014).

This characterization of common ground information does not rule out that some common ground information is the object of outright belief, in addition to acceptance. Obviously, very often the information we rely on, that is, accept, is genuinely believed, if not known. All that is assumed is that, minimally, common ground information is information that is accepted for the purpose of the conversation.

I adopt this characterization of common ground information. So the view of assertion that I think should be used to define lying is the following: To assert that p is to say that p and thereby propose that p become common ground, where common ground is understood in the way just described. In other words, to lie is to say something one believes to be false and thereby propose that it be accepted by the participants and commonly believed to be accepted.

3.3. Bald-Faced Lies

We saw above that thinking about the common ground in terms of acceptance is needed in order to account for the phenomenon of lying without intentions to deceive, since this involves asserting without aiming to be believed. To flesh this out more, consider again the cheating student. I take it to be clear that the student says something she believes to be false, that is, that she did not cheat. Moreover, I claim that the student proposes that it become common ground that she did not cheat. In other words, according to this view, the bald-faced liar is asserting what she says.

The shared intuition about the case of the cheating student is that the reason the student makes her utterance—despite the fact that both she and the Dean know full well that what she says is false—is that she wants to "go on the record." This idea lends itself readily to be explained in terms of the common ground. Namely, to say that the student wants to go on the record is just to say that the student wants it to be common ground that she did not cheat.

There are two immediate questions to be asked here. Namely, should we assume that the information that the student did cheat is common ground from the outset, and if so, is that a problem for our account of lying?

One suggestion is that, given that the Dean and the student both know that the student cheated, that information is common ground between them when the conversation in the Dean's office begins. Indeed, as we saw in Chapter 1, it is straightforward to assume that it is *common knowledge* that the student cheated, that is, that each of them knows that she cheated, and each of them knows that the other knows that she did, etc.

The fact that a proposition p is common knowledge very often means that p is also common ground in conversations among the relevant parties. However, it is important to note that this relation does not always hold. A proposition p might be common knowledge, even though it is not common ground, in the Stalnakerian sense. The main reason is that a proposition can be common ground even if its negation is common knowledge. That would be impossible if common knowledge automatically became common ground, since the common ground of a conversation cannot contain both a proposition and its negation. To illustrate this, consider Keith Donnellan's (1966) classic example:

Martini

At a cocktail party, Alice says to Bob,

(3)   The man drinking a martini is a philosopher.

As Stalnaker points out, successful communication in this case does not depend on mutual knowledge (or even belief) that the man is drinking a martini:

perhaps it is mutually recognized that it is not a martini, but mutually recognized that both parties are *accepting* that it is a martini. The pretense will be rational if accepting the false presupposition is an efficient way to communicate something true—information about the man who is falsely presupposed to be the man drinking a martini.   (Stalnaker, 2002, 718)

In this case it is common knowledge (let us assume) that what the man is drinking is not a martini and yet it is common ground that it is a martini.

It cannot be assumed, therefore, that simply because it is common knowledge between the Dean and the student that the student cheated, that information is common ground. Indeed, it is natural to describe this case as one in which there is a difference between what the parties commonly know to be the case, and what they are taking for granted for the purpose of their conversation. The point of the interview is not to find out the truth about the cheating, nor to question what they already believe. Rather, the point is that, given the circumstances, it matters what the student does or does not say (indeed, assert) regardless of what is known to be the facts about the case.

But moreover, even if we assume (although, I think, implausibly) that it is initially common ground that the student cheated, this does not threaten the prediction that the student is lying when she makes her utterance. The reason is that it is nevertheless clear that the student is proposing to update the common ground with what is said. The reason she says what she does is to make sure that the common ground comes to include the false information that she did not cheat. The student wants herself and the Dean to mutually accept that she did not cheat. And this may come about as the result of altering previous common ground information, or of updating with new information.

As I suggested above, in general, situations in which it is advantageous to tell bald-faced lies are situations in which it makes a difference that a particular assertion is made, regardless of whether anyone believes it or not. The crucial part of Carson's example of the cheating student is that the student is privy to the fact that the Dean does not punish someone who explicitly denies their guilt. That is, the student knows that it will be enough to get off the hook to simply assert that she did not cheat.

Here is (an adaptation of) another of Carson's examples, which makes the point even more vivid.[7]

Intimidated Witness
A man on the witness stand in a courtroom has witnessed a murder. Because there is CCTV footage that clearly shows the man witnessing the murder, and this footage has been presented to the jury, everyone knows that everyone knows that the man saw the crime take place. But, for fear of reprisals, when asked whether he saw the murder, the witness says,

(4)   I did not see the murder.

The witness, in this example, is clearly lying. Yet, just as in the case of the cheating student, the witness does not intend to deceive anyone. In particular, I assume that the same dialectics that we went through in Chapter 1 applies to this case. That is, ultimately, one cannot deny that there are versions of this example in which the witness cannot be said to have intentions of deceiving, or indeed of being deceitful in the sense of Lackey (2013).

---

[7] See Carson (2010, 20).

As in the case of the cheating student, the reason it is advantageous to the witness to tell the bald-faced lie is that the situation is such that it makes a difference which assertion is made, regardless of whether it is believed or not.

The view that assertion centrally involves making a bid to include what is said in the common ground is particularly apt to account for this trait shared by bald-faced lies. As we have seen, on this view, assertion does not necessarily involve intending to make people believe what one says, even though, of course, it often does. Rather, what assertion essentially involves is the aim of making what is said part of the information that is mutually taken for granted.

3.4. Bald-Faced False Implicature

It is important to note that the weak conception of common ground information in terms of what is (believed to be) accepted also gives the right results with respect to other phenomena. In particular, we should note that lying is not the only kind of insincere speech that may occur unaccompanied by intentions to deceive. There are also cases of *bald-faced false implicature*.

First, a bald-faced false implicature may be derived from a bald-faced lie. Here is an example.

Thelma and Louise
Thelma knows that Louise knows that Thelma has been drinking.
(5) Louise. Are you OK to drive?
     Thelma. I haven't been drinking.

It is a datum that Louise will infer from Thelma's utterance that she wants to convey that she is OK to drive. And moreover, this is what Thelma both intended and expected to happen. Of course, Louise will not come to *believe* that Thelma is OK to drive as a result of the utterance and her inference from it. But she will still infer that Thelma wanted to convey that she is, and indeed, Louise will recognize (correctly) that Thelma wanted her to recognize that she wanted her to do so. In other words, Thelma implicates that she is OK to drive.[8]

---

[8] For more detailed arguments for this claim, see Stokke (2016c).

Again, the same points we made in relation to non-deceptive lying in Chapter 1 apply to this case of bald-faced implicature. In particular, since Thelma knows that Louise knows she is not OK to drive, Thelma is not trying to get Louise to believe that she is OK to drive, that is, she has no intention of deceiving Louise by implicating that she is. Even so, that Thelma is OK to drive becomes common ground as a result of Thelma's implicature.

There are also more complex cases of bald-faced false implicatures. A bald-faced implicature might be inferred from a true assertion, as in the following situation.[9]

Applicant

Mr X has submitted a job application. The committee members, Maude, Jack, and Gene, all think that Mr X's application is excellent, and it is common knowledge among them that they all think so. However, the committee members each have personal reasons for not wanting to hire Mr X, and it is common knowledge among them that they do. Yet outright lying about one's opinions of the qualifications of candidates would be grounds for dismissal.

(6) Maude. So what do you think of Mr X's application?
     Jack. I like the font.

Jack implicates that he thinks that Mr X's application was not very good. This is both what he wants the others to infer from his utterance, and what they do infer from his utterance. Yet since it is common knowledge that everyone thinks the application excellent, he is not trying to deceive anyone into believing that he thinks it is not good. Still what he said, and asserted, was true. So even though he is not lying, he is clearly conveyed a bald-faced false implicature.

3.5. Asserting and Pretending

It is now time to consider some potential problems for the view of lying, and insincerity more broadly, in terms of Stalnakerian common ground that I have been sketching. The first of these problems concerns the way the view deals with bald-faced lies.

---

[9] Adapted from the well-known example in Grice (1989, 33).

Some critics of my view of lying have objected that the very fact that common ground information is characterized in terms of the weak attitude of acceptance has the result that bald-faced lies are not adequately represented as assertions. Here is how James Mahon (2015) describes the objection:

> Either, in the case of a non-deceptive lie, the speaker does propose that the believed-false proposition become common ground, but becoming common ground is too weak to count as asserting, or becoming common ground is strong enough to count as asserting, but, in the case of a non-deceptive lie, the speaker does not propose that the believed-false proposition become common ground.
>
> (Mahon, 2015, Sec. 2.4)

Mahon notes that, as we saw above, Stalnaker describes the Martini situation as one in which the participants *pretend* that the man is drinking a martini, even though it is common knowledge that he is not. He then writes:

> However, if proposing that a believed-false proposition become common ground can mean engaging in and sustaining a "pretence," possibly in order to communicate truths, then it is not clear that this counts as making an assertion [. . .]. Hence, a non-deceptive liar may be proposing that her believed-false proposition become common ground without this being an act of making an assertion.
>
> (Mahon, 2015, Sec. 2.4)

So the worry is that, for example, when the student makes her statement she is merely proposing that what she says become subject of pretense. That is, that the Dean and herself henceforth pretend that she did not cheat. But this, the objection goes, is not plausible as a description of the act of asserting that she did not cheat.[10]

It is important to emphasize that, for the Stalnakerian, the bald-faced liar is not pretending to say something, nor is she pretending to propose that what she says become common ground. For instance, the intimidated witness in the example above is not pretending to say that she did not see the murder, nor is she pretending to propose that this information become part of what is mutually taken for granted. In other words, on the view I favor, the bald-faced liar is not pretending to make an assertion.

---

[10] Keiser (2015) raises a similar objection. See also section 3.10 for more discussion of Keiser's criticism.

What is in dispute is the significance of the kind of pretense that will sometimes be involved in the subsequent conversation as a result of a bald-faced lie. Since the bald-faced liar is making a *bona fide* assertion, on this view, cases of successful bald-faced lies are analyzed as cases in which the circumstances are such that, because someone has asserted something everyone knows to be false, the participants are obliged to conduct the ensuing discourse under the pretense that it is true. This, however, seems to be precisely what we want to say about situations like the Intimidated Witness and the Cheating Student. It is a datum about these cases that no one comes to believe the lie told. And yet, it is straightforward to describe these cases as ones in which everyone is obliged to act as if they did, that is, to pretend that the lie is true.

Perhaps the objection should be understood as maintaining that since the kind of pretense involved is unserious or frivolous, proposing that a particular piece of information be the object of it does not adequately reflect the force of assertion. However, it would be a mistake to think that the kind of pretense that, on this view, ensues from bald-faced lies cannot be a very grave matter. To see this, consider a show trial during a totalitarian regime. Someone is called on to go on the stand and testify to something that is commonly known to be false. That is, to go on the stand and tell a bald-faced lie. People in such circumstances have chosen to be executed, or to commit suicide, rather than do so.[11] In many cases where people prefer such dire alternatives, they do so in order to avoid having to engage in the kind of pretense that follows the assertion of a bald-faced lie. Given that it can take on importance of this magnitude, it is hard to see how this kind of pretense is insufficient to account for bald-faced lies *qua* assertions.

3.6. Official and Unofficial Common Ground

Another type of problem for the view is brought out by the following story.

The Confused Politician
A politician is invited to give a humorous speech at a festive banquet and a serious speech at a formal banquet. She confuses the dates, and

---

[11] I first heard this point made by David Owens during a workshop on *Lying and Deception* at King's College London in November 2015. For some relevant discussion, see Saul (2012, 9–11).

ends up delivering the humorous speech at the formal banquet and the formal speech at the festive banquet. During the humorous speech the politician tells a story about the President having "broken wind" during a meeting with some ambassadors. The politician knows that this event did not actually happen and is only relating it to make a joke. During the serious speech she says that the President withheld important information, even though she knows this to be false.

Many commentators have had the reaction to this example that, while the politician is not lying at the first event, she is lying at the second event.[12] The reasoning behind this is something like the following. Although her audience were expecting something else, when the politician gives her humorous speech, she is only joking. However, at the second event, she is speaking in earnest, and she is therefore lying when she says something she believes to be false, even though the audience was expecting her to be informal.

In order to handle this type of example, we need to make a qualification about common ground information. Once it is in place, we will be in a position to say that, during the humorous speech, while the politician says something she believes to be false, she is not proposing that it become common ground, while during the serious speech, she is saying something she believes to be false with the aim of making it common ground. The motivation for these claims about the confused politician is based on a distinction between what I shall call *official* and *unofficial* common ground.

The distinction between official and unofficial common ground is independently motivated. Consider for instance a play being performed on stage. One plausible thought is that during the performance of a play, a common ground is active, which stores information about the characters and situations that the play is about. This unofficial common ground is used to keep track of presuppositions, determine indexical content, etc., expressed by the characters in the play.

Here is one way of motivating such a picture. Imagine we are in the US, witnessing the performance of a play set in a monarchy. We are in the middle of an intense scene, where, after the exit of her husband, the hero is declaring his love for the heroine. Indexicals are being used in lines such as, "I love you." And presuppositions are being invoked by utterances

---

[12] See, e.g. Carson (2006), (2010), Fallis (2009), Stokke (2013).

involving "the King." Without even thinking about it, we are taking these indexicals to refer to the characters in the play, which suggests that the common ground we are using to evaluate these utterances is one that corresponds to the reality of the play. And similarly, we are resolving presuppositions by using this common ground of the play.[13]

Suppose now that in the middle of this scene, the cuckolded husband suddenly bursts in, runs to the edge of the stage and shouts in a distressed tone of voice:

(7)   Ladies and gentlemen! I have just received word that the President has been shot!

Most likely, we will all take this utterance to express the proposition that the actor has just received word that the real President has been shot. In particular, we will not be puzzled by the fact that there is no president in the play. And we will take *I* to refer to the actor, not the character he was playing a few minutes ago.

A plausible way of modelling what happens in cases like that of the interrupted play, then, is in terms of two common grounds being operative at the same time. Of one of these common grounds we know that it is the official one, namely the one that contains information such as that there is a president, that the person on the stage is an actor, and not a jealous husband from a distant era, etc. (Yet even the official common ground may contain information that everyone knows to be actually false.) It is likely, therefore, that the complex ways in which we smoothly move from discourse to discourse is to be explained by interactions with different common grounds, some more official than others.

---

[13] This view is compatible with more than one analysis of fictional discourse. According to Lewis (1978), sentences of fiction contain a hidden intensional operator "In fiction f ..." defined as follows: "a prefixed sentence 'In fiction f, ϕ' is true (or, as we shall also say, ϕ is true in the fiction f) iff ϕ is true at every possible world in a certain set, this set being somehow determined by the fiction f." (1978, 39) Familiarly, the common ground of a conversation is taken to determine a set of possible worlds w s.t. for all propositions p in the common ground, p is true at w. It is then straightforward to take the set of worlds determined by f to be what I have called the unofficial common ground. Similarly, the view I am sketching is compatible with accounts such as the one proposed by Predelli (2005, 66–73) according to which the hallmark of sentences of fiction is that they are evaluated at fictional worlds, although this shift is not triggered by a hidden operator. See Recanati (2000, ch. 15) for an alternative view of utterances inside fictions.

3.7. Lying and Official Common Ground

The notion of common ground in our definition of lying is intended to be that of the official common ground, that is, it is intended to rule out cases in which information is stored for temporary purposes such as play acting, etc. The actor in the example above is clearly lying if he believes that it is false that the President has been shot, when he bursts in and makes his announcement. The reason for this, I am suggesting, is that in this case he is proposing to update the official common ground.

We can now explain the example involving the confused politician. In the case where she is delivering her humorous speech, the politician is not proposing to add the information that the President broke wind to the official common ground, but merely to the unofficial common ground of her joking speech. Hence, she does not count as lying. By contrast, when she delivers her serious speech, she is intending to update the official common ground, and she therefore counts as lying when she says something she believes to be false.

It does not matter that the audience, in each case, is expecting the opposite mode of speech. Our definition of lying merely requires that the politician is *proposing* to add to the (official) common ground. In general, lying does not require that the information which the speaker believes to be false be *in fact* included in the common ground; even if the other participants refuse to accept the speaker's false information, she still counts as lying just for proposing to update with something she knows to be false.

So we account for our intuition that the politician is not lying when she is joking by the independently motivated assumption that the common ground of fiction and jokes is seen as unofficial.

Finally, I want to consider a potential worry concerning what I have just said in relation to bald-faced lying. Someone might object that, given the distinction between the official and the unofficial common ground, the bald-face liar should be taken as proposing to update a merely unofficial common ground, and hence will not be counted as lying after all.

However, this suggestion is clearly not what we are committed to. As emphasized repeatedly, bald-faced lying is characterized by the speaker's desire to be on the record. The cheating student is not joking, she is not play acting, nor is her speech act comparable to mere assumption. She is sincerely asserting her innocence. So it seems natural to say that she is putting forth her statement for the official common ground, and not for some merely temporary purpose.

This suggestion can be corroborated in the following way. Both assertions and presuppositions added to an unofficial common ground can later be unproblematically revoked. For example, suppose that, after the politician has given her humorous speech, someone charges her with having lied. She can defend herself by saying:

(8)   No, no, you didn't realize that I was just joking.

And although the politician will be expected to apologize for having made this mistake, she is not obviously reproachable for having lied.

Significantly, the parallel is not the case for the cheating student. If later charged with lying, she cannot claim to have merely been joking, speaking unseriously, or the like. In particular, even though the cheating student *can* admit later on that she only said what she said in order not to get punished, someone can equally well point out that, even so, she lied.

3.8. Proposing and Intending

The case of the Confused Politician shows that assertion, and hence lying, do not require that what one says in fact becomes common ground. In neither of the two scenarios does what the politician says become common ground, but that does not mean that she is not lying in the case where she gives her serious speech.

It is important to emphasize that something weaker is true, on the Stalnakerian view I am assuming. In particular, lying, and hence assertion, does not require that the speaker *believes* or *expects* that what she says will become common ground. You can lie even if you know that what you say will be rejected by your audience. This is another reason for characterizing assertion and lying in terms of proposing to update the common ground with what is said.

This point is emphasized by Stalnaker:

A person may make an assertion knowing it will be rejected just as Congress may pass a law knowing it will be vetoed, a labor negotiator may make a proposal knowing it will be met by a counterproposal, or a poker player may place a bet knowing it will cause all the other players to fold.   (Stalnaker, 1999 [1978], 87)

Further, Stalnaker points out that this means that assertion cannot be characterized in terms of *intentions* to update the common ground:

> My suggestion about the essential effect of assertion does not imply that speakers INTEND to succeed in getting the addressee to accept the content of the assertion, or that they believe they will, or even might succeed. (Stalnaker, 1999 [1978], 87)

As we saw in Chapter 1, most philosophers accept some version of the principle we called the Belief-Intention Constraint, that is, the idea that one cannot intend to do something that one does not believe one can do. Correspondingly, one cannot intend to make people accept one's statement if one knows one will not succeed.

Some critics of Stalnaker have objected that this view does not succeed in ensuring that one can make an assertion even when one knows it will be rejected. Mikhail Kissine argues that Stalnaker's example of the negotiator, quoted above, does not show what it is supposed to show. He writes:

> [E]ven though the negotiator expects his proposal to be met with a counter-proposal, such an expectation presupposes that he also expects that his intention to make the proposal will succeed, for only if a proposal is made can the other party put a counter-proposal on the table. (Kissine, 2013, 66)

However, the Stalnakerian can, and should, *agree* with this. In particular, in the case of assertion, we should agree that someone who makes an assertion while knowing that it will be rejected still intends to make the assertion.

The crucial point is that, given the Stalnakerian view, to intend to make an assertion is *not* to intend that its content become common ground. Rather, to intend to make an assertion is to intend to *propose that* its content become common ground. Kissine's objection conflates these two different kinds of intentions. This is evident from his further remarks. He says:

> recall that according to Stalnaker asserting *is* attempting to add the propositional content to s [i.e. the common ground]. It follows that if S's intended effect in uttering a sentence with the content p is not to augment s with p, by definition what she intends is not to perform an assertion that p. (Kissine, 2013, 66)

Kissine is right that the Stalnakerian view is that asserting is attempting—in our terminology, proposing—to add the contents of the assertion to the common ground. But it does not follow from this that you intend to assert that p only if you intend to add p to the common ground. What follows is that you intend to assert that p only if you intend to propose (or attempt) to add p to the common ground. In other words, what follows from the Stalnakerian view is that if the speaker does not intend to propose p for common ground uptake, she is not making an assertion.

More generally, to assert that p, on the view I favor, is not to make p common ground, even though asserting that p typically has the effect of making p common ground. Rather, to assert that p is to put p forward for the common ground. Correspondingly, when someone speaks ironically, or is winking an eye, what they are signaling is that they are not putting what they say forward in that way, that is, they are not proposing that what they say become common ground.

3.9. Support Potential and Propriety

It is worth commenting more on what is involved in proposing to add information to the common ground. In particular, in this connection, it is important to bring out some features of what it means for information to be common ground, as this is understood here. To do so, it is useful to look at situations where it might at first sight look like the speaker is not proposing that what she says become common ground, while at closer examination that is not in fact a plausible description of the conversation.

One such situation has been described by Don Fallis (2013).[14] He gives the following example:

> In a deserted parking garage in our nation's capital, a devious Deep Throat attempts to mislead a journalist by saying, "I am saying this only to you. And I am going to say it only once. If you repeat it (or say anything that presupposes it), I will deny it. The Attorney-General himself was behind the cover-up."
>
> (Fallis, 2013, 350)

Fallis concludes:

> Deep Throat does not seem to be proposing that the claim that the Attorney-General was behind the cover-up be added to the common ground of the conversation. [. . .] Even so, Deep Throat seems to be lying as he knows that the Attorney-General was *not* behind the cover-up. (Fallis, 2013, 350–1)

---

[14] See also my reply in Stokke (2016b).

As this suggests, Fallis thinks that this kind of situation is a counter-example to my view of lying. According to him, the Deep Throat case shows that "while most liars propose that what they say be added to the common ground, we can imagine liars that do not." (Fallis, 2013, 350)

I agree that Deep Throat is lying in this case, and hence I agree that Deep Throat is making an assertion. But I do not agree that Deep Throat is not proposing to update the common ground with what he says. Deep Throat is making his utterance because he wants to communicate the information in question to the journalist. He wants the journalist to believe what he says, to use it in drawing inferences, and most likely he even hopes the journalist will tell other people. Typically, what speakers try to communicate to others in this sense, they try to make part of the conversational common ground, and typically they succeed in doing so.

Fallis acknowledges that Deep Throat's utterance of (9) has the effect of making what it says common ground.

(9)   The Attorney-General himself was behind the cover-up.

The main evidence for thinking that Deep Throat's utterance of (9) has the effect of making what it says common ground is the observation that, as a result of his utterance, it can felicitously be presupposed that the Attorney-General was behind the cover-up. It is worth stressing that, on the Stalnakerian view, that p can be felicitously presupposed is not a necessary condition on p being common ground. In particular, the fact that p is common ground does not guarantee that no one will object to p, if presupposed. Correspondingly, the fact that p is common ground is perfectly compatible with there being strong reasons not to say things that presuppose that p. However, there is a clear sense in which the fact that p can be felicitously presupposed is good evidence that p is common ground, on the Stalnakerian view.

Imagine that, in reply to Deep Throat's utterance of (9), the journalist asks the question in (10).

(10)   How did the Attorney-General arrange the cover-up?

Given the reasonable assumption that there is no relevant difference between being behind something and arranging it, in this case, this question presupposes what is asserted by (9). The question is felicitous as a response to Deep Throat's utterance. That a presuppositional utterance is felicitous means, at least, that it does not require the kind of repair strategies that are typically prompted by unfamiliar presuppositions.

There are two main types of such repair strategies. An unfamiliar presupposition can be accommodated, that is, it can be allowed to become common ground.[15] Alternatively, an unfamiliar presupposition can be questioned or rejected. The need for accommodating, rejecting, or questioning a presupposition is a sign that it was not common ground when the relevant utterance was made.

There is no intelligible sense in which Deep Throat can be said to have the option of accommodating what is presupposed by (10). To be sure, the journalist's question might make Deep Throat believe that the journalist believes, or at least accepts for present purposes, that the Attorney-General was behind the cover-up. In general, hearing someone presuppose what one has previously asserted is an indication that what one asserted has become common ground. But even if one's beliefs about what is common ground change as a result, such a process is not to be confused with the process of accommodation. That is, the process by which a hearer accepts without comment a new presupposition she is presented with.

Yet it might be said that there is a sense in which Deep Throat can reject or question the presupposition that the Attorney-General was behind the cover-up. For example, Deep Throat might react to (10) with responses like those in (11).

> (11)   a. What are you talking about?
>   b. What makes you think the Attorney-General was involved?
>   c. He didn't.
>   d. I never said he did.

Indeed, it is natural to think that, in a situation like the one Fallis describes, Deep Throat would react to (10) in this way.

However, for Deep Throat to respond to (10) with replies like those in (11) involves a significant degree of *pretense*. The familiar kind of stony, poker-faced effect of replies of this sort arguably owes a lot to this

---

[15] The notion of accommodation was introduced by Lewis (1979). See Stalnaker (1999 [1998]) and von Fintel (2008) for details about accommodation in a Stalnakerian framework.

feature. By contrast, no pretense is needed for questioning or rejecting a presupposition in standard cases.

The fact that one can react to a presupposition by pretending that it is not already common ground is not evidence that it did not become common ground when it was originally introduced. So we have strong reasons to think that what Deep Throat tells the journalist becomes common ground, as witnessed by the fact that it can felicitously be presupposed in subsequent conversation.

Yet Fallis does not think that the fact that what Deep Throat says becomes common ground vindicates the common ground account of lying. He writes:

> However, even if the information does affect the future progress of the conversation in this way, that does not show that Deep Throat is *proposing* that it be added to the common ground. This sort of reply from the journalist [i.e. (10)] is precisely what Deep Throat was trying to prevent.   (Fallis, 2013, 351)

Why would one think, as Fallis does, that Deep Throat is signaling that he is not proposing that what he says become common ground? One reason might be the thought that proposing that what one says become common ground involves agreeing to others repeating it or saying things that presuppose it. There is a sense in which this is true. Making something common ground makes it possible for others to repeat it or to say things that presuppose it without thereby triggering surprise or requiring repair. Call this the *support potential* of common ground information. Common ground information has support potential in discourse in the sense that it can be repeated or presupposed without the need for repair.

It is important to note that the fact that common ground information has support potential does not imply anything concerning the *propriety*, broadly construed, of repeating such information or saying things that presuppose it. The fact that something is common ground means that one can felicitously repeat it or say things that presuppose it. But, as noted earlier, that does not rule out that there may be reasons not to do so. For example, doing so might be imprudent, it might be disrespectful or impolite, it might be uninteresting, it might be morally problematic, or there might be still other considerations against it.

Correspondingly, proposing to make something common ground is compatible with forewarning others of the impropriety of repeating it or saying things that presuppose it. One can tell a friend or a spouse about a medical condition because one wants someone to know about it in case of an emergency, while at the same time explicitly requesting that it not be talked about again.

Hence, the fact that Deep Throat warns the journalist against repeating what he tells him, and against saying things that presuppose it, does not show that Deep Throat is not proposing to make what he says common ground. Another way to put this is to say that Deep Throat gives the journalist a reason not to repeat or presuppose what he tells him during their subsequent conversation. Indeed, it is natural to think that it would be imprudent for the journalist to do so. Perhaps there are even moral considerations against it. But this in no way implies that Deep Throat is not proposing to update the common ground of the conversation with what he is telling the journalist.

Another potential way of motivating Fallis's claim is to emphasize the fact that Deep Throat declares that, if repeated or presupposed, he will deny what he tells the journalist. We have already seen that for Deep Throat to later deny what he tells the journalist requires him to pretend that it did not become common ground when he said it. But an explicit decision to later pretend that what he says is not common ground does not show that Deep Throat is not putting that information forward for the common ground in the first place.

Just as there may be reasons for not repeating something that is common ground or saying things that presuppose it, there may be reasons for pretending that something is not common ground should someone repeat or presuppose it. Stalnaker emphasizes the point that there may be considerations that require one to engage in pretense of this kind:

> If one is talking for some other purpose than to exchange information, or if one must be polite, discreet, diplomatic, kind, or entertaining as well as informative, then one may have reason to act as if the common background were different than one in fact knows it to be.   (Stalnaker, 1999 [1974], 51)

Similarly, it is easy to see why Deep Throat would need to pretend that it is not common ground that the Attorney-General was behind the cover-up, should the journalist bring this up again. But that does not mean that he was not trying to make that information common ground when he said it.

We should not be surprised, therefore, that there might be reasons for pretending that something one has previously proposed to make common ground is not in fact part of the mutual background information of the conversation. Moreover, one might be aware of such reasons prior to making one's statement in the first place, and one might explicitly let others know that one will act on them. But none of this implies that one is not proposing to make the relevant information common ground when saying it.

Proposing to make something common ground is merely to propose that it be added to the stock of background information with support potential. But doing so is compatible with being aware of, and making explicit, reasons concerning the impropriety of subsequent reiterations of the information one contributes. And it is compatible with forewarning others that, given such reiterations, one will feign unfamiliarity with what one is proposing to make common ground.

3.10. Metaphor

Another potential objection to my account of lying in terms of Stalnakerian common ground is that it fails to give the right results concerning non-literal speech. Jessica Keiser (2015) has argued that:

> acceptance is too weak a notion to ground the distinction between lying and non-literal speech. Since acceptance of p does not involve believing p, it is unclear how the provided definition is going to be able to rule out certain cases of non-literal speech as instances of lying. (Keiser, 2015, §5.2)

The core of this worry is that there are cases of non-literal speech where information that is believed to be false is made common ground. Hence, so the complaint goes, all such utterances will count as lies, on my view.

For example, according to this objection, when someone uses a metaphor, disbelieved information becomes common ground, and hence such utterances will invariably count as lies. This would be a serious problem, since whether or not one thinks that it is possible to lie with a metaphor, one surely does not want to accept that metaphors are always lies. However, as we will see below, this blanket judgment on metaphorical speech is not a consequence of the common ground view of lying.

For concreteness, take Grice's (1989, 34) example in (12).

(12)   You're the cream in my coffee.

According to my view of lying, you lie when you say something you believe to be false and thereby propose to make that thing common ground. Hence, my view invariably counts (12) as a lie only if the view is forced to accept that the following two claims are true for all instances of (12):

(a) The speaker of (12) says that the addressee is the cream in her coffee.

(b) By saying that the addressee is the cream in her coffee, the speaker of (12) proposes to make it common ground that the addressee is the cream in her coffee.

First, consider (a). There are broadly two ways of thinking about metaphors in relation to what is said. The first is the classic Gricean view, according to which metaphors are instances of conversational implicatures, and in particular, cases in which the speaker says—or strictly speaking, for Grice, "makes as if to say"—something false in order to implicate something true.[16] As we noted in Chapter 2, on the Gricean view, these are cases in which the speaker flouts the First Maxim of Quality, "Do not say what you believe to be false."

The other school of thought is that the literal meaning of a metaphor is not said, and hence the metaphorical meaning is not something that is conveyed by way of a Gricean inference. Instead the metaphorical meaning is expressed directly as what is said, and is not arrived at via an antecedent literal interpretation.[17] For convenience, call the latter stance the "anti-Gricean" view of metaphors.

So, according to the Gricean view, the speaker of (12) literally says that the addressee is the cream in her coffee. In doing so, she flouts the First Maxim of Quality, thereby inviting the hearer to infer the metaphorical meaning—that is, that the speaker is fond of the addressee, or the like—as a conversational implicature. By contrast, according to the anti-Gricean view, the speaker of (12) directly expresses the metaphorical meaning as what is said by the utterance.

---

[16] See Grice (1989, 34). Note that, if one follows Grice's strong view of non-literal speech as cases in which the speaker merely "makes as if to say" the literal meaning of her utterance, my view straightaway is not saddled with (a). For discussion, see Neale (1992) and Stokke (2013).

[17] For relevant discussion, see, e.g. Sperber and Wilson (1981), Stern (2000), Bach (2001), Bezuidenhout (2001), Camp (2011), Saul (2012).

As we will see next, regardless of which of these two views of metaphor is right, my theory of lying is not forced to accept both (a) and (b).

If the anti-Gricean view of metaphor is right, then (a) is false. If the speaker of (12) does not say the false literal meaning of her utterance, my theory of lying does not automatically count metaphorical utterances as lies. Still, if the metaphorical meaning of utterances like (12) is said by the speaker, my theory of lying does count such utterances as lies if the speaker believes the metaphorical meaning to be false. For instance, (12) will be a lie if the speaker is aware of not being fond of the addressee. Whether or not this is the right result is an open question—namely, the question of whether one can lie with metaphors or not.[18] But what we wanted to establish was that my theory does not *invariably* count metaphorical utterances as lies. Given an anti-Gricean view of metaphor, it does not.

On the other hand, if the Gricean view of metaphor is right, then (a) is true. But (b) is not. What is proposed for common ground uptake by an utterance of (12), in the right context, is not that the addressee is (literally) the cream in the speaker's coffee. Hence, on my view, even if the literal meaning of metaphorical utterances is said, it is not asserted. The whole point of uttering (12) is to communicate something else, for example, that the speaker is fond of the addressee. This may or may not be what the speaker takes to be the truth about her sentiments toward the addressee. But either way, she is not lying, since, on the Gricean view, the metaphorical meaning is not said. Even if the speaker is using (12) to communicate something she believes to be false, such an utterance will be a case of merely implicating disbelieved information.

To corroborate the suggestion that the literal meaning of metaphorical utterances does not become common ground—even in the sense of being accepted for the purpose of the conversation—we can note that it cannot subsequently be felicitously presupposed. Suppose, for example, that Mona utters (12) to Jack, but that Jack does not hear her. Then consider the following utterance by one bystander to another both of whom did hear the utterance, and both of whom know that the other one heard it, etc.

(13)   #Jack doesn't realize that Mona thinks he's a dairy product.

[18] For discussion, see Saul (2012) and Fallis (2014b).

The only way to hear this utterance is as a joke. By contrast, unsurprisingly, the metaphorical meaning can be felicitously presupposed, as illustrated by (14).

(14)   Jack doesn't realize that Mona is crazy about him.

Since (14) felicitously presupposes that Mona is crazy about Jack, this is evidence that the metaphorical meaning of (12) becomes common ground, when uttered in normal contexts.

Moreover, one can keep talking in the same metaphorical terms once a metaphorical utterance has been made. For example, the following utterance is also felicitous:

(15)   Jack doesn't realize that Mona thinks he's the cream in her coffee.

However, the felicity of (15) does not support the claim that the literal meaning of (12) becomes common ground. What is presupposed by (15) is the metaphorical meaning of "Mona thinks he's the cream in her coffee."[19] That is, on the relevant reading, (15) does not presuppose that Mona thinks Jack is a dairy product. The infelicity of this kind of presupposition is demonstrated by (13). The felicity of (15), therefore, does not support the suggestion that the literal meaning of (12) becomes common ground. And moreover, the fact that common ground information is characterized in terms of (belief about) what is accepted does not prevent the Stalnakerian from accepting these facts.

So, to sum up, the common ground view of discourse does not have to accept that the literal meaning of metaphorical utterances becomes common ground, regardless of whether one's view of metaphors implies that the literal meaning is said or not.

3.11. Malapropism

Whether or not one is sympathetic to the Gricean view of metaphor, it is hard to deny that we often speak in a way that aims at making common

---

[19] The fact that metaphorical meaning survives embeddings—as in this case, under attitudes—is one major piece of evidence against the Gricean view of metaphors as cases of (particularized) conversational implicatures. As noted, if the Gricean view is wrong, my view of lying has an even easier time not counting all metaphorical utterances as lies.

ground information that diverges from what is said by our utterance. We have already looked at irony as a key instance of this. I want to end this chapter by noting that our account handles other cases of this kind, too. One such type involves *malapropism*.

As discussed by Marga Reimer (2004) and Roy Sorensen (2011), malapropism gives rise to cases in which speakers arguably say things they do not intend to say. Indeed, in cases of malapropism, speakers may say things they do not believe and still intuitively they are not lying. For example, suppose that Dave, who is mistaken about the conventional meaning of *suppository*, utters:

(16)   The library is a suppository of wisdom.

Following Reimer (2004), I assume that in this case Dave *says* that the library is a suppository of wisdom.[20] Yet, Dave does not believe this proposition. Hence, it might seem that his utterance will be counted as a lie on our account. But, intuitively, while Dave is misspeaking, he is not lying.

However, the proponent of the Common Ground Definition of Lying is not committed to this verdict on the case. In fact, there is a natural way of avoiding it. It is intuitively compelling to describe Dave's utterance as a case in which what the speaker said was not what she proposed to make common ground. The information that Dave hopes will become common ground as a result of his utterance is not that the library is a suppository of wisdom, but, presumably, that the library is a repository of wisdom. So, while the former proposition is what he said, it is not the one that is relevant for evaluating whether he is lying.

There are also cases of malapropism in which the speaker says something she does believe. Consider, for example, (17), which was allegedly uttered by Al Gore in an attack on President Bush.[21]

(17)   A zebra does not change its spots.

---

[20] The contrary view was held by Davidson (1986).

[21] The story is widely circulated, sometimes with the quote being, "We all know the leopard can't change his stripes." The latter version can illustrate the same point I make with respect to the zebra version. Either way, the story that Gore ever said something along these lines may be apocryphal.

Since what Gore said is trivially true (because zebras do not have spots), Gore does believe what he said. Yet, Gore might have intended to mislead with his utterance.

Our proposal handles this type of case, as well. Abstracting away from the further complication of Gore's use of metaphorical language, whether he is being misleading or not arguably turns on whether he believes the proposition that a leopard does not change its spots (or perhaps the proposition metaphorically associated with it, or the like.) And correspondingly this is the proposition that is most naturally taken to be what Gore proposed to make common ground, despite what he said. And since the proposition he proposes for the common ground in this case is one that he believes (we may assume), he does not count as being misleading.

To be sure, cases like this are very likely to result in what Stalnaker (1999 [1978], 85) calls a "defective" common ground. Particularly, if the hearer is not aware of the speaker's mistaken grasp of the meanings of the words she is using, it is likely that the hearer's beliefs about what is proposed for the common ground will be false, and hence what the hearer will take to be common ground is not what the speaker will take to be common ground. Yet, it is simply a further advantage of the common ground framework that it provides an intuitively plausible way of analyzing complex cases of this kind.

4

What is Said

We have seen that my definition of lying relies on two central notions, namely the notion of common ground in (L2) and the notion of what is said in (L1).

The Common Ground Definition of Lying
A lies to B if and only if there is a proposition p such that

(L1)   A says that p to B, and
(L2)   A proposes to make it common ground that p, and
(L3)   A believes that p is false.

In Chapter 3, I fleshed out the notion of common ground involved in (L2). In this chapter I will propose a theory of the notion of what is said on which (L1) relies.

4.1. Lying and Misleading

One important purpose of clauses such as (L1) in characterizations of lying is to rule out various forms of non-linguistic deception, such as Kant's (1997 [1784–5]) often-cited example of packing your bags in front of someone else in order to deceive them into thinking you are going on a trip.[1] But although actions like these are intended to deceive, they are not lies. (L1) rules them out insofar as they do not involve saying the things they are designed to make people believe. Packing your bags in front of someone else might deceive them into thinking that you are going on a trip, but you have not lied unless you *say* that you are going on a trip.

Furthermore, theories of lying typically rely on the possibility of specifying the notion of saying (or some relative of it) so as to avoid

---

[1] See Kant (1997 [1784–5], 202–3). Cf. Fallis (2009, 37–8), Mahon (2009, 204).

counting as lies utterances that are misleading, or deceptive, but not lies. The classic contrast between lying and merely misleading speech is the contrast between asserting or saying something one believes to be false vs. asserting or saying something one believes to be true in order to conversationally implicate something one believes to be false.[2]

Take, for instance, the story of Abraham and the king from Chapter 2. As we saw, most philosophers since Augustine (1952 [395]a) have held that Abraham's utterance of (2), referring to Sarah, was not a lie.

(1) She is my sister.

But even though Abraham did not lie, he was clearly being misleading; indeed, to mislead the king into thinking that Sarah was not his wife was the purpose of his utterance of (2). As we noted, the reason Abraham did not lie, while he was being misleading, is that although Abraham conversationally implicated disbelieved information, that is, that Sarah is not his wife, what he *said* was merely that Sarah is his sister, which is something he knows to be true. Here is another example. Consider the following situation and the contrast between the dialogues in (1) and (2).[3]

Work
Dennis is going to Paul's party tonight. He has a long day of work ahead of him before that, but he is very excited and can't wait to get there. Dennis's annoying friend, Rebecca, comes up to him and starts talking to him about the party. Dennis is fairly sure that Rebecca won't go unless she thinks he's going, too.

(2) **Rebecca.** Are you going to Paul's party?
     Dennis. No, I'm not going to Paul's party.

(3) **Rebecca.** Are you going to Paul's party?
     Dennis. I have to work.

---

[2] It is worth noting that a similar distinction can be drawn for the realm of non-linguistic insincerity. Suppose, for example, that you have a friend who looks exactly like Gordon Ramsey. Your friend approaches a company that produces frozen dinners and agrees to have them put his picture on their boxes with a legend that says, "I recommend!" This might be thought to be a non-linguistic parallel of the contrast between lying and merely misleading. Thanks to Renaud Gagné for this example.

[3] Adapted from Davis (2010).

In both cases Dennis conveys the misleading information that he is not going to Paul's party. But while Dennis's utterance in (1) is a lie, his utterance in (2) is not a lie.

This distinction between lying and merely misleading is important to us. We often take pains to stay on the right side of it in everyday matters. We build it into law codes, and it is a basic distinction in many religious systems of belief. There are famous cases of presidents and saints having exploited the difference dexterously, as do the rest of us with varying degrees of regret.

As the 1865 vote on the 13th Amendment was due to take place, Confederate representatives were traveling north for peace negotiations. On January 31, James Ashley wrote to Lincoln: "The report is in circulation in the House that Peace Commissioners are on their way or are in the city, and is being used against us. If it is true, I fear we shall loose [sic] the bill. Please authorize me to contradict it, if not true." Lincoln wrote back: "So far as I know, there are no peace commissioners in the city or likely to be in it."[4] In fact, the commissioners were on their way not to Washington, but to Fort Monroe, where Lincoln met them a few days later. Or consider the often-cited case of Saint Athanasius who, when asked by pursuers sent by the Emperor Julian to persecute him, "Where is the traitor Athanasius?", replied, "He's not far away."[5]

4.2. Direct and Indirect Deception

Writers on lying often use *mislead* and *deceive* interchangeably, and sometimes the distinction we have just noted is described as a difference between lying and other forms of linguistic deception, or the like. I follow this practice insofar as I will not be concerned with proposing distinctions in meaning between these words. (I tend to use *mislead, misleading,* etc. when speaking of the contrast between lying and deceptive speech that is not lying.)

Rather, what is important is to capture the distinction between the two different phenomena we noted above. Considering our examples,

---

[4] See Lincoln (1953 [1865]).

[5] See, e.g. Williams (2002, 102) who quotes a version on which Athanasius's reply is, "Not far away." I include the pronoun because it allows me to discuss ways of misleading with the person features of pronouns. See also MacIntyre (1995, 336).

a natural thought is that what distinguishes lies from utterances that are misleading but not lies is that the former convey misleading information with a certain kind of directness or explicitness. Accordingly, the standard approach has been to argue that lying involves *saying* something misleading, as opposed to conveying it in some other, more indirect way. Similarly, (L1) in my definition of lying is intended to rule out utterances that are misleading but not lies.

Put differently, the difference is between, on the one hand, utterances that are intended to deceive about what they say, and on the other hand, utterances that are intended to deceive about something they do not say. Let us call the first kind of deception *direct* and the second *indirect*. We can spell out this difference as follows:

Direct Deception
In making an utterance u, a speaker S is directly deceptive if and only if u says that p and S intends to deceive with respect to p.

Indirect Deception
In making an utterance u, a speaker S is indirectly deceptive if and only if u communicates that p, p is not said by u, and S intends to deceive with respect to p.

By intending to deceive with respect to a proposition p I mean being deceptive with respect to p in one or more of Chisholm's and Feehan's (1977) eight ways of deceiving someone, which we looked at in Chapter 1. By an utterance communicating that p, I mean that making u involves proposing to make p common ground, in the sense of Chapter 3.

Consider how paradigmatic cases of deceptive lies work. For example, Dennis's reply in (1) says that he is not going to Paul's party, and that is the proposition with respect to which he wants to deceive, i.e. that is the disbelieved information he wants Rebecca to believe. Hence, on our way of speaking, Dennis is being directly deceptive in (1).

By contrast, Dennis's reply in (2) says that he has to work, which is something he knows is true. This is why we think Dennis is not lying, in this case, and moreover, he is not being directly deceptive. Nevertheless in virtue of saying that he has to work, he wants to deceive Rebecca with respect to another proposition, namely the proposition that he is going to the party. Hence, in (2) Dennis is being indirectly deceptive. Such indirectly deceptive utterances are what we also call *merely misleading* utterances.

Sometimes utterances are both directly and indirectly deceptive. One may say something one believes to be false in order to implicate something else that one also believes to be false. For example, suppose that Dennis knows that he does not have to work at all. In that case he is clearly lying if he tells Rebecca, "I have to work." This lie is a classic, directly deceptive lie, since it is intended to make Rebecca believe what is said. But the utterance is also intended to convey to her the further false information that Dennis is not going to the party, and hence the utterance is also indirectly deceptive.

In more intricate cases, a lie can be indirectly, but not directly deceptive. Here is an example that Don Fallis gives:

> A crime boss, Tony, has discovered that one of his henchmen, Sal, has become an FBI informant. But Tony does not want Sal to find out that his treachery has been uncovered. So, to keep his disloyal henchman at ease, Tony says with pride to Sal one day, "I have a really good organization here. There are no rats in my organization." (Fallis, 2010, 9)

Tony's utterance is a lie. What he says is something he believes to be false. But he does not intend to deceive Sal about what he says. That is, Tony does not intend Sal to believe that there are no rats. Tony knows that Sal knows that there are rats. After all, Tony knows that Sal is himself a rat. So Tony's lie is not directly deceptive. But the lie is nevertheless indirectly deceptive. It is intended to deceive Sal into thinking that Tony does not think there are any rats. So there is a proposition—namely, that Tony believes there are no rats—with respect to which the lie is intended to deceive.

By contrast, a bald-faced lie, such as the one the cheating student tells the Dean, is neither directly nor indirectly deceptive. As we said in Chapter 1, we can imagine situations in which the student lies to the Dean but does not intend to deceive the Dean about *anything*. Here is another example, from the movie *The Godfather: Part II* (Paramount Pictures, 1974):[6]

Pentangeli
Frank Pentangeli is interrogated about the Corleone family in a senatorial hearing. Pentangeli has given a written statement of his knowledge

---

[6] Also cited by Keiser (2015, §2).

of the crimes of Michael Corleone, and it is clear to everyone that he has been intimately involved with the godfather for a long time. But during the hearing, the Corleones bring in Pentangeli's brother as an audience member. When Frank sees this, he is disheartened. So he suddenly answers one of the questions with the undisguised lie,

(4)   I never knew no godfather.

Pentangeli is not intending to deceive anyone about what he says. But nor is he intending to deceive anyone about anything else, for example, about what he believes. Pentangeli's lie is therefore neither directly nor indirectly deceptive. Bald-faced lies are purely non-deceptive.

The notion of indirect deception we have spelled out above is deliberately broad. In particular, it allows that an utterance may be indirectly deceptive about things that are completely unrelated to the contents of the utterance. This is appropriate. For example, someone skilled enough might change the tone of their voice in order to convey false information about themselves. Suppose, for instance, that a male salesperson is hired to call people and try to sell them a line of women's underwear. Imagine that studies have found that customers are more likely to buy the underwear if a woman calls. If the salesperson is skilled enough, he might change his voice in order to deceive the customers into thinking he is a woman. In doing so, he would clearly be intending to deceive the customers. On our account, he would be indirectly deceptive.

In this way, utterances can be indirectly deceptive, even if they do not say anything at all. In particular, we will see that non-declarative utterances, such as questions and orders, can be misleading, even though they cannot be lies, since they do not say things.

4.3. Inquiry and Discourse Structure

In order to have a full characterization of the difference between lying and merely misleading, we need a precise way of understanding the notion of what is said. The main goal of this chapter is to provide a detailed theory of this kind. But unlike previous approaches, on my view, what is said will be sensitive to *discourse structure*. More plainly, on my view, whether or not you have said that p sometimes depends on the state of the conversation you are engaged in.

In particular, I will argue that whether an utterance is a lie or is merely misleading depends on the topic of conversation, understood as the *question under discussion* (henceforth, QUD) in the sense of Craige Roberts (2004), (2012). More specifically, according to this view, what is said by a sentence in a context is the answer that it provides to a relevant question that is antecedently accepted as the topic of discussion.[7] In the tradition from Stalnaker (1999 [1978]), (1984), (1999 [1998]), (2002), a discourse is taken to be a cooperative activity of information exchange aimed at the *goal of inquiry*, that is, to discover how things are. In this setting a QUD is a subinquiry, that is, a strategy for approaching the goal of inquiry.

I propose that to mislead is to disrupt the pursuit of the goal of inquiry, that is, to prevent the progress of inquiry from approaching the discovery of how things are. On the view I will argue for, the difference between whether doing so counts as lying or as merely misleading depends on how one's utterance relates to the QUD one is addressing.

We will see in this chapter that, once we look beyond classic cases like those above, we need discourse-sensitive notions of saying and asserting in order to capture the difference between lying and merely misleading. Some accounts of the lying–misleading distinction, like the one put forward by Jennifer Saul (2012), allow what is said to go beyond what is linguistically encoded by an utterance. Yet, as we will see, such views are still unable to account for the way the distinction depends on the state of the discourse.

The view of what is said I defend agrees that what is said may go beyond linguistically encoded meaning. Yet I argue that what is said is nevertheless strictly constrained by a minimal kind of compositional meaning. As a result, on this view, what is said by a sentence in a context is determined systematically by the linguistic meaning of the sentence and the configuration of QUDs in the context.

4.4. Committing to Misleading Answers

Consider the following story:[8]

Christmas Party

At an office Christmas party, William's ex-wife, Doris, got very drunk and ended up insulting her boss, Sean. Nevertheless, Sean took the

---

[7] This view was defended in Stokke (2016a), Schoubye and Stokke (2016).
[8] This example was first mentioned to me by Anders Schoubye.

incident lightly, and their friendly relationship continued unblemished. More recently, the company was sold, and Doris lost her job in a round of general cutbacks. But, despite this, Doris and Sean have remained friends. Sometime later, William is talking to Elizabeth, who is interested in hiring Doris. However, William is still resentful of Doris and does not want Elizabeth to give her a job.

(5)   **Elizabeth.** Why did Doris lose her job?
       William. She insulted Sean at a party.

(6)   **Elizabeth.** How is Doris's relationship with Sean?
       William. She insulted him at a party.

I think that William's utterance in (5) is a lie and that his utterance in (6) is not a lie, even though it is clearly misleading.[9] The reason for the difference seems clear. In both cases William's utterance provides a misleading answer to the question it is addressing. In the first case it provides the answer that the reason Doris lost her job was that she insulted Sean at a party. In the second case it provides the answer that her relationship with Sean is not good. Yet we have a strong sense that, whereas in the first case the answer is provided directly, or explicitly, in the second case the misleading answer is supplied indirectly, or implicitly.

At the same time, the only substantial difference between the dialogues in (5) and (6) is which question is being addressed. So the same utterance (*modulo* the pronoun) is, in one case, a lie and, in the other case, merely misleading. This suggests that the difference between lying and merely misleading is sensitive to previous discourse structure, and in particular to the topic of conversation, or QUD. In other words, whether you lie

---

[9] I use "utterance" to mean what Stanley and Szabó (2000, 77–8) call "grammatical sentence", that is, roughly, disambiguated phonological form (or the equivalent, for written sentences.) Hence, an utterance, in this sense, does not include pragmatic enrichments or implicatures, and does not include saturation of indexicals such as the pronouns, demonstratives, or indexical adverbs of space and time. An utterance, in this sense, is not identical to what I call *minimal content*, since the latter includes saturation of indexicals. In terms of the account I propose, utterances, on this terminology, determine minimal contents, in context, which in turn determine what is said, given a QUD. I allow myself to not strictly distinguish between utterance tokens and utterance types, and I do not always distinguish between "an utterance" in the sense of an act and in the sense of the object of such an act. By locutions such as *a's utterance u was a lie* I mean that *a* lied by making *u*.

or merely mislead depends on which question you are interpreted as addressing.

These observations can be corroborated by considering possible continuations of the discourses. In general, it is characteristic of utterances that are misleading but not lies that one can subsequently retreat from the misleading information one conveys. That is, one can deny that one intended to convey the relevant misleading information, while this does not involve retracting one's utterance completely. Correspondingly, when one is lying, one is typically committed to the misleading information one conveys in a particular sense.[10] Part of the reason the contrast between assertion and conversational implicature has typically been used to exemplify the difference between lying and merely misleading is arguably that it represents a contrast between a committing and a less committing way of communicating.

To illustrate, consider the continuations of our previous examples in (1') and (2').

(1') **Rebecca.** Are you going to Paul's party?
      Dennis. No, I'm not going to Paul's party.
      Rebecca. Oh, don't you think he'll be disappointed?
      Dennis. #No, I'm going to the party.

(2') **Rebecca.** Are you going to Paul's party?
      Dennis. I have to work.
      Rebecca. Oh, don't you think he'll be disappointed?
      Dennis. No, I just meant I have to work now.

In both cases Dennis's initial utterance conveys the misleading information that he is not going to the party. When this is done by lying, as in (1'), the speaker is committed to this information, as witnessed by the infelicity of attempting to retreat from it in subsequent discourse. By contrast, when misleading while avoiding outright lying, as in (2'), the speaker is not so committed in that he can subsequently retreat from the misleading information.[11]

---

[10] I am not suggesting that the impossibility of retreating in the way illustrated in the text is either necessary or sufficient for having lied, but merely that such impossibility is good evidence.

[11] Given that the contrast between (1) and (2) is the contrast between assertion and conversational implicature, this is just the standard observation that conversational implicatures are cancellable. However, the fact that misleading (vs. lying) in general allows for

It is important to emphasize that we are not claiming that retreating subsequent to having been merely misleading is not, in an obvious sense, marked or infelicitous. For instance, by the retreat in (2'), Dennis openly signals having been uncooperative in the preceding discourse, so it is not surprising that his response is seen as annoying, exasperating, or the like. Yet the contrast with the corresponding response in (1') is clear.

As noted earlier, misleading while avoiding lying typically correlates with the possibility of subsequently claiming that one did not intend to convey the relevant disbelieved information—however obnoxious doing so may be. By contrast, lying typically correlates with a marked unintelligibility of this kind of subsequent retreat. I take this as evidence that lying involves commitment to the misleading information one conveys, whereas this type of commitment is avoided by utterances that are misleading but not lies.

This pattern is borne out by our case from above. Consider the continuations in (5') and (6').

(5')   **Elizabeth**. Why did Doris lose her job?
       William. She insulted Sean at a party.
       Elizabeth. Oh, so he fired her because of that?
       William. #No, that wasn't the reason.

(6')   **Elizabeth**. How is Doris's relationship with Sean?
       William. She insulted him at a party.
       Elizabeth. Oh, so they're not on good terms?
       William. No, they're still friends.

As before, the retreat in (6') is clearly seen as annoying due to its signaling that the speaker has previously been uncooperative. Yet, again, the contrast with (5') is clear. In (5') there is no possibility for the speaker to claim that he did not intend to convey the misleading information that Doris lost her job because she insulted Sean at a party.[12] In other words,

cancellation, or retreat, does not mean that misleading is always a matter of conversationally implicating disbelieved information. Although cancellability is generally thought to be a necessary condition for a proposition to count as a conversational implicature, few would argue that it is a sufficient one.

[12] The speaker can claim that he was not addressing the question that was asked, that is, that he was intending to contribute to a different topic of conversation. However, such a defense is tantamount to opting out of the conversation altogether. In particular, if William claims, in (5), that he was not addressing Elizabeth's question, this is significantly not analogous to cancelling the implicature in (6). In the latter case the reply is still claimed to

in (5'), William is committed to the misleading information he conveys. By contrast, in (6'), he is not committed to the misleading information he conveys, i.e. that their relationship is not good.

Another difference exhibited by classic cases of lying vs. merely misleading concerns the possibilities for denials by hearers. A lie can be met with an explicit denial, while a merely misleading utterance does not permit such denials, but typically requires questioning the speaker's intentions instead. This difference is illustrated by (1") and (2").

(1")   **Rebecca.** Are you going to Paul's party?
        Dennis. No, I'm not going to Paul's party.
        Monica. Yes, you are!

(2")   **Rebecca.** Are you going to Paul's party?
        Dennis. I have to work.
        Monica. #Yes, you are!/Wait, are you trying to make her believe you're not going?

The same difference is exhibited by (5) and (6), as shown below.

(5")   **Elizabeth.** Why did Doris lose her job?
        William. She insulted Sean at a party.
        Garry. No, that wasn't the reason!

(6")   **Elizabeth.** How is Doris's relationship with Sean?
        William. She insulted him at a party.
        Garry. #No, their relationship is fine!/Wait, are you trying to make her believe they're not on good terms?

I think this is sufficient to group (5) with (1), and (6) with (2), with respect to the lying–misleading distinction. Dennis's utterance in (5) involves the same kind of committing mode of communicating as in classic cases of lying. By contrast, in (6), the speaker does not incur such a commitment.

I conclude that the case of (5)–(6) shows that the difference between lying and merely misleading sometimes depends on whether the speaker commits herself to a misleading answer to a question she is addressing. Next, we will see that this kind of question-sensitivity also occurs in cases involving incompleteness.

---

have been intended to be relevant to the question, although what it was most naturally taken as contributing is claimed to have been unintended. By contrast, to claim, in (5), that one was not addressing the question is to claim that one was not taking part in the conversation at all. I am not concerned with such anomalous cases here.

4.5. Exploiting Incompleteness

As pointed out by Saul (2012), one can sometimes exploit particular kinds of incompleteness in navigating the lying–misleading distinction. Here is an example:

Logic Book
Larry is keen on making himself seem attractive to Norma. He knows she's interested in logic—a subject he himself knows nothing about. From talking to her, Larry has become aware that Norma knows that he has just finished writing a book, although she doesn't know what it's about. In fact, the book Larry wrote is about cats. Recently, Larry also joined an academic book club where the members are each assigned a particular book to read and explain to the others. Larry has been assigned a book about logic. But he hasn't even opened it.

(7)   **Norma.** What's the topic of the book you wrote?
  Larry. My book is about logic.

(8)   **Norma.** Do you know a lot about logic?
  Larry. My book is about logic.

I think Larry's utterance in (7) is a lie, while his utterance in (8) is merely misleading. Moreover, it is natural to say that the reason is that, whereas in both cases Larry's utterance conveys the misleading information that he wrote a book about logic, only in the first case does this information constitute a direct answer to the question.

In support of these judgments we can consider continuations of the dialogues, as in (5') and (6').

(5')   **Norma.** What's the topic of the book you wrote?
  Larry. My book is about logic.
  Norma. Oh, you wrote a book about logic?
  Larry. #No, I just meant that the book I'm assigned to read is about logic.

(6')   **Norma.** Do you know a lot about logic?
  Larry. My book is about logic.
  Norma. Oh, you wrote a book about logic?
  Larry. No, I just meant that the book I'm assigned to read is about logic.

As this shows, these cases behave in a manner parallel to the ones examined earlier. In (5') the speaker cannot claim that he did not intend to convey the relevant misleading information. By contrast, this is possible in (6'), although the speaker is again seen as uncooperative. As with the previous cases, lying correlates with commitment to the misleading information, while merely misleading does not. And again, the contrast between (5) and (6) suggests that whether the speaker incurs commitment of this kind turns on which question is being addressed.

Similarly, these cases exhibit the behavior we should expect with respect to the possibilities for denials by hearers, as illustrated by (5")–(6").

(5") **Norma.** What's the topic of the book you wrote?
      Larry. My book is about logic.
      Julie. No, the book you wrote is about cats!

(6") **Norma.** Do you know a lot about logic?
      Larry. My book is about logic.
      Julie. #No, you don't know anything about logic./Wait, are you trying to make her believe that you know a lot about logic?

As before, this is evidence that (5) behaves like classic cases of lying, as in (1), while (6) behaves like classic cases of merely misleading, as in (2). In other words, the case of (5)–(6) demonstrates that one can sometimes rely on semantic incompleteness in order to mislead, while avoiding outright lying.

4.6. The Need for a Discourse-Sensitive Account

The cases we have examined suggest that an account of the lying–misleading distinction that relies on notions of saying or asserting that are not sensitive to discourse structure is likely to be inadequate. Importantly, this is so even given accounts on which what is said is allowed to go beyond linguistically encoded meaning.

Such an account is provided by Saul (2012). Agreeing that lying requires saying something one believes to be false, Saul argues that what is said is constrained by the principle (NTE) below.

(NTE) A putative contextual contribution to what is said is a part of what is said only if without this contextually supplied material, S would not have a truth-evaluable semantic content in C.[13]

However, this principle is unable to account for examples such as (5). William's utterance is truth-evaluable without supplementation. It is true if and only if Doris insulted Sean at a party. Hence, (NTE) cannot count the utterace as *saying* that Doris lost her job because she insulted Sean at a party, and hence, Saul's account cannot agree with the judgment that the utterance is a lie. The reason is clear. Namely, (NTE) is not sensitive to discourse structure.

On the other hand a particular virtue of Saul's account is that it pays close attention to the semantics–pragmatics distinction, and as such is able to handle cases like (6).[14] Arguably, in this case, the speaker exploits the fact that his utterance allows for different completions. The most salient interpretation of his utterance is that Larry wrote a book about logic. Clearly this is the completion Larry hopes the hearer will fasten on, since it is the one that will in turn furnish an answer to the QUD, i.e. that he knows a lot about logic. At the same time, Larry is not committed to this contribution, and moreover there is a possible completion that he believes to be true. It is natural to think that this feature of the example is what exempts Larry from lying. As Saul's account makes explicit, one may avoid lying if one or more available completions are believed to be true.[15]

So, although Saul's account makes explicit the fact that what is said, in the sense that is relevant for the lying–misleading distinction, may go beyond what is linguistically encoded in a sentence, her view retains the traditional conception on which the sentence is the basic unit of analysis. Yet, as we have seen this picture is unable to account for the way in which the lying–misleading distinction depends on discourse structure.

More generally, we can take from this section two desiderata for our account of the lying–misleading distinction. First, it must be sensitive to discourse structure, and in particular, to QUDs. Second, it must take into

---

[13] Saul (2012b, 57). For discussion of this principle, see also Recanati (1993, 242), Bach (1994, 160–2). Saul (2012b, x) is explicit that her discussion of what is said does "not aim to show that any theory of saying is *the right theory* (or the wrong theory) of saying" but instead attempts to "discern which is the right theory of saying for a particular purpose—drawing the intuitive distinction between lying and misleading."

[14] By contrast, e.g. neither Adler (1997) nor Williams (2002) considers examples beyond the classic contrast between assertion and conversational implicature.

[15] See Saul (2012b, 65).

account the ways in which one can exploit incompleteness concerning what one can be construed as saying. In the rest of this chapter, I provide an account that meets these criteria.

4.7. Saying and Asserting

It will be useful to remind ourselves of the basic structure of my account of lying, which I set out in the beginning of Chapter 2. As advertised, my account endorses the commonly held view that to lie is to assert disbelieved information:

The Assertion-Based Definition of Lying
A lies to B if and only if there is a proposition p such that

(LA1)   A asserts that p to B, and
(LA2)   A believes that p is false.

In the tradition from Stalnaker (1999 [1970]), (1999 [1978]), (1984), (1999 [1998]), (2002), we think of a discourse as proceeding against a background of common ground information. Furthermore, a discourse, on this view, is directed toward the goal of inquiry—to discover how things are, or what the actual world is like—by incrementally collecting true information in the common ground.

As I have been emphasizing, I assume that assertion requires *saying* something, and that assertion requires proposing that what is said become common ground. We spelled this out as the necessary conditions on assertion in (A1)–(A2).

In uttering a sentence S, A asserts that p only if

(A1)   S says that p, and
(A2)   by uttering S, A proposes to make it common ground that p.

So, in asserting that p, a speaker makes an utterance that says that p and thereby proposes to make it common ground that p.[16]

We have already seen many reasons for distinguishing between what is said and what is asserted in this way. As we noted in Chapter 3, one standard consideration involves cases of irony. Consider again our example of an ironic utterance of (1).

---

[16] I use "sentence" to mean grammatical sentence, in the sense of footnote 9, this chapter.

(9) [Ironically] Oh yeah, *Titanic* is a great movie!

As I said in Chapter 2, on my view, an utterance of (1) *says* that the movie was great.[17] We will see that this is a consequence of the theory of what is said I propose. But, uncontroversially, an utterance of (1) does not assert that *Titanic* is a great movie. Hence, saying that *p* is not sufficient for asserting that *p*. Nor does an utterance of (1) assert that *Titanic* is not a great movie—even though to communicate this content is the point of the utterance. Hence, proposing to communicate that *p*, or to make it common ground that *p*, is not sufficient for asserting that *p*. Rather, assertion requires making a bid to add information to the common ground by saying it.

4.8. Questions under Discussion

The account of what is said I favor relies on the framework for understanding discourse structure developed by Roberts (2004), (2012). I now go on to set out the components of this framework.[18]

Roberts's central insight is that, to approach the Stalnakerian goal of inquiry, the discovery of how things are, "we must develop strategies for achieving this goal, and these strategies involve subinquiries."[19] Such subinquiries are aimed at answering questions that have been accepted as being under discussion.

There are two kinds of questions, those that can be answered by a yes or a no, and those that cannot. The first are *polar questions* like those in (10), the latter are *wh-questions*, also sometimes called *constituent* questions, as in (11).

---

[17] On some ways of using the notion of *saying*, this assumption is false. For example, as Neale (1992, 523) points out, "If *U* utters the sentence 'Bill is an honest man' ironically, on Grice's account *U* will not have said that Bill is an honest man: *U* will have made as if to say that Bill is an honest man." The reason for this is that on a Gricean understanding, saying that *p* is more akin to how we are understanding asserting that *p*. Such an account uses different notions to make similar distinctions, e.g. "making as if to say" vs. "saying," or the like.

[18] I am not concerned with giving an exhaustive summary of the details of this model of discourse structure, but just with providing the requisite background for the characterization of the notion of what is said that will generate my account of the lying–misleading distinction. Here I follow the presentation in Roberts (2012). A similar framework was developed by Ginzburg (1995a), (1995b).

[19] Roberts (2012, 4).

(10) a. Is Mary working?
     b. Does Mary like peanuts?
     c. Is Mary in Rome?

(11) a. Who is working?
     b. What does Mary like?
     c. Where is Mary?

I adopt the semantics for questions given by Roberts (2012), which in turn draws on the works of Hamblin (1973), Karttunen (1977), Groenendijk and Stokhof (1984), and others. As on the account in Hamblin (1973), a question is taken to denote a set of propositions—intuitively, the set of its possible answers. We call these the *alternatives* of the question. Roughly, the set of alternatives for a question q is the set of propositions obtained from first abstracting over all the wh-elements in q, if any, and then applying the resulting property to each entity of the appropriate sort in the domain of the model.[20]

Consider, for example, the wh-question (11a). Abstracting over the wh-element *who* in (11a) yields the following property:

$$\lambda x.\ x \text{ is working}$$

Accordingly, the set of alternatives for (11a) is the set of propositions corresponding to

$$[\lambda x.\ x \text{ is working}](x)$$

for each x of the appropriate sort in the domain. Suppose the domain only contains Mary, Kelly, and Jim. Then the alternatives of (11a) will be the set corresponding to

$$[\lambda x.\ x \text{ is working}](\text{Mary})$$
$$[\lambda x.\ x \text{ is working}](\text{Kelly})$$
$$[\lambda x.\ x \text{ is working}](\text{Jim})$$

In accordance with the familiar Stalnakerian view, we think of propositions as sets of possible worlds.[21] So the question in (11a) receives the following interpretation:[22]

---

[20] See Roberts (2012, 10) for a precise definition.
[21] See especially Stalnaker (1984).
[22] As usual $[\![\cdot]\!]$ is a function that assigns denotations to linguistic expressions.

$[\![(11a)]\!] = \{\{w: \text{Mary is working in } w\}, \{w: \text{Kelly is working in } w\},$
$\{w: \text{Jim is working in } w\}\}$

Now consider the polar question (10a). Since (10a) does not contain any wh-elements, its set of alternatives is just the singleton of the proposition corresponding to it:[23]

$$[\![(10a)]\!] = \{\{w: \text{Mary is working in } w\}\}$$

So a question denotes the set of its alternatives. A wh-question is analyzed as abstracting into a property and in turn denoting the set of propositions obtained from applying that property to each of the relevant items in the domain. A polar question just denotes the singleton of the proposition corresponding to it.

The alternatives of a question can be seen as corresponding to a range of polar subquestions. Given the narrow domain of our toy example, the subquestions of (11a) are those in (12).

(12)   a. Is Mary working?
       b. Is Kelly working?
       c. Is Jim working?

Given this, we can distinguish between *partial* and *complete* answers. A partial answer to a question is an answer that constitutes a yes or a no to one or more of its subquestions. A complete answer is an answer that constitutes a yes or a no to each of its subquestions.

Following Groenendijk and Stokhof (1984), we can represent the set of complete answers to a question as a *partition* on logical space, that is, the set of all possible worlds. A question partitions logical space into cells, i.e. sets of worlds, corresponding to each of its complete answers. Wh-questions determine partitions corresponding to all the possible distributions of truth-values to their alternatives. Polar questions determine partitions with two cells corresponding to their positive and negative answers.

For example, (11a) partitions logical space into eight cells. Let m, k, and j be the propositions that Mary is working, that Kelly is working, and that Jim is working, respectively. Then the partition set up by (11a) is represented by Figure 4.1.

---

[23] See Roberts (2012, 10).

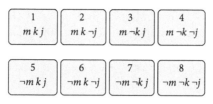

Figure 4.1

Cell 1 covers worlds in which Mary, Kelly, and Jim are all working, Cell 2 covers worlds where Mary and Kelly, but not Jim, are working, and so on. Formally, a partition is therefore a set of sets of worlds.

Each cell represents a complete answer to (11a), that is, an answer that affirms or denies each of its subquestions. Correspondingly, we will say that a complete answer *rules in* a unique cell in the partition. In turn, a partial answer rules in at least one cell (but not all), and hence all complete answers are also partial answers. The cells that are ruled in represent the possibilities that are still live, given the answer to the question.

For convenience, let us henceforth use [q?] to denote the partition determined by q. We then characterize "answerhood" more formally, as follows:

Answerhood
An answer (partial or complete) to a question q is the union of a non-empty, proper subset of [q?].

As above, intuitively, an answer is a statement that rules in at least one cell, but not all. We therefore specify that an answer to a question q must be the union of a *proper, non-empty* subset of the partition determined by q, since neither a statement that rules in no cells nor a statement that rules in all cells of [q?] is intuitively an answer to q.[24]

To illustrate, consider the replies to (11a) in (13).

(13) a. Mary is working.
      b. Mary and Kelly are working.
      c. Only Jim is working.

(13a) is a partial answer to (11a), since it is a positive answer to one of its subquestions, (12a), but remains neutral on the others. Correspondingly,

---

[24] I refrain from discussing this in detail here. See Schoubye and Stokke (2016) for details.

(13a) rules in cells where Mary is working, i.e. Cells 1–4. (13b) is a positive answer to two of the subquestions, but remains neutral on the third. So (13b) rules in cells where both Mary and Kelly are working, i.e. Cells 1–2. Finally, (13c) is a complete answer in being an answer to each subquestion and rules in a unique cell, namely the cell where only Jim is working, that is, Cell 7.

Finally, since polar questions only have two answers, the "yes"-answer and the "no"-answer, they determine partitions with only two cells. For example, as illustrated by Figure 4.2, (10a) partitions logical space into worlds in which Mary is working and worlds in which she is not working.

There are only two non-empty, proper subsets of this partition, namely Cell 1 and Cell 2, respectively. Correspondingly, there are only two answers to (10a), namely, that Mary is working and that she is not.

4.9. Misleading and the Big Question

In the previous chapters of this book, we have assumed a Stalnakerian model of communication, and most importantly, we have made use of the notion of common ground information. We now need to make this model more formal in order to show how the account of what is said in terms of QUDs is placed in relation to the Stalnakerian view of inquiry and information exchange.

Following Stalnaker, common ground information can be formally represented by a set of possible worlds, called *the context set*—the set of worlds that are compatible with the information in the common ground.[25] The possibilities included in the context set are the possibilities that are live given what has already been collected in the common ground of the discourse. Further, Roberts points out that the context set at any given time in a discourse can be thought of as the alternative set for the

Figure 4.2

[25] See in particular Stalnaker (1999 [1998]), (2002).

general question that corresponds to the Stalnakerian goal of inquiry, i.e. discovering what the actual world is like:

> Stalnaker's goal of discourse can itself be viewed as a question, the Big Question, What is the way things are?, whose corresponding set of alternatives is the set of all singleton sets of worlds in the context set at a given point in discourse.
>
> (Roberts, 2012, 5)

In other words, inquiry can be understood as the pursuit of a complete, true answer to the Big Question—in Stalnakerian terms, of narrowing the context set to just the actual world. Accordingly, a QUD is a subinquiry, that is, a strategy toward the goal of answering the Big Question. In answering a QUD, one advances the discourse and thereby reduces the context set. That is, one effectively claims that the actual world is among the worlds one rules in.

Given this framework, to mislead is to disrupt the pursuit of the goal of inquiry, that is, to prevent the progress of inquiry from approaching the actual world. If one answers (11a) with (13a), one reduces the context set to a set from which worlds in which Mary is not working are eliminated. (Here, as throughout, I focus for convenience on cases in which the relevant speech act is accepted by the other discourse participants.) If one effectuates this change while disbelieving that Mary is working, one reduces the context set to a set that, according to one's own beliefs, excludes the actual world. Thereby one steers the narrowing of the context set that is unfolding through the discourse away from the actual world.

There are many ways of contributing information to a discourse. Information can be contributed by assertion, conversational implicature, or by other means. There are equally many ways of contributing misleading information. One may do so by asserting something one believes to be false, by conversationally implicating it, or in some other way. Asserting that one is not going to a party and implicating that one is not going are both ways of contributing this information to the common ground of the discourse, and both effectuate a narrowing of the context set. If one believes that one is not going, both are ways of disrupting the pursuit of the goal of inquiry.

In the classic cases exemplified by (1)–(2), a speaker avoids lying, while still misleading, by contributing disbelieved information as a conversational implicature. According to the standard Gricean understanding, a proposition counts as a conversational implicature only if it is derived (or at least derivable) from information available to the hearer about what is said by the speaker.[26] In other words, on the orthodox Gricean conception, implicature-derivation must take as its input a content that the hearer recognizes as what is said. The derivation then proceeds along familiar lines appealing to the cooperative principle and the maxims and to available information about the context.

We will see that contributing disbelieved information by means of classic conversational implicatures of this kind is not the only way of being misleading, while avoiding lying.

4.10. Minimal Content

The central part of my account of the lying–misleading distinction is its characterization of the notion of what is said. On this characterization what is said by an utterance depends on QUDs. Briefly, what is said by a sentence in a context is the answer it provides to the QUD it is addressing. But moreover, this view also assumes that what a sentence can be used to say is constrained in a precise way by a species of *compositional* meaning.

For example, on the view I will argue for, while (14a), given the right QUD, can be used to say (14b), the same utterance cannot be used to say (14c) or (14d).

(14) a. [Uttered by Larry] My book is about logic.
b. The book Larry wrote is about logic.
c. The book Larry wrote is about cats.
d. Larry knows a lot about logic.

To implement this, I assume that any grammatically complete, declarative sentence determines what I shall call a *minimal content* as a result of composition of the lexical meaning of its constituents, in context.

In many cases the minimal content of a declarative sentence is a proposition. In the terminology of Recanati (1989), Bach (1994), Cappelen and Lepore (2004), and others, such a proposition can be identified as a so-called *minimal proposition*, i.e. a proposition that is determined solely by composition of the constituents of the relevant sentence. For example, it

---

[26] See in particular Grice (1989, 31). For relevant discussion and for a view according to which what is said is sometimes derived by way of Gricean maxims, see Soames (2008).

is safe to assume that (15) determines the minimal proposition that Mary is working.

(15)   Mary is working.

But moreover, even sentences that contain uncontroversial examples of context-sensitive expressions and constructions will often determine minimal propositions.

In particular, I follow Cappelen and Lepore (2004) in assuming that there is a *basic set* of context-sensitive expressions and constructions that are typically saturated before determination of minimal content. I take this set to include, at least, the pronouns (*I, you, he, she, it, we, they*, etc.), demonstratives (*that, this, those*, etc.), and the recognizable adverbs of space and time (*here, now, there, yesterday*, etc.), that is, roughly the set of expressions for which Kaplan's (1989) formative treatment was designed to account.

As mentioned in Chapter 3, Stalnaker often suggests that the referents of indexicals like the personal pronouns are determined by common ground information. This contrasts with the Kaplanian view that such contents are determined by facts concerning the utterance situation such as who is speaking, when, and where. The two approaches give different results in some cases.[27] For example, it might be common ground that the person speaking is Jim, even though the speaker is in fact Tom. In this case the Stalnakerian view predicts that an occurrence of *I* refers to Jim whereas the Kaplanian view predicts that such an occurrence refers to Tom. If one furthermore thinks that referents determined in this way are what is contributed to what is said, we can see that the two approaches may have different results for what is said by a particular utterance.

However, the two views diverge only in cases where there is a discrepancy between what is common ground and the relevant facts about the utterance situation. Even though this difference is important, I will set it aside here. So I will only be looking at examples in which the common ground information that is relevant for determining referents for indexicals, on the Stalnakerian view, corresponds to the facts about the utterance situation that the Kaplanian view will take as relevant. Given

---

[27] For detailed discussion of this, see Huvenes and Stokke (2016).

this restriction, I will not take a stand on how the contents of the elements of the basic set are determined.

So, for example, I assume that (16) determines the minimal proposition that Mary is working.

(16)   [Demonstrating Mary] She is working.

Beyond the obvious candidates mentioned above, however, the issue of which expressions and constructions to include in the basic set is highly contentious and non-trivial.[28] Yet, for our purposes, it is not necessary to decide on a definite list of basic set elements. What is needed is the assumption that composition of lexical meaning, in context, determines constraints on what is said.

For a range of context-sensitive expressions and constructions in natural language, it is plausible to think that these will very often be saturated prior to determination of this minimal content. This class of obvious context-sensitive elements, we may take it, largely coincides with Cappelen and Lepore's basic set. But we do not need to assume that such expressions and constructions are always assigned values before minimal content emerges.

In particular, on the view I will defend here, minimal content may fall short of complete propositionality. There are many ways in which this can come about. Two of these are, first, due to unclarity concerning how particular context-sensitive elements are to be saturated, e.g. in cases of vague demonstrations or where there is no determinate salient value for a particular context-sensitive parameter, and second, due to indeterminacies in the boundaries of the lexically encoded conditions of ingredient expressions.[29]

But even in such cases, what a sentence can be used to say is constrained by its minimal content. In cases where the compositionally determined constraints on what is said fall short of propositionality, we can construe the minimal content as a range of candidate minimal propositions. As we

---

[28] Cappelen and Lepore (2004, 1) provide a list that extends beyond the three basic categories mentioned in the text.

[29] The notorious statement by Bill Clinton, "I did not have sexual relations with that woman," was claimed not to be a lie because, it was argued, Clinton was using the term *sexual relations* in a way such that its extension did not include the relevant acts. This is arguably an example in which indeterminacy arises due to lexical non-specificity. Here I focus on indeterminacy arising from contextual underdetermination.

will see, on my view, such cases allow for particular ways of exploiting the lying-misleading distinction.

As this suggests, my view disagrees with so-called *Radical Contextualists*, such as Travis (1985), Sperber and Wilson (1986), Carston (2002), and Recanati (2004), (2010), who claim that compositional meaning always falls short of propositionality. On the other hand I refrain from adopting the strong position of so-called *Semantic Minimalists*, such as Cappelen and Lepore (2004), according to which all grammatical, declarative sentences express propositional contents that are determined purely by lexical meaning and compositional procedures.[30] Instead, my view agrees with so-called *Moderate Contextualists*, such as Bach (1994), in granting that compositional content, although sometimes fully propositional, may fall short of complete propositionality.[31]

4.11. What is Said

I can now state the definition of what is said that my account of the lying–misleading distinction turns on. Using $\mu_c(S)$ to denote a minimal proposition expressed by a sentence S in a context c, I adopt the following definition of what is said:[32]

What is Said

What is said by S in c relative to a QUD q is the weakest proposition p such that (i) p is an answer (partial or complete) to q and (ii) either $p \subseteq \mu_c(S)$ or $\mu_c(S) \subseteq p$.

So, what is said, according to this proposal, is the weakest answer to a QUD that either entails or is entailed by a minimal proposition expressed by the utterance in question, given the context. As before, we understand an answer to a question q to be the union of a non-empty, proper subset of $[q?]$, or intuitively, a statement that rules in at least one cell, but not all.

---

[30] For a different type of Semantic Minimalism, see Borg (2004).

[31] The view I argue for also disagrees with Cappelen and Lepore's *Speech Act Pluralism* according to which "an utterance can assert propositions that are not even logical implications of the proposition semantically expressed. Nothing even prevents an utterance from asserting (saying, claiming, etc.) propositions incompatible with the proposition semantically expressed by that utterance." (Cappelen and Lepore, 2004, 4).

[32] This proposal is defended in detail in Schoubye and Stokke (2016). See also Gauker (2012) for a view that has some similarities to this one.

Let me first explain the way this characterization of what is said works in cases where the minimal content expressed is propositional. On this view what is said by a sentence S relative to a QUD q is always a proper subset of $[q?]$, that is, a proper subset of the complete answers to q. Specifically, what is said is the weakest such proposition that entails the minimal proposition expressed by S, given the context. In other words, to determine what is said by S relative to q, first find the proper subsets of $[q?]$ that entail the minimal proposition expressed by S, then pick the weakest of them. (By a proposition p being weaker than another proposition r, we mean that p is entailed by r, but not *vice versa*.)

To illustrate, consider our previous example of the reply to (11a) in (13a).

(11a)   Who is working?

(13a)   Mary is working.

The minimal proposition expressed by (13a) is the proposition that Mary is working. So we look for proper subsets of the partition set up by (11a) that entail this proposition. As seen from Figure 4.1, there are several proper subsets of [(11a)] that entail that Mary is working. In general, any proper subset that contains some m-worlds and no $\neg m$-worlds entails the minimal proposition expressed by (13a).

For example, the subset covered by Cells 1 and 2 entails that Mary is working. But if this subset counts as what is said, this amounts to the prediction that, relative to (11a), (13a) says that Mary and Kelly are working, which is clearly incorrect. However, this proposition is not the *weakest* of the propositions in [(11a)] that entail the minimal proposition expressed by (13a). Rather, the weakest of them is just the set of all worlds where Mary is working, that is, the worlds covered by Cells 1–4. So, in this case, what is said is just the minimal proposition itself, that is, the proposition that Mary is working.

What about cases in which minimal content is not fully propositional? As we said above, in such cases, the minimal content can be construed as a range of candidate minimal propositions. For example, as we will see, (14a) may fall short of determining a fully propositional minimal content, and instead be associated with a range of candidates. In such cases I suggest that the interpretation "looks through" the candidates and tries to find a suitable content for what is said, given the QUD. In each case what is said is evaluated in the same way as above, i.e. as the weakest proposition that is an answer to the QUD and entails the relevant candidate minimal proposition.

We will see that sentences can be used to say things that go beyond their minimal contents. Yet what is said is precisely constrained both by minimal, compositional meaning and by QUDs, and hence so is assertion. I take this to be a natural extension of the Stalnaker–Roberts view of information exchange. The goal of inquiry—to answer the Big Question— is approached via subinquiries, i.e. QUDs. When solving the task of which information to add to the common ground as the result of an utterance, the participants of a discourse will look at the minimal content of the utterance and at which QUD is being addressed in order to determine what the speaker said.

Finally, note that the account of what is said allows for cases in which the relevant answer to the QUD is entailed by minimal content, rather than entailing minimal content, in the way we have just described. To see why, let us consider an example due to Kent Bach (1994). Relative to the right question, (17b) can be what is said by (17a).[33]

(17)   a. You're not going to die.
        b. You're not going to die from that cut.

However, if what is said is only allowed to entail minimal content, our account rules out that (17b) is what is said by (17a), since in this case the opposite seems to hold, that is, (17a) entails (17b). In Stalnakerian terms, worlds in which the addressee does not die (at all) are included in the set of worlds in which the addressee dies from that cut.

The source of the problem in this particular case is the negation in (17a)–(17b). The negation reverses the entailment relations and, as a result, the definition of what is said makes the wrong prediction. The same problem will generally arise whenever the "underdetermined" part of the content is in the scope of a downward entailing operator. Consider for example (18a) and (18b).

(18)   a. Nobody is going to die [from that cut].
        b. You will never die [from those bruises].

---

[33] By contrast, Bach (1994) takes (17a) itself to determine a complete proposition as what is said.

Our account of what is said solves this problem. In cases involving downward entailing operators, it seems that to capture that the meanings of the constituents constrain what a sentence can mean, entailment in the opposite direction is needed. So, instead of the requirement that what is said entails the minimal content, we require that what is said either entail or be entailed by the minimal content.

This suffices to guarantee that there is a constraining relation between minimal content and what is said. In some cases what is said goes beyond minimal content, while in other cases, what is said is circumscribed by minimal content. But in all cases there is a strict and well-defined relation between the two.

5

The Difference between Lying and Misleading

In the last chapter I proposed a theory of the notion of what is said involved in my definition of lying. In this chapter we will see that this account of what is said, given my account of lying, draws the line correctly between lying and other forms of misleading speech.

5.1. The Classic Contrast

Consider first the classic contrast between assertion and conversational implicature, as illustrated by (1)–(2).

(1)   **Rebecca.** Are you going to Paul's party?
      Dennis. No, I'm not going to Paul's party.

(2)   **Rebecca.** Are you going to Paul's party?
      Dennis. I have to work.

We assume that, in (1), Dennis's utterance determines the minimal proposition that Dennis is not going to Paul's party. Rebecca's question is a polar question, and hence its partition contains two cells corresponding to the positive answer and the negative answer, respectively. The negative answer entails (is identical to) the minimal proposition expressed by Dennis's utterance. According to our definition, this proposition is therefore said by the utterance. Moreover, since Dennis is obviously offering this proposition for common ground uptake, it is asserted. So because Dennis, in this case, is asserting something he believes to be false, we explain why he is lying.

Now look at (2). We assume that Dennis's utterance determines the minimal proposition that Dennis has to work. There is no answer to the question that entails this minimal proposition. Neither the proposition that Dennis is going to the party nor the proposition that he is not going to the party entails that he has to work. So our account does not predict that either the positive answer or the negative answer to Rebecca's question is said. Regardless, the classic observation is that Dennis, in this case, conversationally implicates that he is not going to the party. This implicature will typically be explained by appeal to the Maxim of Relation, "Be relevant."[1] Implicatures are offered for common ground uptake. Hence, Dennis is being misleading, since he is making a bid to update the common ground with disbelieved information.

As we noted in Chapter 4, conversational implicatures are standardly seen as derivable from what is said. Intuitively, Dennis's utterance in (2) says that he has to work, and this content is uncontroversially the input to the derivation of the implicature that he is not going to the party. So our account should predict that what is said, in this case, is that Dennis has to work. However, it might not be obvious that we can meet this demand, since we do not predict that this content is said relative to the question in (2). Yet, as I now go on to explain, the QUD framework offers an elegant way of achieving this result.

5.2. Defaulting to the Big Question

We have seen that, given the Stalnakerian understanding of the aim of inquiry, information exchanges are always, ultimately, directed toward resolving the Big Question. In this sense, therefore, the Big Question is always a background QUD (at least in serious conversation.) I suggest that, in cases where an utterance cannot be seen as saying something relative to a more immediate, local QUD, the interpretation typically defaults to seeing the utterance as addressing the Big Question directly. More precisely, when there is no answer to the local QUD that entails any candidate minimal proposition, the utterance is interpreted against the Big Question. (I return to this later in this chapter.)

A complete answer to the Big Question is an answer that rules in one world and rules out all others. So the Big Question is the question that partitions logical space into one cell for each and every possible world, as illustrated by Figure 5.1.

---

[1] See Grice (1989, 27) and Davis (2010, 7).

Figure 5.1

The minimal proposition expressed by Dennis's utterance in (2) is the proposition that Dennis has to work. The weakest non-empty proper subset of the partition in Figure 5.1, i.e. the weakest answer to the Big Question, which entails that Dennis has to work, is simply the set of all worlds where Dennis has to work. Hence, since Dennis's utterance in (2) addresses the Big Question, even if it does not address the local QUD raised by Rebecca, we predict that Dennis's utterance says that he has to work, and moreover, this proposition is asserted. In this way we predict the desired input to the derivation of the implicature that he is not going to the party.

Furthermore, this means that, on our account, if Dennis believes that he does not have to work, he is lying in addition to misleadingly implicating that he is not going to the party. Again, this is clearly the result we want.

5.3. Committing to Misleading Answers

Now let us consider the case of (3)–(4).

(3) **Elizabeth.** Why did Doris lose her job?
    William. She insulted Sean at a party.

(4) **Elizabeth.** How is Doris's relationship with Sean?
    William. She insulted him at a party.

As we saw, discourse-insensitive accounts like Saul's (2012b) are unable to explain why William's utterance in (3) is a lie, while the same utterance, in (4) is merely misleading.

William's utterance, in each case, expresses the minimal proposition that Doris insulted Sean at a party. The weakest non-empty proper subset of the partition set up by Elizabeth's question in (3), which entails this minimal content, is the proposition that Doris lost her job because she insulted Sean at a party. So, given our proposal, this proposition is said, and asserted, by William's utterance in (3). We therefore explain why William is lying.

By contrast, there is no subset of Elizabeth's question in (4) that entails that Doris insulted Sean at a party. In particular, the content that is most naturally taken to be implicated by William's utterance—that the relationship is not good, or the like—does not entail the minimal proposition expressed by the utterance, and therefore, it is not asserted, on our account.

Nevertheless, William's utterance in (4) is misleading because it contributes disbelieved information to the discourse, that is, that the relationship is not good. This contribution is plausibly seen as a conversational implicature. Again, the most likely explanation appeals to a violation of the Maxim of Relation. As above, I take it that William's utterance in (4) is seen as addressing the Big Question, since it does not make an assertion with respect to the local QUD. Interpreted against the Big Question, William's utterance says that Doris insulted Sean at a party. On our account this proposition is asserted by the utterance and hence serves as input to implicature-derivation. This prediction accords with the intuitive judgment that if William believes that Doris did not insult Sean at a party, he is lying.

So we explain why one can lie by committing oneself to misleading answers to QUDs, namely because what one says, and hence what one asserts, depends directly on the QUD one is addressing.

5.4. Lying via Incompleteness

The next type of case we looked at involved exploiting incompleteness, as in (5)–(6).

(5) **Norma.** What's the topic of the book you wrote?
     Larry. My book is about logic.

(6) **Norma.** Do you know a lot about logic?
     Larry. My book is about logic.

As we noted, Larry's utterance in (5) is seen as a lie, while in (6), he is being merely misleading. Intuitively, in both cases, Larry conveys that he wrote a book about logic, which is something he believes to be false. But only in (5) is this information a direct answer to the question. But at the same time, the way in which the information that Larry wrote a book about logic is provided turns crucially on his use of the possessive construction.

What minimal content is expressed by Larry's utterances in these cases? I take it to be sufficiently uncontroversial that the possessive construction requires contextual supplementation of a possession relation. Intuitively, we need to know what relation Larry is supposed to bear to the relevant logic book in order for the utterances to make sense.[2] This is arguably a central part of the reason why one can use this kind of semantic incompleteness to mislead while avoiding lying.

But are possessives to be seen as belonging to the basic set of context-sensitive elements that are saturated prior to determination of minimal content? As I said earlier, I will not attempt to answer this question in this chapter.[3] However, as we will see next, there are good reasons to think that, regardless of how this issue is resolved, our account will be able to offer a plausible explanation of this type of case.

Given the context as described, it is natural to say that the compositional meaning of Larry's utterance, in each case, falls short of determining a minimal proposition. Instead, it is indeterminate between a range of candidates, including, at least, those represented by (7a) and (7b).[4] (We assume that the first person feature of *my* is saturated.)

(7)   a. The book Larry wrote is about logic.
      b. The book Larry is assigned to read is about logic.
      . . .

Moreover, there is no sense in which the utterance is compatible with (8), even though the latter is true.

(8)   The book Larry wrote is about cats.

---

[2] Cappelen and Lepore (2004, 94–5) argue that the possessive construction is not included in the basic set. Since they take minimal content to determine truth-conditions, Cappelen and Lepore therefore do not think that contextual supplementation of the possessive is necessary for truth-conditional content. Yet Cappelen and Lepore are not committed to the view that their minimal truth-conditions should be intuitively recognizable as contents that are communicated.

[3] Recanati (2004) argues that possessives involve a variable that must be "saturated," but that they differ from Kaplanian indexicality, where the value in question is determined via a linguistic rule operating on what he calls "narrow context." Barker (1995) argues that the possessive in English involves an empty determiner that receives its value via a contextually salient possession relation. See also Stanley (2007 [2000], 489) and Carston (2002, 185–6).

[4] Some theorists, e.g. Heim (1992) and Barker (1995, 78–82), take possessives to involve definiteness, yet this view remains controversial, and I will not presuppose it. The paraphrases in (7) employ the definite article merely for convenience, and none of my arguments rely on any substantial assumption about the definiteness of possessives.

So although it is insufficient to fix a fully propositional content, the compositional meaning of the utterance, in context, still specifies a concrete constraint on what it can be used to say.

In terms of the Stalnakerian framework, the compositional meaning of utterance rules out that it can be used to update the common ground with the information that the book Larry wrote is about cats, i.e. that it can be used to assert (8). However, the compositional meaning allows that it may be used to update the common ground with assertions like those in (7). Put differently, even though the incompleteness of the utterance means that it does not determine a propositional minimal content, it still maps out a region of logical space within which to locate what it can be used to say.

There are two main ways to motivate the claim that the utterance fails to determine a minimal proposition. First, it might be argued that the possessive is part of the basic set, but is not sufficiently fixed in this context. Second, it might be argued that the possessive is not part of the basic set. Both suggestions have a claim to being plausible. But we do not need to settle this matter here. With respect to how it exploits the lying–misleading distinction, the important feature of the case is the indeterminacy between different minimal propositions. For our purposes, it is less important to settle for an account of the source of this indeterminacy.

According to what we suggested earlier, the interpretation will attempt to find a suitable content for what is said in terms of the candidate minimal propositions and the space of answers to the QUD. In (5) there are several answers to the QUD that entail (7a). The weakest of these is the proposition that the book Larry wrote is about logic. So, given the QUD, this candidate minimal proposition yields a plausible content as what is said. Furthermore, none of the answers to the QUD in (5) entail (7b). The same is true for other possible completions. For example, consider the candidates in (9).

(9) a. The book Larry is thinking about is about logic.
    b. The book Larry is talking about is about logic.
    c. The book Larry has been working on is about logic.
        . . .

No answer to the question in (5) entails any of these. Rather, since (7a) yields a plausible outcome for what is said, in this case, we predict that Larry is interpreted as saying, and hence asserting, that the book he wrote is about logic. This also accords with our judgment that Larry is lying in this case.

5.5. Misleading via Indeterminate Minimal Content

Now consider (6). Neither of the candidate completions in (7) is entailed by either the positive or the negative answer to the QUD in (6). Nor is any other possible completion. So Larry's utterance in (6) cannot be construed as saying anything relative to the local QUD. So, according to our earlier proposal, the utterance is instead seen as addressing the Big Question. Notice, however, that in cases like this, where there are different candidate minimal propositions in play, the Big Question does not distinguish a particular content as what is said. We could say, therefore, that each of the candidates in (7) and (9) is said. But this is not right. Larry is not lying, in this case, and therefore (7a) cannot be said, or asserted. This conforms to our sense that Larry, in (6), is not asserting any particular completion.

Instead, I propose that, in cases where an utterance is indeterminate between a range of minimal propositions, and moreover cannot be construed as saying anything relative to the relevant local QUD, the interpretation pulls back even further and takes as what is said a particular kind of generalized proposition. This proposition is the union of all possible completions, i.e. not just the most salient ones. In Stalnakerian terms, since the interpretation cannot determine an assertion that situates the actual world within a particular completion, it settles for the observation that the utterance nevertheless locates the actual world somewhere in the region of logical space enclosed by the candidates taken together, i.e. the region of space determined by the compositional meaning of the utterance. In other words, the utterance is seen as making an assertion that is true if and only if at least one completion is true.

In our case, given that Larry's utterance cannot be interpreted as saying anything relative to the QUD, and since the Big Question does not distinguish a particular completion as said, the interpretation takes as what is said the union of all possible completions, i.e. like those in (7) and (9). There are different ways of paraphrasing the resulting generalized proposition, for example, as in (10).

(10)   Larry bears some relation to a book about logic.

Intuitively, this is the content that would be understood by someone who had no access to the contextual information relevant for deciding between the candidate minimal propositions.

(10) is a plausible content for what is said in (6). And furthermore, Larry is naturally seen as proposing to add to the common ground the information it paraphrases. Part of the peculiarity of this case is that Larry makes an assertion that is, on the one hand, sufficiently specific to achieve his misleading purposes and, on the other hand, sufficiently non-committal to avoid lying. Given that (10) is asserted in (6), we predict that Larry is lying if he believes that (10) is false. This is the right result. In particular, we make the same prediction as on Saul's (2012b) account, according to which speakers in cases like this avoid lying if at least one possible completion is believed to be true.

It remains to be explained why Larry is being misleading in (6). Arguably, the reason is that his utterance succeeds in implicating that he knows a lot about logic. As we have seen, implicatures are derived from what is said. According to our account, the hearer, in this case, recognizes that Larry's utterance does not say anything relative to the local QUD, and moreover, that it does not say anything particular relative to the Big Question. Hence, finally, the generalized content in (10) is taken to be what is said. In turn, the implicature that Larry knows a lot about logic is inferred.

This inference is arguably drawn on the basis of, first, Norma's belief that Larry wrote a book about logic, and second, the Maxim of Relation. If Larry had not been aware of this belief of Norma's, he would not have thought that he could mislead her in this way. However, I will not attempt to provide a more precise account of this process here. Doing so is a challenge for any view on which utterances can give rise to implicatures even when their compositional meaning falls short of full propositionality.[5] As before, our account can do no more than make sure it predicts a suitable input for implicature-derivation. I assume that, given the context and the beliefs of the participants, a plausible account can be given of how Larry succeeds in implicating that he knows a lot about logic by asserting (10) in response to the question in (6).

---

[5] For examples of such views, see, e.g. Carston (2002), Recanati (2004).

5.6. Incomplete Predicates

To further illustrate the way this account handles incompleteness, I want to briefly comment on two cases involving so-called *incomplete predicates*. Discussion of utterances involving incomplete predicates have been at the center of the literature on the semantics–pragmatics distinction in philosophy of language. Here are three stock examples, all from Bach (1994):[6]

(11)   a. Steel is strong enough.
      b. Tipper is ready.
      c. Al has finished.

Even though they are grammatically complete, to determine what is said by utterances of sentences like these, we need complements for the predicates *enough*, *ready*, and *finished*, that is, we need to know what steel is supposed to be strong enough for, what Tipper is supposed to be ready for, and what it is that Al is supposed to have finished.

This kind of incompleteness can be exploited for the purpose of navigating the lying–misleading distinction in ways analogous to those we have just considered involving the possessive construction. Here is an example to illustrate this:[7]

Bank Robbers
Russell is an engineer involved in building a bank. Pamela is a consultant who specialized in materials for high-level security buildings. But little does Russell know that Pamela is in league with a ring of bank robbers who plan to break into the bank when it's finished, and Pamela wants to make their job as easy as possible. Pamela thinks steel is strong enough for the roof of the bank, but not for the security booth at the front.

(12)   **Russell.** We need a material for reinforcing the security booth at the front of the building. What's strong enough?
      Pamela. Steel is strong enough.

(13)   **Russell.** We're thinking about using steel. What do you think?
      Pamela. Steel is strong enough.

---

[6] Bach discusses the negation of (11a), but the point is the same.
[7] See also Saul (2012) and Stokke (2016a).

While Pamela is lying in (12), she is not lying in (13), although she is being misleading. We can consider continuations to corroborate these judgments, as in (12')–(13').

(12')   **Russell.** We need a material for reinforcing the security booth at the front of the building. What's strong enough?
Pamela. Steel is strong enough.
Russell. Right, so you think steel is strong enough for the security booth?
Pamela. #No, steel isn't strong enough for that.

(13')   **Russell.** We're thinking about using steel. What do you think?
Pamela. Steel is strong enough.
Russell. Right, so you think steel is strong enough for the security booth?
Pamela. No, I just meant that steel is strong enough for the roof.

As before, while Pamela's response in (13') is clearly obnoxious and uncooperative, it is not marked with the kind of unintelligibility that attaches to her response in (12').

Given this, our account should predict that, in (12), Pamela says that steel is strong enough for the security booth, while in (13), this information is not what she says, although she conveys it indirectly. To see that these are indeed the results we get, consider first the minimal content of Pamela's response, in each case. As with the incompleteness engendered by possessives, we take it the compositional meaning of sentences containing incomplete predicates like those in (11) do not determine propositional minimal contents. Instead, they will be indeterminate across a range of potential minimal propositions.

In both of the cases above, this range includes at least the candidates in (14).

(14)   a. Steel is strong enough for the roof.
b. Steel is strong enough for the security booth.
c. Steel is strong enough for the counter.
. . .

Next, we assume that in (12), the QUD that Pamela is addressing is the question in (15).

(15)   What is strong enough for the security booth?

There is an answer to this question that entails (14b), namely that steel is strong enough for the security booth. Hence, we predict that this proposition is what is said in (12). So, since Pamela, in this case, says something she believes to be false, she is lying. Indeed, she is being directly deceptive.

However, in (13), there is no answer to the QUD that entails a candidate minimal completion. Given the above, therefore, what is said by Pamela's utterance is the proposition that is the union of all the candidates. This content can be paraphrased as (16).

(16)   Steel is strong enough for something.

Hence, since Pamela believes that (16) is true, since she believes that steel is strong enough for the roof, she avoids lying in this case. Nevertheless she is being misleading, since she manages to implicate that steel is strong enough for the security booth. Again, while I do not pretend to have a fully worked-out story of how this kind of implicature is generated, I take it that we have succeeded in predicting a suitable input to this process in the form of what is said, that is, (16).

5.7. Incomplete Questions

Before moving on, I want to address a potential concern that might arise at this point. The objection concerns the way our account deals with cases in which a question is itself incomplete. For example, Russell's question in (12), "What's strong enough?" itself involves the incomplete predicate *enough*. It might be asked, if we allow incomplete questions like this one to be filled out as completed QUDs, as in (15), why not just do the same for incomplete utterances, in the first place? Why not just argue that Pamela's reply in (12), in this context, gets completed as (14b), instead of going the roundabout way via QUDs?

In response to this, we should emphasize that the issue of how (15) gets to be the QUD for this context is a different issue than the issue of what is said by Pamela's utterance, *given* the assumption that (15) is the QUD it is addressing. That is, one task is to give an account of how uttering the English interrogative sentence, "What's strong enough?" given the context and the previous discourse, manages to determine the QUD that partitions the relevant worlds according to which material is strong enough for the security booth. We have not provided an account of this mechanism. Rather, we have been concerned with giving a theory of what is said by declarative sentences that relies on the assumption that discourses are structured around specific QUDs of this kind. This assumption we have taken to be independently motivated.

More immediately, our aim has been to point out that the lying–misleading distinction is sensitive to discourse structure due to the relationship between what is said and which question is addressed. As we have seen, in the case of (3)–(4), one and the same, grammatically complete, declarative sentence can be used to say different things depending on the question it is addressing. This is evidence that any adequate account of what is said must be sensitive to discourse structure in this way. The suggestion made above concerning the example of (12)–(13) demonstrates how such an account can handle cases in which a question explicitly asked is incomplete. Moreover, as we will see later in this chapter, there are further reasons for thinking that QUDs can be introduced in other ways than by being explicitly asked in conversation.

5.8. Lincoln's Letter to Ashley

To illustrate further the power of this account, we can consider the case of Lincoln's reply to James Ashley's letter, mentioned in Chapter 4. The exchange was as in (17).[8]

(17)   **Ashley**. The report is in circulation in the House that Peace Commissioners are on their way or are in the city, and is being used against us. If it is true, I fear we shall loose [sic] the bill. Please authorize me to contradict it, if not true.

   Lincoln. So far as I know, there are no peace commissioners in the city or likely to be in it.

I take it that Lincoln's reply is not a lie. We want to say that the craftiness of the reply is that it succeeds in misleading without lying. Here is how our account delivers this result. We assume that Ashley's letter introduces the QUD in (18).

---

[8] See Lincoln (1953 [1865]).

Figure 5.2

(18)   Are peace commissioners either in or on their way to
          Washington?

It is commonly observed that, semantically, disjunctive questions of the
form *(p or q)*? are more akin to wh-quesitons than to polar (yes/no)
questions.[9] Following these suggestions, I assume that questions like this
determine partitions corresponding to their alternatives, rather than two-
cell partitions corresponding to yes/no answers. Let me explain this by a
simpler example than the one before us. Consider the question in (19).

(19)   Did John or Mary pay the bill?

We represent the partition determined by (19) as in Figure 5.2 (where m
is the proposition that Mary paid the bill and j is the proposition that John
paid the bill.)

The replies in (20) are all felicitous answers to (19).

(20)   a. John paid the bill.
          b. Mary paid the bill.
          c. They both did.
          d. Neither of them did.

Consider (20a). It is standard to observe that (20a) will, almost always,
be taken to mean that *only* John paid the bill. It is controversial how
to account for this effect, and we need not propose a solution to this
problem here.[10] We can note that our framework, as it is set up, allows
for broadly two ways to go. First, it might be argued that the minimal
proposition expressed by (20a), in this context, is that only John paid the
bill. If so, then since the only non-empty proper subset of the partition

[9] See e.g. Krifka (2011, 1749–50), Groenendijk and Roelofsen (2011).
[10] For discussion, see, e.g. Carston (1998), Levinson (2000), Groenendijk and Stokhof
(1984), van Rooij and Schultz (2004), Krifka (2011).

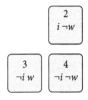

Figure 5.3

in Figure 5.2 that entails this proposition is just Cell 3, the latter will be what is said. Second, it might be argued that the exhaustive interpretation is an implicature—sometimes called an *only*-implicature—and hence we will be able to predict as input to its derivation that what is said by (20a) is the union of Cells 1 and 3.

Further, it is typical to note that, given the right setting, one can felicitously answer a question like (19) with a "yes" or a "no." For example, suppose that what is at issue is whether the bill has been paid or not. In that case, answering "yes" will be seen as saying the proposition that is the union of Cells 1, 2, and 3. In turn, answering "no" is tantamount to supplying the complete answer consisting solely of Cell 4.

There is more to be said here, but this will suffice for showing how we will handle Lincoln's reply to the QUD in (18). Letting i be the proposition that the commissioners are in Washington, and w the proposition that they are on their way to Washington, we can represent the partition set up by this QUD as in Figure 5.3.

As illustrated here, since there are no worlds, so we assume, in which the commissioners are both in Washington and on their way to Washington, the corresponding cell of the partition, i.e. the one containing both i-worlds and w-worlds, does not exist.

Now consider Lincoln's reply in (17). We can safely ignore the rider, "So far as I know." The minimal proposition expressed by the reply is therefore that no peace commissioners are in Washington and no peace commissioners are likely to be in Washington. Assuming that, given the common ground, if peace commissioners are on their way to Washington, peace commissioners are likely to be in Washington, the only non-empty proper subset of the partition in Figure 5.3 that entails the minimal content is just Cell 3. So, according to our account, the latter is what is said by Lincoln's reply. That is, Lincoln's reply says that there are no peace commissioners in Washington and no peace commissioners on their way to Washington. Analogously to what we saw above, this answer corresponds to responding to (18) with, "no."

Since Lincoln believes that what is said is true—that is, it is true that there are no commissioners in or on their way to Washington—he is not lying. But clearly he is being misleading. In particular, Lincoln's reply is misleading because it manages to implicate that no peace negotiations are imminent, which is something that Lincoln knows to be false, given the upcoming meeting at Fort Monroe. As before, I do not propose to have an account of how this implicature is generated. Yet I take it that by predicting that Lincoln said that no peace commissioners are in or on their way to Washington, we have predicted the right kind of input to the implicature-derivation.

5.9. Misleading with Presuppositions

As noted earlier, since conversational implicature is not the only way of adding information to the discourse without saying it, conversationally implicating disbelieved information is not the only way of being misleading while avoiding lying. One of the most prominent sources of non-asserted information in natural languages are presuppositions. According to the Stalnakerian view, the hallmark of a presupposition is that it places a requirement on the common ground of a conversation. We can say that if a sentence S presupposes that p, S is felicitous, in a context c, only if p is either already common ground in c or is accommodated. As we will see below, this allows for two ways of being misleading with the use of presuppositions. First, if the common ground contains information one does not believe, one can sometimes serve one's communicative goals by presupposing the disbelieved common ground information. Second, one can offer presupposed information that one does not believe for accommodation.

Both ways of misleading are also possible with other kinds of presuppositions. For example, if Allan knows that Kyle falsely believes that his wife cheated on him, Allan may exploit that fact in uttering (21).

(21) Your wife really regrets that she cheated on you.

Allan is being misleading in allowing the false information that Kyle's wife cheated to remain common ground. But moreover, Allan is lying. Since *regret* is a factive verb, if Allan believes that Kyle's wife did not cheat, he must also believe that it is false that she regrets cheating. So, in this case, Allan is both presupposing and outright asserting disbelieved information. And moreover, if it was obvious that Kyle did not believe, or suspect, that his wife cheated, Allan would be offering disbelieved, presupposed information for accommodation while at the same time offering disbelieved, asserted information for common ground uptake. Finally, if Allan knew that the wife did cheat but that she does not regret it, this would be a case of exploiting a true presupposition in order to facilitate a lie.

In general, then, one can employ presuppositions for misleading purposes either by knowingly allowing disbelieved information to remain common ground, or by directly aiming for disbelieved information to be accommodated. Since presuppositions are not said, both of these are ways of misleading while not lying, even though such maneuvers may be accompanied by outright lying if what is asserted is likewise disbelieved.

5.10. Athanasius, Nathan, and the Henchman

To illustrate the first of these possibilities, let us return to the stock example of Saint Athanasius, mentioned earlier. Consider a modernized version:

Nathan and the Henchman
Nathan is sitting in the office, when suddenly a henchman of a loan shark he owes money to bursts in. As he questions him, Nathan realizes that the henchman does not know that he is Nathan.

(22)   **Henchman.** Where's Nathan?
Nathan. He's not far away.

There are arguably two ways in which Nathan is being misleading in this case. First, he is non-standardly using the third person to refer to himself. And second, he conveys that Nathan is not in the office, while avoiding outright asserting that. We will discuss each in turn.

According to one standard view, the so-called *phi-features* of pronouns (person, gender, and number) are presupposition triggers.[11] Specifically,

---

[11] See, e.g. Cooper (1983), Heim and Kratzer (1998), Heim (2008), Sauerland (2008).

the third person feature is seen as triggering the presupposition that the referent of the pronoun is neither the speaker nor the hearer.[12]

What role does this kind of presupposition play in a common ground model of conversation? It is obvious that at least one function of the features of pronouns is to facilitate reference-identification. Stalnaker (1999 [1998]) is explicit:

> If certain information is necessary to determine the content of some speech act, then appropriate speech requires that the information be presumed to be shared information at the time at which that speech act is to be interpreted.
>
> (Stalnaker, 1999 [1998], 101)

Stalnaker observes that a use of the first person, singular pronoun *I* requires that the speaker "must be presuming that the information that she is speaking is available to her audience—that it is shared information." (1999 [1998], 101)[13] If this is right, the analogous observation should hold for the third person. When someone uses the third person, they must be presuming that the information that the intended referent is neither speaker nor hearer is available to the audience. In particular, someone using the third person is relying on common ground information about who the speaker and addressee are in order to allow the audience to identify the intended referent.

Furthermore, as Stalnaker (2002) emphasizes, common ground information need not be true, and need not even be believed by the participants:

> Successful communication is compatible with presuppositions that are recognized to be false, but the information that they are being presupposed must be actually available, and not just assumed or pretended to be available.
>
> (Stalnaker, 2002, 716)

---

[12] There is debate about the source of this presupposition. On some views the third person feature triggers the requirement that the referent be neither speaker nor hearer as a semantic presupposition. On others the first and second persons encode semantic presuppositions, while the third person feature is empty, and the presupposition concerning the participant role of the third person is derived as an implicature. On these options, see Heim (2008), Sauerland (2008).

[13] It is not required that this information be available before the utterance was made. See Stalnaker (1998, 101).

Along these lines, Stalnaker (1999 [1998]) points out:

> Sometimes the most effective way to communicate something true is to presuppose something false. For example, if you are presupposing something false but irrelevant, I may presuppose it as well, just to facilitate communication. (You refer to Mary's partner as "her husband," when I know that they are not married. But I might refer to him in the same way just to avoid diverting the discussion.)
>
> (Stalnaker, 1999 [1998], 100)

These observations make it possible to explain the way in which the use of the third person pronoun in cases like (2) is misleading.

As in Stalnaker's example, Nathan is presupposing something false in order to serve his communicative purposes. (As we will see later, he is doing so in order to assert something true, and thereby avoid lying.) What Nathan is presupposing is that the referent of *he* is neither the speaker nor the hearer. Moreover, since it is obvious from the utterance and the context that *he* is intended to refer to Nathan, the presupposition of the pronoun is that Nathan is neither the henchman nor the person speaking. This presupposition is felicitous because it is obvious that the henchman thinks it is common ground that the person speaking is not Nathan.[14] Since it is advantageous to him, Nathan goes along with this.

On this analysis, then, Nathan's use of the third person to refer to himself does not mislead by adding disbelieved information to the common ground. The disbelieved information that he is not Nathan is already common ground when he makes his utterance, and he is relying on that fact in using the third person. Rather, Nathan's use of the third person is to be seen as the kind of misleading by which one allows others to continue to hold a false belief for disingenuous purposes. This is what Chisholm and Feehan (1977) called omissive, positive deception *secundum quid* (see Chapter 1.) Since one thereby deliberately prevents the common ground from approaching the truth, this constitutes another way of disrupting the pursuit of the goal of inquiry.

The same points apply to Stalnaker's own example of going along with the false presupposition concerning Mary's partner. Again, the speaker

---

[14] Well-known complications concerning the representation of necessarily false propositions in terms of possible worlds will arise here. In particular, the set of worlds in which Nathan is not Nathan is the empty set. However, I assume that there are ways of accommodating the obvious fact that discourse participants may entertain false presuppositions about the identity of other participants, or of people in general. For relevant discussion, see Stalnaker (1999 [1978]).

may later be accused of having been misleading, not by getting the hearer to accept false information, but by allowing the hearer to continue holding a false belief. As in all other cases, the perceived severity of this kind of breach will vary.

Presuppositions can also be used to mislead in the second sense distinguished above, that is, the sense of aiming for disbelieved information to become common ground as a result of one's utterance. One can offer presuppositions that one believes to be false for accommodation.[15]

In the case of pronouns this is most obvious regarding the gender features of pronouns. Suppose, for instance, that Marion replies as in (23) in order to make Mick think that Tim's baby is a girl, even though she knows it is a boy.

(23)   **Mick.** Have you seen Tim's baby yet?
       Marion. Yes, she's lovely.

The feminine feature of the pronoun triggers the presupposition that the referent is female. Since it is obvious that the referent is Tim's baby, Marion's use of the pronoun will—unless something out of the ordinary happens—have the effect of making it common ground that the baby is female.[16] Hence, if Marion believes this is false, she is being misleading by contributing disbelieved information without asserting (or saying) it.

We can now explain the sense that Nathan contributes misleading information—that is, that he is not in the office—to the discourse, while avoiding lying. This requires an explanation of what is said by utterances involving negations. As we will see, this is straightforward, given our proposal.

The henchman's question partitions logical space into cells corresponding to its complete answers. A complete answer is an answer that constitutes a yes or a no to each place Nathan could be. Clearly, the list will be very long. Moreover, some of the places will exclude each other, while some will not. And furthermore, for some of the places, it will be vague whether they are far away or not. Let us assume that there are five salient places Nathan could be: the office, the mall, the bar, his home, and the

---

[15] On accommodation, see Stalnaker (1998, 102–4).

[16] As before, this point is independent of the contrast, discussed in Chapter 4, between whether one thinks that the referents of pronouns are determined by Stalnakerian common ground information or by Kaplanian assignments of values.

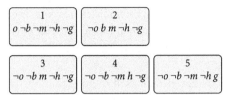

Figure 5.4

garage. Moreover, assume that the bar is in the mall, and hence there are no worlds where Nathan is in the bar but not in the mall. So the question determines the partition in Figure 5.4.

Suppose further that (i) Nathan's home is nearby, (ii) the mall, and hence the bar, are far away, and (iii) the garage is neither near nor far. In other words, the places that are not far away are the office, home, and the garage. Consequently, there are many proper subsets of the question that entail the minimal content that Nathan is not far away—for example, the subset covered by Cell 1, the one covered by Cells 1 and 5, etc. The weakest of these is the subset covered by Cells 1, 4, and 5. So this proposition counts as what is said.

Given the way things are set up in this simplified example, this proposition can be paraphrased in more than one way, as in (24).

(24) a. Nathan is neither at the bar nor in the mall.
      b. Nathan is either in the office, at home, or at the garage.
      c. Nathan is not far away.

These are all correct ways of describing what Nathan said, that is, of describing the proposition consisting of the worlds covered by Cells 1, 4, and 5. But on any of them, what is said is clearly something Nathan believes to be true. Hence, he is not lying.

We can now ask why Nathan is seen as misleading—apart from the features we noted above concerning his use of the third person. It is plausible to say that his utterance implicates that Nathan is not in the office. One way of suggesting how this implicature arises starts from the observation that what Nathan says, on any description, is weaker than the proposition that Nathan is in the office. The proposition that Nathan is in the office, i.e. the worlds covered by Cell 1, entails the proposition that is said, i.e. the worlds covered by Cells 1, 4, and 5. Correspondingly, on either of the descriptions in (24), what is said is entailed by the proposition that Nathan is in the office. Hence, the latter is a stronger statement than what Nathan asserted. Given a principle like Grice's (1989, 26) First Maxim of Quantity, "Make your contribution as informative as is required (for the current purposes of the exchange)," the speaker can be expected to contribute the strongest available content. According to this idea, then, since what was asserted is weaker than the proposition that Nathan is in the office, the utterance implicates that Nathan is not in the office.

5.11. Presuppositions of Interrogatives and Imperatives

Having explained these various ways in which people can say things and thereby succeed in misleading while avoiding outright lying, I want to turn to a different group of examples. Given our account of what is said, there are utterances that cannot be used to say anything. If an utterance does not express a minimal content, there will be no content that is determined as what is said relative to any question.

In fact, a large number of the utterances we use to communicate with each other have this particular feature. These are *non-declarative* utterances. This includes utterances of interrogative sentences used to ask questions, and utterances of imperative sentences used to issue orders, invitations, or suggestions.

I will devote the bulk of Chapter 10 to giving an account of how non-declaratives interact with common ground information and of the ways in which utterances of such sentences can be insincere. What I want to bring out here is that non-declaratives sometimes presuppose things. And, like other presuppositions, presuppositions carried by non-declaratives can be exploited for misleading purposes. For brevity, I will focus here on sentences in the interrogative and imperative moods.

Interrogatives and imperatives generally share the presuppositions of their assertive counterparts.[17] Here are some simple examples:

(25)   a. Will Ronny ever stop stealing candy bars from the store?
       b. Ronny, stop stealing candy bars from the store!

---

[17] See e.g. Levinson (1983, 184), Roberts (2012, 23).

(26)   a. Did you see the fake Eiffel Tower when you were in
          Las Vegas?
       b. When you're in Las Vegas, go see the fake Eiffel Tower!

Both the question in (25a) and the imperative in (25b) presuppose that Ronny has been stealing candy bars from the store.[18] Similarly, both the question in (26a) and the imperative (26b) presuppose that there is a (unique) fake Eiffel Tower in Las Vegas. Yet none of these sentences say anything, in our sense, since they do not express minimal contents.

Still, since non-declaratives can carry presuppositions, they can be used to mislead in any of the ways we mentioned earlier. For example, all of these examples can be used with the aim of making their presupposed information common ground as a result of accommodation. For instance, if the speaker of either of the non-declaratives in (25) knows that Ronny has not been stealing candy bars from the store, but is trying to make someone else believe he has, she is clearly being misleading. The same applies to the non-declaratives in (26). And similarly, non-declaratives can also be used to mislead in other ways. For example, the presuppositions of non-declaratives can be aimed at allowing someone to continue holding a false belief.

5.12. Implicit Questions and Prosodic Focus

The cases we have looked at until now have, for the most part, been cases in which the relevant QUDs are explicitly asked. Yet much communication does not proceed like this. We very often say things, even though there is no question explicitly asked. We can lie or be merely misleading in such cases, too. This might be thought to be a potential problem for my view, since its notion of what is said is only defined relative to QUDs. However, as I explain below, the fact that no question has been made explicit in the previous discourse does not mean that there are no QUDs.

Roberts (2012, 8) stresses that "questions are often only implicit, inferred on the basis of other cues." Specifically, Roberts's suggestion is that questions are often accommodated by the interlocutors in much the same way as presuppositions are. Retrieving the right question to accommodate, however, is arguably a much more complicated process than that

---

[18] These examples arguably also presuppose other things, such as that there is a (unique) salient store to be referred to.

of presupposition accommodation.[19] Even so, there are mechanisms that speakers use to indicate which questions they are addressing.

Roberts argues that one of these mechanisms, in English, is prosodic focus:

> prosodic focus in English presupposes the type of question under discussion, a presupposition which enables the hearer, with some other contextually given clues, to reconstruct that question and its relation to the strategy being pursued.
>
> (Roberts, 2012, 8)

Roberts's discussion of this phenomenon is rich and highly detailed. My aim here is merely to sketch a rudimentary way of understanding the relation between focus and question accommodation as a way of suggesting one way in which QUDs can be in place even if they are not made explicit.[20]

To take an example given by Manfred Krifka (2011), (27) can be used to address either of the questions in (28).

(27)   Fritz will go to Potsdam tomorrow.

(28)   a. Where will Fritz go tomorrow?
       b. When will Fritz go to Potsdam?
       c. Who will go to Potsdam tomorrow?
       d. Who will go where tomorrow?
       e. Who will go where when?

But, as Krifka points out, which question is being addressed will typically be indicated by intonational pattern. Representing focus by an f-subscript and stress using capitals, each intonational pattern in (29) is only felicitous relative to the corresponding question in (28).

(29)   a. Fritz will go [to POTsdam]$_f$ tomorrow.
       b. Fritz will go to Potsdam [toMORrow]$_f$.
       c. [FRITZ]$_f$ will go to Potsdam tomorrow.
       d. [FRITZ]$_f$ will go [to POTsdam]$_f$ tomorrow.
       e. [FRITZ]$_f$ will go [to POTsdam]$_f$ [toMORrow]$_f$.

---

[19] Presupposition triggers differ with respect to the facility with which their presuppositions can be retrieved for accommodation. In some cases the process requires considerable contextual information. For example, this is notoriously the case with the iterative *too*, as noted by Kripke (2009).

[20] As such, my discussion of focus and question accommodation diverges from Roberts (2012).

In a case where there is no suitable QUD already in place, choosing one of the intonational patterns in (29) will indicate to the listener which of the questions in (28) is being addressed. In other words, prosodic focus—as expressed by intonational pattern—is one way in which speakers provide cues that allow other participants to accommodate QUDs. For example, uttering (29a) in a context in which no suitable question has previously been accepted as a QUD will typically have the effect that the participants will assume that the speaker is addressing (28a), and thereby accommodate that question as a QUD.

Focus can be used for misleading purposes in this way. Here is an example:

Rome
Melissa knows that Fritz is first going to Potsdam and then on to Rome tomorrow.

(30)   **Jack.** Will Fritz go to Potsdam tomorrow?
       Melissa. Fritz will go to [ROME]$_f$ tomorrow.

Melissa's utterance is not felicitous with a flat intonation. In other words, Melissa's utterance in (30) must be seen as addressing, not the question about Potsdam that was explicitly asked, but a different question, namely (28a). Relative to (28a), and ignoring the indexical *tomorrow*, we predict that what is said is that Fritz will go to Rome tomorrow. Therefore, Melissa is not lying, since she is asserting something she believes to be true.

However, there is a clear sense that Melissa is being misleading in the Rome example above. We feel that her utterance conveys that Fritz is not going to Potsdam tomorrow, and this sense is particularly explicit due to the presence of Jack's question. I take it to be plausible that this effect can be explained on the basis of our prediction that what is said, in this case, is merely that Fritz is going to Rome tomorrow. Yet the issue of *how* to explain this effect is vexed and highly controversial. Even though I will not offer anything like a complete account of this issue here, it is worth gesturing at one way this kind of case might be explained within a framework of the kind we are presupposing.[21]

---

[21] For other relevant discussion, see, e.g. Carston (1998), Levinson (2000), Sauerland (2004), Spector (2007).

On the Stalnaker–Roberts view of discourse, the goal of a discourse is to answer the Big Question—that is, to reach the goal of inquiry—and this overarching goal is approach via the attempt to answer more local QUDs. Following Carlson (1982), Roberts uses the analogy of games, that is, interactions involving goals, rules, moves, and strategies, to describe this endeavor. One type of rule that governs this kind of game, that is, the game of reaching the goal of inquiry via subinquiries, are conversational rules like the Gricean maxims, arising from rational considerations concerning the goal of the game. Along these lines, Roberts suggests that "Quantity 1 [follows] from the desire to maximize the payoff of a move in view of commitment to the ultimate goal [...]." (2012, 4) In particular, she argues that, when a QUD is raised, participants are generally expected to provide complete answers, if possible (see Roberts, 2012, 6.) So, if we are right that Melissa's utterance in (30) addresses (28a), there will be a presumption that she try to provide a complete answer to the latter question. Consequently, it will be presumed that Melissa wants to convey that Rome is the only place Fritz will go tomorrow. This might therefore be a way of explaining the inference that Fritz will not go to Potsdam as well. However, much more work is needed to flesh out this kind of account, let alone to determine its overall viability.

In other cases there is more room for maneuver concerning which question is to be accommodated, as in the following story:

Memo
In an office memo Barbara sees Doris's name on a list of recent lay-offs. Surprised, she shows the memo to William and points to Doris's name on the list while making a quizzical, puzzled face.

(31) **William.** She insulted Sean at the Christmas party.

Suppose, as in the previous scenario, that William knows that, while Doris did insult Sean, this is not the reason she got fired. Did he lie?

I think intuitions are unclear here. In particular, I think the degree to which one will judge William to be lying correlates with the degree to which one will judge that he can only be seen as addressing the question of why Doris got fired. To support this, suppose that the situation is as described above, but that Barbara, while pointing to the list, utters, "Why?", "What?", or the like. I think that, in these cases, intuitions that William is lying become stronger, and that the reason is that the degree to which his utterance can only be seen as addressing the question of why Doris got fired is strengthened.

One can avoid lying, while still being misleading, if one can exploit which question the hearers can be expected to accommodate, while remaining in a position to claim that one intended to address a different QUD.

5.13. Multiple Questions

The final issue I want to turn to concerns the fact that realistic contexts invariably contain multiple QUDs. Moreover, the different QUDs in a context are tyically related to each other. One important way QUDs can be related is by specific kinds of entailment relations. I will look at two such relations and the way in which they influence ways of lying and misleading.

One notion of entailment between questions is the following.

Strict Question-Entailment
A question q_1 strictly entails a question q_2 if and only if completely answering q_1 yields a complete answer to q_2.[22]

Following Roberts (2012, 16), let us consider a simplified example of Strict Question-Entailment. Imagine a discourse concerning only two individuals, Hilary and Robin, and concerning only two kinds of foods, tofu and bagels. Then consider the following questions:

(32) Who ate what?

    a. What did Hilary eat?
       i. Did Hilary eat bagels?
       ii. Did Hilary eat tofu?
    b. What did Robin eat?
       i. Did Robin eat bagels?
       ii. Did Robin eat tofu?

Given the narrow domain described above, (32) strictly entails both (32a) and (32b), which in turn strictly entail the questions below them.

---

[22] Cf. Roberts (2012, 7), Roberts (2012, 12), Groenendijk and Stokhof (1984, 16).

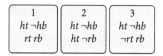

Figure 5.5

A complete answer to (32) yields complete answers to both (32a) and (32b) and to their subquestions. This is easily illustrated by considering a fragment of the sixteen-cell partition determined by (32). Consider, for example, the three randomly selected cells from [(32)] in Figure 5.5 (where *ht* means 'Hilary ate tofu,' *rb* means 'Robin ate bagels,' and so on.)

If one answers (32) by specifying that Hilary ate tofu but not bagels and Robin ate both, one's answer is represented by Cell 1 of Figure 5.5. As seen, this answer also yields complete answers to the subquestions, i.e. it also completely answers what Hilary ate, what Robin ate, and whether each of them ate tofu, bagels, both, or neither.

We can now see that our definition of what is said has the consequence that saying, and hence assertion, is preserved from subquestions to superquestions under Strict Question-Entailment. This can be spelled out as follows:

Upwards Preservation of What is Said
If a question q_1 strictly entails a question q_2, then
If a proposition p is said relative to q_2, p is said relative to q_1.

To see that what is said is preserved in this way, observe that (33) says that Robin ate tofu relative to all of (32b$_{ii}$), (32b), and (32).

(33)   Robin ate tofu.

However, even though (33) says that Robin ate tofu relative to (32), it says nothing relative to (32a), (32a$_i$), (32a$_{ii}$), and (32b$_i$). That is not a counterexample to Upwards Preservation of What is Said. Yet it shows that assertion is not preserved downwards from superquestions to subquestions under Strict Question-Entailment. That is, a proposition may be said relative to a question q_1 but not relative to a question q_2 it entails.

Earlier we assumed that when an utterance does not make an assertion with respect to a local QUD, the interpretation typically defaults to the Big Question. For example, if the only QUD available is (32b$_i$), (33) will be seen as addressing the Big Question, and thereby as saying that Robin ate tofu.

Since the Big Question is the most general question of all, it strictly entails all other questions.[23] The proposal that interpretations default to the Big Question can therefore be seen as a special case of a more general principle according to which, when there is no way of obtaining an assertion for an utterance from a local QUD, the interpretation moves up the hierarchy of strictly entailing QUDs until it reaches a QUD relative to which the utterance makes an assertion. Once this is achieved, since assertion is preserved upwards, the same proposition will be asserted relative to all strictly entailing super-QUDs, and ultimately the Big Question itself.

This means that if one lies relative to a question, one lies relative to all questions that strictly entail it. Moreover, since the Big Question is always available, whether one can lie or not does not depend on which local QUDs are in place. As such, lying is always an option—namely, one can always utter a sentence that says something one believes to be false. Yet, as we will see next, the option of misleading without lying does depend on which QUDs are available.

If one conveys a misleading answer to a question, one will thereby also be conveying a misleading answer to all questions that strictly entail it. This is clear from (34).

> (34) **Mark.** Who ate what?
> **Kevin.** Well, let's see—did Robin eat tofu?
> **Albert.** Robin ate bagels.

Albert's response to Kevin's question is most naturally seen as conveying that Robin did not eat tofu.[24] Suppose Albert believes that Robin ate both bagels and tofu. In that case he is being misleading, but is not lying. He conveys disbelieved information without saying it. This misleading

---

[23] See Roberts (2012, 7).

[24] In accordance with what was said in section 5.1, there is a clear preference for the intonational pattern in (i) for Albert's utterance in (34).

> (i) Robin ate [BAgels]$_f$.

As such, the utterance might be taken to indicate that it is addressing (32b). This does not detract from the point I am making concerning the way lying and misleading behave under Strict Question-Entailment.

information is also a partial answer to Mark's superquestion, and hence Albert is also misleading with respect to this question.

However, this only holds *if* there is a subquestion against which one is being misleading. If, for example, the discourse in (34) only contained Mark's question, then Albert's utterance would not have been misleading—it would just have said that Robin ate tofu. In other words, whether or not one can succeed in misleading while avoiding outright lying depends on which QUDs are in place, and which QUD one is seen as addressing. But if one does contribute a misleading answer (even if one does not assert it) to a QUD, the same information will be a misleading answer to each strictly entailing QUDs.

It is of course implausible to think that QUDs are always (perhaps even often) related to each other by the relation of Strict Question-Entailment. Still, it is a natural thought that, in well functioning, truth-pursuing discourses, QUDs are related in ways that are similar to this. In particular, QUDs are arguably often ordered such that answering them in turn will, step by step, be a way of progressing toward the goal of inquiry.

This idea is captured by Roberts's (2012) model of discourse structure. Roberts assumes that the QUDs of a discourse are totally ordered by a precedence relation $<$, which is simply the relation of one utterance having been made before another.[25] She then defines the following relation on the QUDs of a discourse:

Contextual Question-Entailment
For all QUDs q, q' of a discourse, if $q < q'$, then the complete answer to q' contextually entails a partial answer to q.[26]

One way in which Contextual Question-Entailment can be satisfied is if the QUDs of a discourse stand in the relation of Strict Question-Entailment. For example, a complete answer to (32b) yields a partial answer to (32), and so on. But Contextual Question-Entailment also allows for cases in which the relation between the QUDs of a discourse is more subtle than Strict Question-Entailment. To take an example from Roberts (2012, 19–20), consider the questions in (35).

---

[25] See clause (10d) in Roberts (2012, 14). To be sure, this is arguably too simple in that QUDs can be hierarchically ordered with respect to each other, independently of the order in which they were uttered, and furthermore. I ignore this here, though.
[26] This is a slight simplification of clause (10g$_{iii}$) in Roberts (2012, 15).

(35) a. What kinds of seafood will John eat?
      b. Isn't he allergic to clams?

As Roberts (2012, 19) observes, completely answering (35b) does not straightforwardly entail a partial answer to (35a). Suppose that the answer to (35b) is *yes*. Even so, John might still eat clams for other reasons, e.g. out of politeness, or because he cannot resist. On the other hand, suppose the answer to (35b) is *no*. Even so, that does not directly entail that John *will* eat clams, since there might be other reasons why he will not. However, Roberts proposes that in many contexts in which this kind of discussion takes place, it will be common ground that (a) one will not eat anything one is allergic to and (b) one will eat something unless one has reason not to. (a) takes care of the case in which the answer to (35b) is *yes*. (b) takes care of the case in which the answer is *no*, given the further observation that an answer to (35b) is a partial answer to (36).

(36) What reasons would John have for not eating clams?

In other words, Contextual Question-Entailment appears to be a promising way of explaining at least some of the intricate ways in which QUDs are related. Briefly, we try to order our QUDs such that those raised will deliver partial answers to the previous ones, given the common ground, and perhaps via bridge-questions.

Now consider the following situation:

Clams
Maria knows that John is allergic to clams, but that he will eat them anyway because he can't resist.

(37) **Kelly**. What kinds of seafood will John eat?
      Eric. Isn't he allergic to clams?
      Maria. Yes, John is allergic to clams.

Intuitively, Maria is being misleading, since she conveys that John will not eat clams, and yet she is not lying because all she is asserting is that he is allergic to clams.

The reason Maria is not lying in (37) is clear. Her utterance expresses the minimal proposition that John is allergic to clams. The latter is entailed by the corresponding answer to Eric's question, and is therefore asserted by Maria. So we explain why she is not lying.

How do we explain the sense that Maria is being misleading in (37)? That is, how do we explain that Maria succeeds in adding to the discourse the information that John will not eat clams? As noted, Roberts suggests that it is reasonable to assume that it is common ground that one will not eat something one is allergic to. It is natural to explain Maria's strategy for misleading as trading on a fact of this kind. The reason she can mislead Kelly and Eric into thinking that John will not eat clams by asserting that he is allergic to clams is because she can rely on a general assumption to the effect that people typically avoid eating what they are allergic to. In other words, the operation of Contextual Question-Entailment, and the configuration of the common ground, help explain the misleading nature of Maria's utterance.

As before, that Maria can succeed in misleading is due in part to which QUDs are in place—in this case, the misleadingness is due to the presence of Kelly's question. For example, suppose the question of what kinds of seafood John will eat is not a QUD, neither explicitly nor implicitly, for example, as in (38).

(38)   **Kelly**. What ailments does John have?
       Eric. Isn't he allergic to clams?
       Maria. Yes, John is allergic to clams.

In this case Maria does not convey that John will not eat clams, or any other misleading information. So, whether one misleads or not depends on the constellation of QUDs in the context, and furthermore, on how they are related to each other.

As seen from (37), Contextual Question-Entailment is not sufficient to ensure that what is said is preserved from subquestions to superquestions, as Strict Question-Entailment is. Nevertheless, as demonstrated by (38), Contextual Question-Entailment does ensure something weaker. If one asserts a complete answer to a subquestion, in a discourse satisfying Contextual Question-Entailment, one will thereby be contributing a partial answer to its superquestions. Therefore, in such a discourse, one way of contributing a disbelieved partial answer to a QUD, while avoiding lying, is to assert a complete answer to a subquestion that one believes to be true but which, given the context, will be a way of achieving one's goals with respect to the superquestion.

PART II
Attitudes

6

Bullshitting and Indifference Toward Truth

At the beginning of Part I, in Chapter 1, I made an assumption that has so far been left unchallenged. The assumption was that lying, and insincerity more broadly, involves conveying information that one believes to be false. We have been assuming that what is involved in misleading speech, whether direct or indirect, is that the speaker communicates information that she believes to be false, and we have understood lying as asserting disbelieved information. As has hopefully been apparent from the examples we have looked at, this assumption is justified for a wide range of cases. Very often, perhaps even typically, lying and misleading do involve communication of disbelieved information. Yet, as we will see throughout the chapters in Part II, once we dig a bit deeper, things unsurprisingly begin to look more complicated.

In cases of lying the speaker says something she believes to be false. Similarly, in typical cases of misleading while avoiding lying, the speaker communicates something she believes to be false, even if she asserts something she believes to be true. But there are other ways in which people speak insincerely. Sometimes people say things without really caring about what they say. People are sometimes indifferent toward what they are saying, in particular ways. In this chapter and the next we will explore some of the ways in which we sometimes speak with indifference, and the relation between this kind of insincerity and lying.

6.1. Frankfurt on Indifference Toward Truth

In his celebrated essay, "On Bullshit" (2005 [1986]), Harry Frankfurt identified the phenomenon of bullshitting as a category of non-alethic speech distinct from lying.[1] While lying is plausibly thought of as commonplace in most human cultures, Frankfurt saw bullshitting as particularly characteristic of the modern way of life:[2]

One of the most salient features of our culture is that there is so much bullshit.
(Frankfurt, 2005 [1986], 1)

According to Frankfurt's influential analysis, bullshitting is a mode of speech characterized by a particular kind of indifference toward truth. In particular, for Frankfurt, the phenomenon of bullshitting is marked by the speaker being indifferent toward the truth or falsity of what she says. As illustrated by Frankfurt's discussion, speaking with indifference toward truth and falsity is common in many areas of contemporary culture, including advertising and politics. One of Frankfurt's main examples of bullshit was a certain kind of political speech-making, as in the following example:

4th of July Orator
Consider a 4th of July orator who goes on bombastically about "our great and blessed country, whose Founding Fathers under divine guidance created a new beginning for mankind."
(Frankfurt, 2005 [1986], 16)

But even outside such areas of public discourse, people sometimes engage in talk characterized by this kind of indifference. Even in our private lives, we are familiar with the fact that people sometimes say things without caring whether what they say is true or false. There are many reasons people might do so. They may be trying to present themselves in a certain way or they might think (perhaps correctly) that the situation calls for certain things to be said regardless of their truth or falsity. Or there might be other reasons.

For example, it has been claimed that part of what is achieved by certain statements by President Trump that are arguably instances of bullshitting is that they function to test the loyalty of subordinates by requiring them to accept and even repeat such bullshitting statements, and in so doing,

---

[1] The essay first appeared in *Raritan* (vol. 6, no. 2) in 1986. It was reprinted in Frankfurt (1988), and later as the monograph Frankfurt (2005 [1986]). Frankfurt's analysis of bullshit explicitly owed much to Max Black's (1983) ideas about what he called humbug.
[2] For some discussion of cross-cultural prevalence and significance of lying, see Barnes (1994, ch. 5).

bullshitting utterances of this kind create a kind of tribal relation between Mr Trump and his aides.[3]

According to Frankfurt, the central characteristic of bullshitting of this kind is that the bullshitter is indifferent toward the truth or falsity of what she says. In an often-quoted passage Frankfurt describes the bullshitter as follows:

> Her statement is grounded neither in a belief that it is true nor, as a lie must be, in a belief that it is not true. It is just this lack of connection to a concern with truth—this indifference to how things really are—that I regard as of the essence of bullshit. (Frankfurt, 2005 [1986], 33–4)

So, for Frankfurt, the key characteristic of the kind of talk he wants to identify as bullshitting is indifference toward whether what one says is true or false.

In this chapter I will argue that indifference toward truth is a more differentiated phenomenon than both Frankfurt and his critics have assumed. One may care about the truth-value of what one is saying and yet at the same time be indifferent toward truth and falsity in other ways. Frankfurt was right that there is an interesting phenomenon that is characterized by indifference toward truth and falsity on the part of the speaker. But whereas Frankfurt originally claimed that the bullshitter lacks concern for the truth-value of her assertions per se, I will argue that the broader phenomenon can be characterized in terms of a different kind of indifference toward truth and falsity.

Rather than understanding the kind of indifference toward truth involved in bullshitting and neighboring modes of insincere speech as indifference toward the truth-value of one's assertions, I propose to think of indifference toward truth in terms of indifference toward inquiry. In particular, the central kind of indifference involved in these modes of speech is indifference toward contributing true or false answers to QUDs. This allows us to understand speakers who are not indifferent toward the truth or falsity of what they say but who are nevertheless bullshitting, or speaking with indifference toward truth and falsity. We will see that one may be indifferent toward making a true or a false contribution to a particular QUD, or subinquiry, even if one is not indifferent toward the truth or falsity of one's assertions per se.

---

[3] See Cowen (2017) and Yglesias (2017).

6.2. Two Ways of Caring about Truth

Against Frankfurt's original idea, it has been suggested that bullshitting does not always involve indifference toward truth. In particular, a number of philosophers have argued that people are sometimes bullshitting even though they care about the truth or falsity of what they say (e.g. G. Cohen, 2002, Kimbrough, 2006, Carson, 2010, Wreen, 2013, Fallis, in press, Stokke and Fallis, 2017).

Here is an example that Thomas Carson gives:

Careful Exam Taker

A student who gives a bullshit answer to a question in an exam might be concerned with the truth of what [s]he says. Suppose that she knows that the teacher will bend over backwards to give her partial credit if he thinks that she may have misunderstood the question, but she also knows that if the things she writes are false she will be marked down. In that case, she will be very careful to write only things that are true and accurate, although she knows that what she writes is not an answer to the question.   (Carson, 2010, 62)

The bullshitting student cares about the truth of what she says in the sense that she cares about saying true things, while she is not particularly concerned with what they are. Even though the student is concerned with making true statements, she is not trying to answer the exam questions correctly, since she knows that she is unable to do so.

It is not difficult to find more examples of the same type of attitude toward one's speech. Consider, for instance, the case of filibusters. Some filibusters parallel the Careful Exam Taker's strategy of bullshitting while being careful to only say true things. Roy Sorensen cites an instance from ancient Roman history:

Cato

When opposing Caesar, the Roman senator, Cato the Younger, delayed votes with rambling speeches that violated the maxims of quantity ("Say only as much as needed"), relation ("Be relevant") and manner ("Be clear"). As a Stoic, Cato condemned lying. This principle was not violated by him bullshitting until dusk (the time at which the Senate was obliged to conclude its business).   (Sorensen, 2011, 406)

As in the Careful Exam Taker case, Cato was careful to only say things he believed to be true, thereby avoiding lying. Yet at the same time his filibustering tactic involved not being concerned with the particular things he said, as long as they were true. Like the student in Carson's example, Cato was merely concerned with the truth of what he said in one sense, while he was indifferent toward truth in another sense. While Cato was concerned with saying true things, he was not particularly interested in what they were.

As these examples suggest, one way in which one can be concerned with the truth of what one says is to have a general concern that is not directed at particular propositions. People sometimes try to make sure that their utterances are true, even if they are not concerned with the truth-value of any particular propositions. This kind of speech is usefully characterized as bullshitting while caring about the truth of what one says.

A different kind of example of this mode of speech has been suggested by Jonathan Webber. He writes:

one can communicate bullshit conversational implicatures. If one's intention is to instil in one's audience a particular belief that one neither believes nor disbelieves, then one can pursue this aim by making assertions that carry the target proposition as a conversational implicature. One could implicate it by asserting only truths, which might be a wise strategy for politicians or advertisers.
(Webber, 2013, 655–6)

Webber suggests that one can sometimes communicate bullshit implicatures. In particular, another way of bullshitting while caring about saying true things is to say something one believes to be true in order to conversationally implicate something the truth-value of which one does not care about.[4]

For example, imagine an advertisement for a toothpaste saying:

(1)   Used by dentists!

That the toothpaste is used by dentists may be true, and the advertiser might care about its being true, perhaps for fear of being sued should the ad say something false. At the same time the slogan may be intended to implicate that the toothpaste is good, or perhaps that it is better than toothpastes not used by dentists. Yet the advertiser might not care whether such implicatures are true or false.

---

[4] Webber is discussing cases in which the speaker communicates something she is agnostic about. I discuss such cases in Chapter 7.

The examples considered above are all cases in which someone cares about truth in the sense of having a goal of saying true rather than false things. Yet there is also another way in which one might care about the truth of what one says. This is the sense in which one might care about the truth of one or more specific propositions. This kind of concern for the truth is also compatible with bullshitting, that is, with being indifferent toward truth and falsity in a different sense.

Consider the following story:

Wishful Thinker
Jack and Julia are going to Chicago. They have tickets to a Cubs game, and being a big Cubs fan, Julia hopes the game will not be rained out. A few days before their departure, they are talking about their trip. Jack says, "I'm really looking forward to that Cubs game. I hope it won't rain." Julia replies with a confident air, "This time of year, it's always dry in Chicago." But she has no evidence about the weather in Chicago, and she has no idea whether it's likely to rain or not.

There is a clear sense in which Julia is not indifferent toward the truth-value of what she says. But unlike the speakers in the previous examples, Julia's goal is not simply to say something true, while being less concerned about the particular proposition she utters. Rather, she cares particularly about the truth of the proposition she utters. She is not indifferent to whether it is always dry in Chicago at that time of year. She wants it to be true that it is always dry in Chicago at that time of year. Or, if one prefers, she hopes or wishes that it is. Even so, Julia is speaking with indifference toward truth in another sense. In particular, as I will argue, speakers like Julia are characterized by a particular kind of indifference toward QUDs.

6.3. Bullshitting and Gricean Quality

To be able to capture these ways of speaking with indifference toward truth, we need a theory that allows that one may be speaking with indifference toward truth, in one sense, while one is not correctly described as being indifferent toward the truth or falsity of what one says.

One proposal is to analyze bullshitting in terms of conversational norms. In Chapter 2 we considered attempts to characterize lying in terms of Grice's maxims of Quality (see Grice, 1989, 27).

Supermaxim of Quality: Try to make your contribution one that is true.

First Maxim of Quality: Do not say what you believe to be false.

Second Maxim of Quality: Do not say that for which you lack adequate evidence.

Similarly, it has been suggested that bullshitting can be characterized in terms of Quality maxims.

Marta Dynel (2011) and Don Fallis (2009), (2012) have proposed accounts of bullshitting in terms of (versions of) the Second Maxim of Quality. For example, Dynel claims:

The violation of the second Quality maxim "Do not say that for which you lack adequate evidence" [. . .] gives rise to *bullshit* which the hearer takes to be truthful. (Dynel, 2011, 152)

And according to Fallis:

you bullshit if and only if you intend to violate the norm of conversation against communicating something for which you lack adequate evidence by saying that thing. (Fallis, 2012, 575)

These views imply that someone is bullshitting if they say that p and thereby intend to communicate that p, while lacking adequate evidence for p.

Perhaps it might be argued that this kind of view can accommodate the phenomenon of bullshitting while caring about truth. Roughly, one idea might be that one may be ignoring the Second Maxim of Quality while taking care to satisfy either the First Maxim of Quality or the Supermaxim of Quality. For example, the careful exam taker might be said to be saying what she does while ignoring the fact that she has no evidence for them, while at the same time she is trying to make true contributions. In turn, other bullshitters might be characterized as ignoring all three maxims. It might be argued, for instance, that the orator is best described as ignoring all three quality maxims.

However, even independently of whether this kind of account can capture the ways of speaking with indifference while caring about truth that we looked at above, there are other reasons for thinking that it will ultimately be inadequate. Problems arise due to the fact that one may believe that one has adequate evidence for a proposition, even though one does not. Typically, if someone says what they believe they have adequate evidence for, they are not bullshitting. Here is an example:

Science Fiction Reader

Joan has read a science fiction novel in which one of the characters states that there is life on Saturn. Joan thinks science fiction novels are a reliable guide to facts about extraterrestrial life. So she comes to believe firmly that there is life on Saturn, and she also believes that she has adequate evidence for that claim, that is, the novel's say-so. Indeed, Joan thinks she knows there's life on Saturn. Sometime later, her younger brother asks her whether there's life anywhere else than on Earth. Joan replies:

(2)   Yes, there's life on Saturn.

Joan is not bullshitting. She is not engaged in the kind of mindless talk that arguably characterizes Frankfurt's orator, as well as Julia and the careful exam taker in Carson's example. Joan's response is motivated by her wish to inform her brother of what she believes to be the truth. But in saying something for which she lacks adequate evidence, and thereby intending to communicate that thing, Joan is violating the Second Maxim of Quality, and likewise the slightly modified norm that Fallis appeals to.

In response to this, one may want to argue that the Second Maxim of Quality should be understood as prohibiting statements made while one *believes* that one lacks adequate evidence for them. This would make the norm parallel to the First Maxim of Quality, which prohibits saying something one believes to be false. So one might propose that someone is bullshitting if and only if they say that p and thereby intend to communicate that p, while believing that they lack adequate evidence for p.

This proposal can likewise be seen to be inadequate. In particular, it can be rejected by considering the kind of speakers that have been described by Jennifer Lackey and others. Consider, for example, the case of Stella from Lackey's "Creationist Teacher" case:

Creationist Teacher

Stella is a devoutly Christian fourth-grade teacher, and her religious beliefs are grounded in a deep faith that she has had since she was a very young child. Part of this faith includes a belief in the truth of creationism and, accordingly, a belief in the falsity of evolutionary theory. Despite this, she fully recognizes that there is an overwhelming amount of scientific evidence against both of these beliefs. Indeed, she readily admits that she is not basing her own commitment to creationism on evidence at all but, rather, on the personal faith that she has in an all-powerful Creator. (Lackey, 2008, 48)

Suppose that Stella is asked, in a private conversation, outside school, what she thinks about the origin of species. She replies:

(3)   God created the species.

In this example, despite the fact that Stella says and intends to communicate something for which she believes she lacks adequate evidence, she is surely not bullshitting.[5] She says what she does because she is convinced of its truth, and she is motivated by a wish to convey that truth to her interlocutor. This clearly distinguishes her from speakers like the orator.

In other words, it seems doubtful that one can identify a sufficient condition for bullshitting in terms of (a version of) the Second Maxim of Quality. As I now go on to argue, the same applies to the other Quality maxims.

As we have seen in Part I, you lie when you say something you believe to be false, and thereby try to communicate that thing to the audience. In Chapter 2 we noted that this means that when someone tells a lie, they violate both the Supermaxim of Quality and the First Maxim of Quality. Furthermore, even if critics of Frankfurt like Carson (2010) are right that lying is not incompatible with bullshitting, it is reasonable to think that Frankfurt was correct in thinking that at least some lies are not instances of bullshitting. (I return to this later in this chapter.)

Consider, for instance, the following example:

Unprepared Exam Taker
Parker wants to convince his parents that he's ready for his chemistry exam. Even though Parker hasn't studied, when asked by his parents, he tells them:

(4)   I have studied really hard, and I'm ready for the chemistry exam.

---

[5] A potential response to this is to argue that, while Stella believes she lacks scientific evidence for what she says, she is not violating the Second Maxim of Quality. Since she believes that what she says is true, the objection goes, Stella is not saying something for which she believes she lacks an adequate basis. However, this response requires reading the Second Maxim of Quality in a broad sense, and it is an open question whether one can justify this kind of interpretation of it. Moreover, it remains true that, in the case at hand, Stella believes that she lacks the kind of evidence for what she says that would be expected and accepted by most of the relevant peers.

Most likely, cases of lying of this kind were the motivation for Frankfurt's claims concerning the distinction between bullshitting and lying. In particular, lies like Parker's are "designed to insert a particular falsehood at a specific point in a set or system of beliefs, in order to avoid the consequences of having that point occupied by the truth." (Frankfurt, 2005 [1986], 54) Accordingly, many will want to say that, even though Parker is lying to his parents, he is not bullshitting. Yet lies like this one violate both the Supermaxim of Quality and the First Maxim of Quality.

Finally, there are reasons to think that one can engage in bullshitting without violating Quality maxims. Consider Carson's exam taker who gives bullshit answers while carefully selecting what to say in order to say only things she believes to be true, because that is how she knows she will get partial credit. Assuming the student has adequate evidence for what she says, she is bullshitting while obeying all the Quality maxims. She is trying to make true contributions, and she says what she believes to be true and has adequate evidence for.

6.4. Bullshitting and Questions under Discussion

In Part I of this book I argued that, instead of characterizing lying and misleading in terms of Gricean norms of conversation, these kinds of non-alethic modes of speech are better understood in terms of their relation to inquiry, and in particular, to subinquiries, or QUDs. We will see that the same framework provides an elegant and illuminating way of accounting for the phenomenon of bullshitting, or speaking with indifference toward truth.

On the view I will defend here, bullshitting is a mode of speech marked by indifference toward providing true or false answers to QUDs. There are many different ways of providing answers to QUDs. We have seen some of these in Part I. When discussing bullshitting we can conveniently confine ourselves to assertion and conversational implicature. As we have done earlier, we can use *contributing that p* as a general term to mean either asserting that p or conversationally implicating that p, that is, to contribute that p to the discourse either by asserting it or conversationally implicating it.

Given that the goal is to advance toward truth, the progress of inquiry is to be served by contributing true answers to QUDs. A contribution that is a true answer to a QUD is a contribution to the progress of the discourse toward the Stalnakerian goal of inquiry. Accordingly, in most cases, participants respond to QUDs by asserting things they believe to be true in order to contribute to the progress of the relevant subinquiry.

As I argued in Chapters 4 and 5, whether or not one lies depends on the QUD one is addressing. Consequently, a lie—just like a truthful assertion—is an answer to a QUD. But unlike the truthful asserter, the liar asserts an answer she believes to be false and thereby steers the subinquiry away from the truth. Later in this chapter I give an account of the difference between truthful assertion, lying, and bullshitting. First I want to spell out my account of the latter.

The bullshitter makes contributions while not caring about their effect on particular subinquiries. More precisely, bullshitting is a matter of contributing to the conversation while being indifferent toward whether one's contributions are true or false answers to QUDs. Like lying, bullshitting is therefore relative to QUDs, or subinquiries. We can spell out this proposal as follows:

Bullshitting
A is bullshitting relative to a QUD q if and only if A contributes p as an answer to q and A is not concerned that p be an answer to q that she believes to be true or an answer to q that she believes to be false.

So, on this account, bullshitting centrally involves disregarding truth and falsity, as Frankfurt suggested. But while, for Frankfurt, bullshitting is marked by disregard for the truth-value of what is said, on this view, bullshitting is characterized in terms of disregard for the alethic effect of one's contributions on QUDs. As stipulated above, by a contribution we mean either an assertion or a conversational implicature.

The kind of bullshitting Frankfurt pointed to is represented by speakers who assert things without caring about the truth-value of what they are asserting. Consider, for example, Frankfurt's 4th of July orator. For concreteness, suppose one of the orator's utterances is the one in (5).

(5)   Under divine guidance our Founding Fathers created a new beginning for mankind.

The first thing to note is that the orator is making what we called a contribution to the conversation. That is, he is putting something forward for the common ground, and in particular, in uttering (5), the orator is making an assertion. In general, we assume that bullshitters are not engaged in non-assertoric speech acts like joking, irony, or play-acting. One piece of evidence for this is that bullshitting does not exempt one from the kind of commitment to what one says that characterizes ordinary cases of assertion. For example, even though the orator is bullshitting, he has no way of later denying responsibility for what he said by claiming that he was not speaking seriously. Correspondingly, the orator's statement can be met with challenges like "Why do you think so?" Such challenges are not appropriate as responses to non-assertoric utterances like jokes or lines spoken during play-acting.

To be sure, there are situations involving non-assertoric utterances that are sometimes spoken of as involving bullshitting but which should nevertheless be regarded as of a fundamentally different kind. Consider, for example, Frankfurt's (2005 [1986], 34–7) discussion of "bull sessions." One kind of bull session is the familiar sort of informal conversation in which it is understood that people tell tall tales for amusement, for example, by saying things like, "I caught a fish this big!" etc.

Frankfurt does not include utterances made as part of the kind of unserious conversation exemplified by bull sessions as instances of the phenomenon he is interested in. His motivation is that, as he says:

> while the discussion may be intense and significant, it is in a certain respect not 'for real.' [. . .] What tends to go on in a bull session is that the participants try out various thoughts and attitudes [. . .] without its being assumed that they are committed to what they say. [. . .]   (Frankfurt, 2005 [1985], 35–7)

I take it that the natural thing to say about such cases is that the participants are not making contributions to the common ground of the conversation, in the relevant sense. In particular, they are not making assertions. Correspondingly, they are not committed to the things they say. For example, if someone later challenges the bragging fisherman with having been inaccurate about the size of his catch, the fisherman is in a position to respond with, "Oh, come on, we were just fooling around!" or something similar. By contrast, as noted above, the 4th of July orator's utterance of (5) incurs the typical commitment characteristic of assertion.

On my view what marks the orator's contribution as a case of bull-shitting is that it is made without regard for its effect on the ongoing subinquiry, that is, without regard for whether it is a true or a false answer to the corresponding QUD.

Which QUD is the orator addressing? The answer depends on the details of the case. Frankfurt's remarks suggest that, as he is thinking of the case, part of the orator's indifference concerns "what his audience thinks about the Founding Fathers, or about the role of the deity in our country's history" (Frankfurt, 2005 [1986], 17). This might point to a question like (6a) or (6b) as the QUD that is being addressed by the orator's utterance of (6).

(6)   a. How should we think of the Founding Fathers?
      b. What is the role of the deity in our country's history?

As this suggests, it is not always easy to specify a particular QUD that is being addressed by a given utterance. But, as I explain below, I do not think this is a problem for my proposal.

As we have seen in Part I, it is not an assumption of this view of discourse structure that QUDs are always explicitly asked. As Roberts says, "questions are often only implicit, inferred on the basis of other cues." (Roberts, 2012, 8) The orator's speech is naturally seen as a case of this kind. In particular, it is natural to think that the occasion—a 4th of July oration—provides obvious cues, to use Roberts's terminology, for inferring one or more QUDs for (5). These may be questions like the ones in (6).

What is characteristic of the orator is that he is not concerned with providing true or false answers to such questions. In fact, the orator is most plausibly seen as disregarding whether he provides answers to QUDs *at all*. Most likely, he is concerned with presenting himself in a particular light. As Frankfurt (2005 [1986], 18) suggests, the orator "wants [his audience] to think of him as a patriot, as someone who has deep thoughts and feelings about the origins and the mission of our country, [...] and so on." He is not concerned with contributing answers to subinquiries. On my view this is what marks the orator as bullshitting. While someone who makes an assertion almost always has some goal in mind in doing so, the phenomenon of bullshitting illustrates that the goal is not always to push a subinquiry closer to the truth.

6.5. Indifference, Minimal Content, and What is Said

The key element of this way of understanding the phenomenon of speaking with indifference toward truth is that it makes it possible to distinguish different levels at which a speaker might care or not care about her contribution to a discourse. The speakers Frankfurt was interested in, like the orator, were characterized by being indifferent toward the truth-value of their assertions. On the view of assertion developed in Part I what is asserted is what is said, where what is said is the weakest answer to a QUD that entails or is entailed by the minimal content of the relevant utterance. Given this, there is a trivial sense in which if one is indifferent toward whether what one asserts is true or false one is indifferent toward providing a true or a false answer to the QUD one is addressing.

But there are other possibilities, given the picture we have been exploring. In particular, someone might take different attitudes toward the minimal content of their utterance vs. what is said by her utterance relative to particular QUDs. In fact, however, we can see that, in most cases, if you are indifferent toward whether the minimal content of your utterance is true or false, you cannot at the same time care about whether what you say (and hence assert) relative to a QUD is true or false. That is, in most cases, if you are indifferent toward whether the minimal content of your utterance is true or false, you are indifferent toward providing true or false answers to QUDs.

To see this, there are three relevant kinds of cases to consider. We will go through each in turn. First, there are cases in which the minimal content of the relevant utterance is identical to what is said. Take, for example, the dialogue in (7).

(7)   A. Who stole my pen?
      B. Mary stole your pen.

Suppose B does not really care about whether Mary stole the pen or not, and does not have any belief either way. Perhaps B just wants to accuse Mary of stealing, regardless of its truth or falsity. (We will consider more speakers like this later.) So B is indifferent toward the truth-value of the minimal content of her utterance, that is, that Mary stole A's pen. But moreover, the answer that is said, and asserted, relative to A's question is also that Mary stole A's pen. If B cared about giving a true answer, she should therefore care about it being true that Mary stole the pen, and if she cared about giving a false answer, she should care about it being false that Mary stole the pen. In other words, since she is indifferent toward whether Mary stole the pen, she must also be indifferent toward providing a true or a false answer to A's question. Hence, in cases where the minimal content of an utterance is identical to what is said relative to a QUD, indifference toward the former implies indifference toward the latter.

Second, in cases where what is said is narrower than the minimal content, the same relation can be seen to obtain. An example of this occurs in the following dialogue.[6]

(8) A. Is steel strong enough to support the roof?
     B. Steel is strong enough.

Even though there is room for discussion on this point, let us assume that the minimal content of B's reply is that steel is strong enough for anything.[7] Given this, our view predicts that what is said by B's reply relative to A's question is that steel is strong enough to support the roof. If she cares about whether steel is strong enough for the roof, she is not indifferent toward whether steel is strong enough for anything, since she cares about at least one of the things steel might be strong enough for, namely the roof. So, in this case, what is said entails the minimal content of the utterance, or put differently, what is said is a narrowing of the minimal content. This I take to be the right result. Now suppose B is indifferent toward whether steel is strong enough for anything. Perhaps she is not interested in the conversation and wants to move on, or perhaps she has some other motivation for speaking with indifference. Regardless, if B is indifferent toward whether steel is strong enough for anything, she cannot at the same time care about whether steel is strong enough to support the roof. So, in cases where what is said relative to a QUD is narrower than minimal content, if one is indifferent toward the truth-value of the latter, one is also indifferent toward providing a true or false answer to the QUD.

Finally, we have also seen that there are cases in which the relation between what is said and minimal content is reversed. That is, cases in which the minimal content of an utterance entails what is said by it relative

---

[6] Adapted from Bach (1994).
[7] See Schoubye and Stokke (2016) for discussion and references.

to a QUD, that is, where what is said is a widening of minimal content. Such cases occur in the presence of downward entailing environments, such as negation. We can see that, in cases of widening of this kind, one can in fact be indifferent toward the truth-value of minimal content while not being indifferent toward what is said. Here is an example:

(9)   A. Will I crash my car by taking this curve at this speed?
       B. You won't crash.

The minimal content of B's reply, so we assume, is that A is not going to crash her car ever. By contrast, what is said by B's utterance relative to A's question is that A will not crash her car by taking this curve at this speed. Hence, in this case, what is said is a widening of the minimal content. Worlds in which A will not crash ever form a subset of the worlds in which she will not crash by taking this curve at this speed. Suppose B is indifferent toward whether A will not crash ever. Perhaps she is just interested in the present situation. She might still care, however, about whether A will crash now. For example, B might hope that A will not crash now, even if she is indifferent toward whether A will not crash ever. Hence, even though B does not really care about whether A will never crash, she might be interested in conveying that A will not crash now by uttering what she does. So, in cases where what is said by an utterance relative to a QUD is a widening of its minimal content, one can be indifferent toward the truth-value of the minimal content while still care about providing true or false answers to the relevant QUD.

6.6. Indifference and Caring about Truth

As we saw earlier (in Section 6.2), there are also speakers who, as opposed to Frankfurt's orator, care about the truth-value of their assertions, while at the same time they seem to be speaking with indifference, in another sense. It is reasonable to suppose that this phenomenon is quite widespread in that people are often indifferent toward what they say while it would be wrong to say that they are indifferent toward whether their assertions are true or false. Our proposal allows for such cases because it takes the mark of bullshitting to be indifference toward the effect of one's assertions on QUDs, and not simply indifference toward truth-value.

We considered two main ways in which speakers might care about the truth-value of what they say. First, sometimes people take care to say true things, while being less concerned with which particular things they say. This kind of strategy was illustrated by the bullshitting student in the Careful Exam Taker case and by the filibustering of Cato the Younger. Neither is interested in asserting particular propositions because they care about the truth-value of those propositions. Rather, they merely have a general concern for asserting true propositions.

Carson imagines that the student is asked the following question in an exam for an applied ethics class:

Briefly describe the facts of the case of Dodge v. Ford and answer the following question: Was Henry Ford morally justified in his actions in this case? Defend your answer.   (Carson, 2010, 61)

But since the student is ignorant about the case, and is unable to construct a coherent argument, she gives a bullshit answer.

As the example is described, the student is nevertheless concerned with the truth or falsity of what she is asserting, since this is the way she thinks she is going to get partial credit. In particular, she is concerned with asserting things she believes to be true. For example, the student might assert things like those in (10).

(10) a. There are many important ethical questions about the role of business in society.
      b. The Ford Motor Corporation had different obligations in this case.
      c. Utilitarians hold that corporations should promote the social good.

However, the Careful Exam Taker is not concerned with whether her assertions are true or false answers to the QUD, that is, the exam question.

The case of the student's answers to the exam question is an instance of the kind of case we considered in Chapter 5 in which an utterance does not constitute an answer to a local QUD. For example, (10a) is not an answer to the question, "Was Henry Ford morally justified in his actions in this case?" I argued that in cases of this kind the interpretation defaults to the Big Question, that is, the question that partitions logical space into one cell for each possible world. Hence, relative to the Big Question, what is said by (10a) is that there are many important ethical questions about the role of business in society. The student cares about the truth of the latter proposition. In other words, she cares about the truth of what she asserts. Yet what is characteristic of her is that she makes this assertion while not caring about thereby contributing an answer to the local QUD, that is, the exam question.

It is important to distinguish this kind of case from the case of implicature. Take our example of (11).

(11)   A.   Are you going to Paul's party?
       B.   I have to work.

B's utterance does not say anything relative to A's question, and hence it is interpreted as addressing the Big Question. Against the latter, B's utterance says that B has to work. B might care about this being true. But, as opposed to the student, B moreover cares greatly about providing an answer to the local QUD, that is, the question of whether she is going to the party. The whole point of asserting that she has to work is to thereby implicate the answer to the QUD that she is not going. By contrast, the student neither cares about, nor does she succeed in, implicating an answer to the exam question by asserting things like those in (10).

On the other hand, on our view, there is a sense in which the student can be said to care about giving a true or false (in particular a true) answer to the Big Question. Consequently, since we have relativized bullshitting to QUDs, we can say that while the student is bullshitting relative to the local QUD—the exam question—she is not bullshitting with respect to the Big Question. It is a strength of our account that it permits us to give this kind of precise description of the salient feature of the case, namely that the student is simultaneously speaking with indifference on one level and speaking with care on another level.

The same points apply to the case of Cato the Younger. While he was concerned with truth in the sense of being careful to only say things he believed to be true, he was not concerned with whether his assertions were true or false answers to local QUDs. As for the case of the 4th of July orator, which questions Cato was addressing may not have been explicit. But, as I argued earlier, this does not prevent us from seeing his assertions as addressing QUDs.

The other kind of bullshitting while caring about truth was exemplified by Julia's assertion of (12) in the Wishful Thinker example:

(12)   This time of year, it's always dry in Chicago.

As in other cases, Julia's utterance is not a reply to a question that has been explicitly asked in the preceding context. But, again, I think that her assertion should nevertheless be seen as addressing a QUD. In particular, in this case, Julia's assertion is a response to Jack's utterance of, "I'm really looking forward to that Cubs game. I hope it won't rain." It is therefore natural to see her assertion as addressing a corresponding question. For simplicity, we can assume that Julia's utterance addresses the question in (13).

(13)   What are the chances of rain when we're going to see the Cubs game?

There are other ways one can try to identify the question addressed by Julia's utterance. Yet what is important for our purposes is that she is addressing one or more QUDs, and the fact that she has a particular kind of attitude toward them.

As we noted, the central feature of this kind of example is that the speaker is not indifferent toward the truth-value of what she asserts. In asserting (12), Julia is not indifferent toward the truth-value of her assertion. Julia cares very much about whether (12) is true or not. She wants it to be true (or hopes or wishes that it is). Correspondingly, there is arguably a sense in which Julia does care about whether her assertion is a true or a false answer to questions like (13). Namely, she hopes it is a true one.

However, as we are understanding the example, Julia does not believe that what she is asserting is true, even though she hopes it is, or she wants it to be. This kind of example motivates our characterization of bullshitting in terms of indifference toward contributing answers that one believes to be true or answers that one believes to be false.

To be sure, there are nearby versions of the case where Julia does believe, perhaps irrationally, that what she asserts is true. Perhaps she has convinced herself of its truth. Yet, in that case, it is no longer right to describe Julia as bullshitting. Rather, in this case, she resembles the creationist teacher we considered earlier. As we said, even though Stella believes that she lacks evidence for her claim, she is not bullshitting when she asserts (3).

(3)   God created the species.

The reason is that Stella firmly believes that what she is asserting is true, even though she might be violating various norms concerning evidence, or perhaps norms of rationality, by having this belief. We can imagine a version of the Wishful Thinker case in which Julia really does believe that it is always dry in Chicago at that time of year. In that case, however, she is no longer bullshitting but is making a contribution to the conversation that she believes to be a true answer to a QUD, even though her belief might be irrationally held.

Alternatively, Julia might even believe that she does have evidence for the claim about the weather, and she might believe it on the basis of this false conception of its being supported by evidence. In that case she is like the science fiction reader who asserts that there is life on Saturn because she believes it and believes she has evidence for it. Again, this is not a case of bullshitting, on our account. Rather, if you assert what you believe to be true because you are concerned with providing it as an answer to a QUD, you are not engaging in the kind of claptrap or hot air that Frankfurt first identified.

Matters are complicated here by the fact that one may hold beliefs unconsciously, and one may hold conflicting beliefs. This complication, and its ramifications for insincerity, will be the subject of Chapters 8 and 9. For now, though, we will ignore it and continue to focus on how to understand speakers who exhibit indifference toward what they say in terms of their beliefs.

Finally, as we saw from Webber's (2013) example, another way of engaging in bullshitting while taking care to assert something one believes to be true is to do so with the object of implicating something one does not care about. This is another way of making a contribution, in our sense of either asserting or conversationally implicating, while being indifferent toward its effect on QUDs. For example, consider again the toothpaste advertisement featuring (1).

(1) Used by dentists!

The advertiser who asserts (1), so we assume, is deliberately asserting something she believes to be true. But she might thereby be implicating something else, such as that the toothpaste is good. In doing so, she is addressing a QUD like (14).

(14) Is this toothpaste good?

The assertion in (1) is made with the aim of implicating an answer to (14). Yet the advertiser is not concerned with whether this implicature constitutes an answer to (14) that she believes to be either true or false.

Hence, while the advertiser is not bullshitting with respect to the Big Question, she is bullshitting relative to a local question like (14).

6.7. Evasion and Changing the Topic

Carson points out that a common reason people engage in bullshitting is in order to evade certain topics of conversation:

Sometimes we are pressured to answer questions that we do not want to answer. When asked such questions, people often produce bullshit responses that do not directly answer the questions. (Carson, 2010, 60)

However, it might be thought that our account implies that evasion is not a form of bullshitting. Typically, someone who is being evasive changes the topic. Given the framework we are assuming, to change the topic is to introduce a new QUD. Someone who evades a topic of conversation by introducing a new QUD might nevertheless be concerned with providing true or false answers to the new QUD. On our account, therefore, this type of evasion does not constitute bullshitting with respect to the new QUD. Still, as I explain below, while some evasion may turn out not to be bullshitting, our account nevertheless leaves room for a large amount of evasive bullshitting.

First, not all evasion involves changing the topic. Sometimes there is no room for introducing alternative QUDs. This is illustrated by the Careful Exam Taker. The student, in this case, is naturally described as evading a QUD, that is, the exam question. She realizes that she has nothing to contribute to this question, and she therefore makes statements that, while she believes them, are not designed to be true or false answers to the exam question.

Yet the exam situation is special, in that, while one can evade an exam question in the way the Careful Exam Taker does, one cannot change the topic. That is, one cannot propose to introduce a different QUD. In such cases evasion implies not addressing the only QUD that could be the topic of conversation. Hence, in such settings, evasion inevitably involves bullshitting.

Second, even if one does succeed in changing the topic, one might not care about providing true or false answers to the new QUD one has introduced. In such cases one is bullshitting, on our account. Imagine, for example, that a politician is asked the question in (15).

(15)   Who is responsible for the deficit?

But because the politician does not want to discuss this question, she changes the topic and starts talking about climate change. She might say something like:

(16)   Well, there are many issues we need to address. I think one of the most pressing one concerns the urgent problems brought about by the impending rise of the sea levels.

She then goes on to expound at length on the causes of global warming, etc. The politician here introduces a new QUD, for example, the one in (17).

(17)   What are the most pressing problems we need to address?

Her assertion of (16) addresses (17) rather than (15). On our account, bullshitting is relative to QUDs. So the politician may or may not be bullshitting with respect to the new QUD, that is, (17), which she has introduced as a way of evading the original question in (15). She might be in earnest about the problems brought about by the impending rise of the sea levels being among the most pressing issues that need to be addressed. Accordingly, that the politician is evading the question she was asked does not necessarily make her a bullshitter, even though, to be sure, she may still be open to criticism for evading the original question.

Conversely, it is not uncommon that someone evades a question by introducing a new topic, which they then go on to bullshit about. For example, the politician who responds to (15) with (16) might be bullshitting with respect to (17). That is, she might be bullshitting in asserting that the rising sea levels are among the most important things that should be addressed. Thereby she would be evading the original question in (15) by bullshitting about (17). As before, it is an advantage of our account that it can capture such differences between cases.

A slightly more subtle type of situation is illustrated by an example that Carson (2010) gives:

In a televised presidential debate, a candidate is asked the following question: "I want to ask you about your criteria for nominating people to the US Supreme Court. Would you be willing to nominate anyone who supports the Roe v. Wade decision? Or, will you make opposition to abortion and Roe v. Wade a requirement for anyone you nominate?" The answer is that the candidate is not willing to nominate anyone who supports Roe v. Wade. [. . .] The candidate wishes that the question had not been asked and gives the following bullshit reply that completely fails to answer or address the question that was asked: "Look, there are lots of things to be taken into account when nominating someone for the Supreme Court. This isn't the only relevant consideration. I want someone with a good legal mind and judicial experience who supports my judicial philosophy of following the constitution as it is written." (Carson, 2010, 60)

In this case the politician is not changing the topic in the same sense as someone who talks about climate change in response to a question about a budget deficit. Rather, it is natural to describe the politician in Carson's example as merely pretending to answer the question he was asked. On our view, this is a form of bullshitting because, while the politician is trying to appear as if he is addressing the original QUD, he is ignoring it. Hence, again, relativizing the kind of indifference toward inquiry that is characteristic of these kinds of speakers to QUDs allows us to account for how people sometimes engage in bullshitting evasion.

6.8. Boosting Inquiry by Lying and Bullshitting

Both lying and bullshitting may sometimes be used to advance inquiry. For example, suppose that a prosecutor knows, through inadmissible evidence, that a suspect is guilty.[8] She is so concerned with getting the suspect convicted that she is willing to say whatever she has to in order to achieve that goal. While the prosecutor lacks a concern for the truth-value of what she says in response to questions like, "Did Smith have a motive?" or "Was Smith nearby at the time of the crime?" she is not indifferent toward the subinquiry concerning the suspect's guilt.

Relativizing bullshitting to QUDs allows us to say that, while the prosecutor is not bullshitting with respect to the subinquiry concerning the suspect's guilt, she is bullshitting with respect to (sub-)subinquiries like those about the suspect's motive and whereabouts. To be more precise about this kind of case, let us picture the discourse structure in this case in a rough-and-ready way, as represented by (18).

(18) Is Smith guilty?

    a. Was Smith at the scene of the crime at the time?

        i. Were Smith's fingerprints found at the scene?

        ii. Did anyone see Smith there at the time?

    . . .

    . . .

---

[8] I owe this example to Roy Sorensen (pers. comm.)

The prosecutor can be described as having the goal of making the yes-answer to (18) common ground. However, she is willing to say what she has to concerning subquestions like those in (18a) in order to get there. As we might say, such situations are cases of boosting inquiry by lying or bullshitting.

Consider first a scenario in which the prosecutor decides to lie about one of the subquestions to (18). Suppose for example that she asserts the yes-answer to (18a$_{ii}$), even though she knows this to be false. Given that the assertion is accepted, it has the effect of adding to the common ground the proposition that Smith was seen at the scene. In turn, this means excluding from the context set all worlds in which Smith was not seen at the scene. Hence, the assertion also excludes the actual world from the context set. Suppose the prosecutor through this and various other arguments manages to make it common ground that Smith is guilty. So she ends up having excluded from the common ground all worlds in which Smith is not guilty. In other words the context set contains only worlds in which Smith was seen at the scene and is guilty. To illustrate, the prosecutor's strategy has the result of adding the worlds in the shaded region of Figure 6.1 to the context set of the discourse. (Here the left-hand rectangle is the set of worlds s where Smith was seen at the scene, the right-hand rectangle is the set of worlds $\neg s$ where he was not seen, the circle is the set of worlds g where Smith is guilty, and @ is the actual world.)

As represented here, among the worlds in which Smith was seen, some are worlds in which he is guilty and some are worlds in which he is not guilty, and similarly, among the worlds where Smith was not seen, in some he is guilty and in others he is not. In turn, the actual world is located in

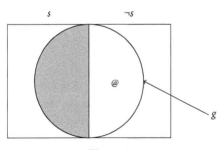

Figure 6.1

logical space among the worlds where he is guilty but was not seen at the scene.

In this case the context set ends up containing only worlds in which Smith is guilty, even though it does not contain the actual world. Hence, this is a way of representing the prosecutor's strategy of lying in order to get to the truth. Since she lies along the way, the result will not be one that incorporates the whole truth, i.e. it contains the false information that Smith was seen. And yet, in this way, we end up with a discourse that is incompatible with the false information that Smith is not guilty. Hence, the prosecutor is not so much getting to the truth by lying, but is more accurately described as excluding falsity by lying.

In other variations of this kind of example, the prosecutor might instead go in for bullshitting about various subquestions in order to achieve the same goal. These will be cases in which the prosecutor makes assertions about subquestions without caring whether her answers are true or false. Instead she makes her assertions simply to make sure that it becomes common ground that Smith is guilty. Doing so, she might end up developing the common ground in a way analogous to the above example, i.e. by adding false information, she might end up excluding the actual world. Alternatively, while bullshitting about subquestions, she might inadvertently end up excluding only false information from the common ground, and hence as a result produce a context set that does include the actual world. (The same can happen if the prosecutor is lying but what she asserts is true, even though she believes it is not.)

So our account is not only compatible with cases in which a particular subinquiry is furthered by bullshitting or lying, it provides an elegant and straightforward way of representing these kinds of situations. In the next chapter I provide a more detailed picture of the relation between bullshitting, lying, and truthful assertion.

7

Bullshitting and Lying

In the last chapter I gave an account of the mode of indifferent speech that Frankfurt identified as bullshitting. I proposed to understand the relevant kind of indifference as indifference toward making contributions to the conversation according to what one believes to be true or false. According to Frankfurt's original analysis, bullshitting was sharply contrasted with lying. Frankfurt argued that, whereas the bullshitter is characterized by not caring about the truth or falsity of what she asserts, the liar is "inescapably concerned with truth-values." (2005 [1986], 51) Yet, as Frankfurt later came to recognize, it is natural to think that the two categories overlap in that speakers sometimes assert something they believe to be false while at the same time exhibiting the kind of indifference characteristic of bullshitting.

In this chapter I will propose a way of understanding the relation between bullshitting and lying, that is, between speaking with indifference toward truth and asserting disbelieved information. In doing so we will see that there are different kinds of lying, differentiated by different attitudes liars might take to what they say and in particular different conversational goals liars might care about.

The view we have argued for here agrees that the categories of lying and bullshitting are not mutually exclusive. On our view someone is bullshitting relative to a QUD if and only if she is indifferent toward whether her contribution is an answer that her evidence suggests to be true or suggests to be false. But, moreover, if someone with this sort of attitude asserts things they believe to be false, they are both lying and bullshitting. We will see that the QUD framework provides a view on which while lying and bullshitting are not mutually exclusive, most lies are not also instances of bullshitting.

7.1. Real Lying and Lying to Discredit Others

In contrast to bullshitters, most speakers do care about the effects of their assertions on QUDs, and in particular, most speakers do care whether their assertions are true or false answers to QUDs. Yet there are different ways in which one can satisfy this condition, that is, there are different ways of avoiding bullshitting in the sense of being concerned with QUDs. It is useful to start by mapping out some of these before returning to the relation between lying and bullshitting.

First, and most obviously, there is the vast range of everyday situations in which people are interested in asserting true answers to QUDs because they are interested in contributing positively to the corresponding subinquiries. Call such speakers honest folks. For example, suppose Mitch asks Sarah what time it is. Sarah wants to help Mitch learn what time it is. So she looks at her watch, sees that it is 4 p.m. and tells Mitch that it is 4 p.m. Assertions like this are not lies, since they are cases in which the speaker believes what she is asserting. Nor are they cases of bullshitting, since they are cases in which the speaker wants her assertion to contribute an answer to the relevant QUD that her evidence suggests to be true. Honest folks neither lie nor bullshit.

Opposed to these are cases in which someone has the specific goal of adding a false proposition p to the discourse, not because she is particularly interested in adding p itself to the discourse but because she is interested in adding something false to the discourse. This is what Augustine called the "real" lie, that is, "the lie which is told purely for the pleasure of lying and deceiving [. . .]." (Augustine (1952 [395]b, 87) Someone who tells you such a lie wants you to believe something false because it is false.

Other examples of Augustinian real lying are instances where someone tells a lie so that she can subsequently discredit the victim when she repeats it. These are likewise instances in which someone wants her victim to believe something false because it is false. A noticeable, nonfictional example of this has been discussed by Peter Ludlow. In describing the group of security teams known as "Team Themis," and the efforts to undermine the credibility of the journalist Glenn Greenwald, Ludlow reports that:

the plan called for actions to "sabotage or discredit the opposing organization" including a plan to submit fake documents and then call out the error.

(Ludlow, 2013)

Ludlow describes several other plans of this kind, including:

> a proposal for the Chamber of Commerce to undermine the credibility of one of its critics, a group called Chamber Watch. The proposal called for first creating a "false document, perhaps highlighting periodical financial information," giving it to a progressive group opposing the Chamber, and then subsequently exposing the document as a fake to "prove that U.S. Chamber Watch cannot be trusted with information and/or tell the truth." (Ludlow, 2013)

Even though, strictly speaking, these cases may not involve lying—in the sense that they do not involve *saying* things that are believed to be false (see Chapter 4)—it is important to note that the Augustinian phenomenon of real lying extends to deception that is not lying. In the cases Ludlow discusses, someone is being given false information simply because it is false.

Real liars are not indifferent toward making true or false contributions to the topic of conversation. I once asked a group of kids directions in an unfamiliar neighborhood of my hometown. They sent me the wrong way. But, since they were clearly locals, I have every reason to believe they did know the right answer. Evidently, they gave me an answer they knew to be false simply because they took pleasure in making me go the wrong way. Such liars are not bullshitters, on my account. They are not indifferent toward whether their assertions are true or false answers to QUDs—they are concerned with their assertions being false answers.

Similarly, suppose that before a big meeting with a foreign client Bill asks Alice the question in (1).

(1)   What's the name of their country's capital?

Alice might give Bill a lying answer, not because she is particularly interested in what he believes about the name of the capital, but because she is planning to discredit him during the meeting by tricking him into blundering about the name. But it is still the case that Alice gives the answer she does because she cares about it being a false answer. She is not indifferent toward whether her assertion moves the subinquiry about the name of the capital toward truth or falsity, and so she is not bullshitting.

7.2. Frankfurt on Lying vs. Bullshitting

Frankfurt (2005 [1985]) originally suggested that the categories are mutually exclusive. One reason for this was Frankfurt's observation that lying involves beliefs about what is true, whereas bullshitting does not require this kind of perspective. As he said:

> It is impossible for someone to lie unless he thinks he knows the truth. Producing bullshit requires no such conviction. A person who lies is thereby responding to the truth, and he is to that extent respectful of it.   (Frankfurt, 2005 [1985], 55–6)

This was also the reason Frankfurt thought that "bullshit is a greater enemy of the truth than lies are." (Frankfurt, 2005 [1985], 61).

Subsequently Frankfurt (2002) nevertheless came to recognize that the two categories overlap in the sense that someone might be telling lies while still being indifferent in the way relevant for bullshitting:

> My presumption is that advertisers generally decide what they are going to say in their advertisements without caring what the truth is. Therefore, what they say in their advertisements is bullshit. Of course, they may also happen to know, or they may happen to subsequently discover, disadvantageous truths about their product. In that case what they choose to convey is something that they know to be false, and so they end up not merely bullshitting but telling lies as well.
>
> (Frankfurt, 2002, 341)

My account agrees that lying and bullshitting are not mutually exclusive. For example, suppose the 4th of July orator, during his speech, tells the story about George Washington cutting down a cherry tree as a child, even though he has considered the evidence for the authenticity of the story and believes it to be false. Since the orator in this case is asserting something he believes to be false, he is lying. But this does not mean that he is not also bullshitting. Even though he asserts something he believes to be false, this does not mean that he makes his assertion with a concern for providing an answer to a subinquiry. In line with how I described the orator earlier, his goal in telling the story might not be to provide an answer to a QUD, but rather to present himself in a particular way. If so, he is lying while being indifferent toward whether his assertion is a contribution to a QUD, and hence he is both lying and bullshitting.

On the other hand, I think my account should be able to limit the amount of overlap between bullshitting and lying, and thereby preserve the core of Frankfurt's (2005 [1985]) original idea that there is a significant and interesting difference between these two kinds of non-alethic modes of speech. There is a difference between most liars and liars who are moreover exhibiting the kind of indifference that is at the core of the phenomenon of bullshitting.

Frankfurt's own remarks on the overlap between lying and bullshitting arguably do not suffice for capturing this difference. As we saw above, according to the way Frankfurt thinks of the bullshitting advertisers, they "decide what they are going to say in their advertisements without caring what the truth is." (Frankfurt, 2002, 341) Yet this characterization is arguably insufficient to distinguish them from many liars, in fact, as we will see next, it is arguably insufficient to distinguish them from most liars.

7.3. Most Lying is Not Bullshitting

Frankfurt points out that most liars are not Augustinian real liars:

Everyone lies from time to time, but there are very few people to whom it would often (or even ever) occur to lie exclusively from a love of falsity or of deception.
(Frankfurt, 2005 [1985], 59)

Arguably, most cases of lying are cases in which someone has the goal of asserting something not because it is false, but because asserting that particular thing serves their purposes, regardless of its truth-value. Consider, for example, the following story.

The Lying Umbrella Saleswoman
Louise wants to sell Tom an umbrella. She knows that Tom is going to Chicago. Even though Louise believes the opposite, she invents the story that it is always raining in Chicago at that time of year, and she tells Tom that in order to make him buy the umbrella.

Unlike the Augustinian real liar, Louise is not telling Tom the lie because it is false, but because she wants to tell him that story, in order to sell him the umbrella. In particular, Louise's goals would have been satisfied, even if she believed the weather in Chicago to be the way she says it is. In that case she could just have told him what she believed. Call liars like Louise *ordinary liars*.

Given that the kind of lie Louise tells is the most common one, it would be desirable not to count such ordinary liars as also bullshitting. However, Frankfurt's suggestion about the bullshitting advertisers applies to ordinary liars, as well. It is plausible to describe Louise as deciding what she is going to say without caring what the truth is. In particular, Louise decides to tell Tom that it is always raining in Chicago at that time of year with the aim of selling him the umbrella but without caring whether it is true or false. So, given Frankfurt's (2002) remarks about the advertisers, ordinary liars like Louise will be seen as bullshitters as well.

This result is an unwelcome one, since not only does it mean that most lying is also bullshitting, but it also appears to obscure a genuine difference between speakers like Louise and speakers like the orator. In particular, there is a kind of indifference that is characteristic of the latter kind of speaker which is not characteristic of ordinary liars like Louise. It would be of interest if we can find a way of describing this kind of indifference and thereby distinguish Louise from bullshitters. As I explain below, our account offers a way of doing so.

There is a sense in which Louise is indifferent toward whether her assertion is something she believes to be a true or a false answer to the QUD—that is, *What is the weather like in Chicago this time of year?* The sense in which Louise is indifferent toward how her assertion relates to this question is the sense in which honest folks and Augustinian real liars are not indifferent to QUDs. Unlike either of these, Louise's opinion of the truth-value of the story does not play a role in why she tells it. Indeed, this is the sense in which ordinary liars satisfy Frankfurt's (2002) characterization of the bullshitting advertisers as deciding what they are going to say without caring about what the truth is.

However, there is also a sense in which Louise does care about whether her assertion is suggested by her evidence to be a true or a false answer. One way to bring this out is by noting the familiar type of ambiguity exhibited by the attribution in (2).

(2)   Louise wants to answer the QUD with something she believes to be false.

On one reading (2) is false. This is the reading on which Louise is being said to be an Augustinian real liar, that is, the reading on which Louise's goal is to assert something false because it is false. Yet on another reading, the attribution is true. This is the reading on which Louise is being said to have the goal of asserting a particular proposition p, while believing that p is false.

It is true of both the real liar and Louise that they want to contribute to the relevant subinquiry with something they believe to be false. There are different reasons why they want to do so. But, for both, what they hope to achieve is for the relevant subinquiry to move away from the truth. Hence, in that sense, neither is indifferent toward whether their assertion is a true or a false answer to the QUD. Both are concerned with giving false answers.

To be sure, the real liar and Louise differ when one considers what they would have wanted, had their beliefs been different. In particular, if the real liar had believed the proposition she asserts to be true, her goal would not be served by asserting that proposition, but would be served by asserting its negation. By contrast, Louise could have asserted the same thing, even if she believed it to be true. But this does not mean that they are not both actually concerned with asserting something false.

It is important to emphasize that the fact that we can distinguish between these two kinds of liars by appealing to different readings of ascriptions like (2) is not an artefact of our account. The analogous claims apply to ascriptions like (3).

(3)   Sue wants to tell Bob something she believes to be false.

Like (2), (3) has two readings. More generally, the difference between the real liar and ordinary liars can be seen as an instance of a familiar phenomenon. Suppose Anna wants to vote for Clinton. Moreover, Anna knows that Clinton wears pantsuits. So it is true that Anna wants to vote for the candidate who wears pantsuits. But of course, the latter statement can be read two ways. On one reading it ascribes to Anna the desire to vote for Clinton, who happens to wear pantsuits. On the other it ascribes to Anna the desire to vote for the candidate who wears pantsuits, who happens to be Clinton. This is the same kind of ambiguity as we are highlighting with (2) and (3).

In other words, on our view, ordinary liars like Louise are not bull-shitting. It is true that ordinary liars may at first sight look very much like the orator, and vice versa. However, the difference is that the orator is not concerned with contributing to a subinquiry. The orator, as we described him earlier, is interested in presenting himself in a particular light. Neither reading of the relevant version of (2) is true of the orator.

Crucially, this characterization of the orator, on our view, holds even in the case where he is lying. When the orator tells the anecdote about Washington, even though he believes it to be false, he is not doing so because he wants to contribute an answer, true or false, to a QUD like Did George Washington chop down a cherry tree as a child? Rather, he tells the story for another reason. Most likely, he wants to present himself as an admirer of Washington, or the like. Hence, when the orator is lying, he is nevertheless also bullshitting, on our view. That is, even though he is lying, he is exhibiting a distinctive kind of indifference toward the state of the discourse. On the other hand, as I have argued, ordinary liars are not indifferent in this way.

Consequently, ordinary liars, like the Augustinian real liar, are not bullshitting. The ordinary liar is concerned with truth-values, albeit in another sense than is the Augustinian real liar. So, since neither real liars nor ordinary liars are bullshitters, on our account, most lies are not instances of bullshitting.

7.4. Agnostic Bullshitting

Finally, I want to return to the Umbrella story we looked at briefly at the beginning of the book, in Chapter 1. (We rename it here in order to avoid confusion with the case from above.)

The Bullshitting Umbrella Saleswoman

Thelma wants to sell Tom an umbrella. She knows that Tom is going to Chicago. Even though Thelma has no idea whether this is true or not, she invents the story that it is always raining in Chicago at that time of year, and she tells this to Tom in order to make him buy the umbrella.

As we saw, on the account of lying I favor, you lie only if you say something you believe to be false. Hence, if you say something of which you are ignorant, or of which you are agnostic, you are not lying.

In accordance with this, I think Thelma is not lying, but bullshitting. Unlike the real liar, Thelma is not concerned with asserting that it is always raining in Chicago because she believes that to be false and she wants to deceive. Like Louise, Thelma is making her assertion because asserting that particular thing serves her purposes. But unlike Louise, she is conscious of being ignorant of the truth-value of her assertion. So there is a natural sense in which she asserts what she does while not caring about whether she is thereby contributing a true or a false answer to the QUD about the weather.

Another way to make the point is to note that *neither* reading of the attribution corresponding to (2), i.e. "Thelma wants to answer the QUD with something she believes to be false" is true. It is not that there is some proposition that Thelma believes to be false and she wants to contribute that proposition as an answer, as is the case for Louise. Nor is her goal simply to assert some proposition that she believes to be false, as is the case for the real liar. Obviously the analogous points hold concerning Thelma's regard for truth, as opposed to falsity. Hence, Thelma is indifferent toward whether her assertion is a true or a false answer to the QUD she is addressing.

Even though lies like Louise's are commonplace, bullshitting is undeniably equally familiar. Frankfurt may not have been right that bullshitting is particular to our own culture—most likely, people in most societies often say things without caring about contributing to the progress of inquiry. Yet it is clear that bullshitting of the kind perpetrated by the 4th of July Orator, by Julia the wishful Cubs fan, or by Thelma is something we frequently encounter.

8

Insincerity and the Opacity of the Self

At the beginning of Chapter 6, I highlighted the assumption from Part I that lying and insincerity in general involves conveying disbelieved information. In the last two chapters we have explored one dimension along which insincerity is a more complex phenomenon than communicating what one believes to be false. As we have seen, speakers sometimes communicate things while being indifferent toward them in various ways.

Yet the fact that disbelief is not the only kind of insincere attitude people can take to what they communicate is not the only complication that arises. Insincere speech is complicated also because what one believes and does not believe is not always transparent to oneself. In this chapter and the following one, I turn to this dimension of complexity in insincere speech.

8.1. Opacity and Deep vs. Shallow Insincerity

It is a platitude in contemporary philosophy and psychology to say that we are not always aware of our own mental states, and that, even when we are concerned with asking ourselves what we think and feel, we are not infallible about our own selves. According to this broad trend, the self is *opaque*. There are many ways of spelling this out, but it is fair to say that (some version of) the following two complementary theses would be endorsed by many:

No Self-Intimation
For some mental states S, that A is in S does not entail that A believes (consciously or unconsciously) that A is in S.

Fallibility

For some mental states S, that A believes (consciously or unconsciously) that A is in S does not entail that A is in S.

Among the kinds of mental states that are typically thought to satisfy theses like these are beliefs, knowledge, desires, intentions, emotions, evaluations, and many others.[1] Many will agree that, even if one has considered the question of whether one is in a state of this kind, one might either not have formed a belief about the matter—perhaps it was too unclear what to believe—or one might, for various reasons, have formed a false belief. Mistakes can be made due to a seemingly endless number of factors, including such things as wishful thinking, unsuspected unreliability, self-deception, carelessness, fallacious reasoning, mental illness, or misinformation obtained from others.

No Self-Intimation and Fallibility are independent of whether the relevant mental states are knowable by way of introspection. If one thinks that some states are opaque but nevertheless, in the right circumstances, if one is in such states, one can come to know this by introspection, one can still hold that introspection is a fallible faculty.[2]

The interest in No Self-Intimation and Fallibility from our perspective is that accepting (versions of) these ideas raises crucial issues concerning the nature of insincerity. Given that insincerity in speech turns on the speaker's attitudes toward the content of her utterance, No Self-Intimation and Fallibility set up an opposition between what we can call *deep* and *shallow* conceptions of insincerity. A deep conception of insincerity is one according to which insincerity turns on attitudes about which the speaker may be in the dark, that is, attitudes that the speaker might fail to recognize that she has, or about which she might be mistaken. By

---

[1] Opinions vary according to the range of states that are thought to be opaque in this way. For example, Timothy Williamson (2000) holds a strong view according to which no mental states are *luminous* in the sense that, if one asks oneself the question, one is always in a position to know whether one is in the relevant state. For discussion, see, e.g. DeRose (2002), Weatherson (2004), Vogel (2010), Greenough (2012), Zardini (2013). I assume here that No-Self Intimation and Fallibility are true for, at least, the kinds of states mentioned in the text. This assumption is largely uncontroversial. For an overview, see Schwitzgebel (2014, Sect. 1.2). See also Shoemaker (1998 [1990], 52). For some dissent, see Lear (1998).

[2] For variations and discussion, see, e.g. Alston (1971), Burge (1988), (1996), Shoemaker (1998 [1990]), (1998 [1996]), Moran (2001), Byrne (2005). For overviews, see e.g. Kim (1998, ch. 1), Schwitzgebel (2014, Sect. 4).

contrast, shallow conceptions of insincerity insist that insincerity turns on the speaker's conscious attitudes, that is, attitudes that she in fact has and is conscious of having.

This chapter argues for a shallow conception of insincerity in speech. I will propose that, in general, an insincere utterance is one that communicates something that does not correspond to the speaker's conscious attitudes. Since beliefs may be unconscious, this means that communicating information one believes to be false is not always a form of insincerity.

8.2. Searle on Expression and Insincerity

It is useful to begin by considering what is often thought to be the orthodox account of insincerity in speech, namely the one given by John Searle (1969), as part of his general theory of speech acts. According to this view, a wide range of speech acts serve to express mental attitudes:

> to assert, affirm, or state that p counts as *an expression of belief* (that p). To require, ask, order, entreat, enjoin, pray, or command (that A be done) counts *as an expression of a wish or desire* (that A be done). To promise, vow, threaten, or pledge (that A) counts as *an expression of intention* (to do A). To thank, welcome, or congratulate counts as an *expression of gratitude, pleasure* (at H's arrival), *or pleasure* (at H's good fortune).   (Searle, 1969, 65)

Against this background, Searle subscribed to the general view that a speech act is insincere if and only if the speaker fails to have the mental state expressed by it.[3] Let us call this *Searlean Orthodoxy*.

When it comes to assertion, Searlean Orthodoxy implies that an assertion is insincere when the speaker does not believe it. Let us spell this out as follows:

Searlean Orthodoxy for Assertions
An assertion that *p* by a speaker *S* is insincere if and only if *S* does not believe that *p*.

---

[3] Accordingly, Searle did not hold that one can only express mental states that one actually has (see Searle, 1969, 65.) The opposite view is held by Owens (2006). For an objection to this, see Chan and Kahane (2011). I am not concerned with giving an account of expression in this paper. See, e.g. Davis (2003), Ridge (2006), Green (2007a), (2007b), Eriksson (2011b) for recent, relevant discussion.

Versions of Searlean Orthodoxy for Assertions have been adopted by many.[4] And indeed the view is plausible for many cases. In all the cases of lying we have looked at so far, the speaker asserts something she does not believe. Take, for example, the case of Parker lying to his parents about having prepared for his chemistry exam from Chapter 6. Parker makes an assertion he believes to be false, namely that he has prepared for the exam. Moreover, since Parker is not confused or irrational, at least on this particular point, he does not believe that he has prepared for the exam. So, according to Searle's view, his assertion is correctly classified as insincere.

However, there are a number of reasons why Searlean Orthodoxy cannot be the full story about insincere speech. First, Searle's view is silent on utterances of declarative sentences that do not assert anything. Our stock example of this is the classic form of irony. Consider the story, from Chapter 2, in which we are discussing movies, and you tell me you think *Titanic* is a great movie. I exclaim in a sarcastic tone of voice,

(1) [Ironically] Oh yeah, *Titanic* is a great movie!

In cases like this the speaker is not making an assertion. The speaker is not asserting the proposition expressed by the sentence she utters, that is, in this case that *Titanic* is a great movie. Given the account of assertion and what is said we have been developing, although ironic utterances like this say things, they do not assert what is said. Nor is the ironic speaker asserting what she aims to communicate by her utterance, that is, in this case, that *Titanic* is not a great movie. One of the main points of speaking ironically is to avoid directly asserting one's opinion.

But even though ironic utterances of declarative sentences do not make assertions, they are nevertheless capable of being insincere. Suppose that, as a matter of fact, I *did* like *Titanic*, but because I am afraid of appearing unsophisticated, I want you to believe I did not. So when I utter (1) in an ironic tone of voice, I do so with the intention of (indirectly) deceiving you into thinking the opposite of what I myself think. In such a case we will want to say that the utterance is insincere. And significantly, the utterance is insincere in a sense in which standard ironic utterances are not.[5]

---

[4] See, e.g. Gibbard (1990), Simpson (1992), Green (2007a).

[5] Kumon-Nakamura, Glucksberg, and Brown (2007) argue that irony always involves a form of "pragmatic insincerity." However, it is clear that what they have in mind is not the kind of insincerity at issue in this book, that is, the notion of insincerity on which all lies are insincere.

Searlean Orthodoxy fails to capture this because it remains silent on non-assertoric uses of declarative sentences. Similarly, as we will see next, Searlean Orthodoxy also remains incomplete with respect to other kinds of indirect deception.

When speaking ironically, speakers assert neither what is said by their utterances, nor what is meant by them. By contrast, the general phenomenon of conversational implicature shows that speakers often assert one thing and mean something else. As we have seen repeatedly in Part I, one may assert something one believes to be true in order to implicate something one believes to be false. Misleading utterances of this kind are clear cases of insincere speech.

Take Abraham's utterance of (2), which we looked at in Chapter 2.

(2)   She is my sister.

While what is said, and asserted, in this case, is that Sarah is Abraham's sister, what is implicated is that she is not his wife. Since the utterance is a case of indirect deception, or misleading without lying, we will want to judge the utterance as insincere. Implicating something one believes to be false is a form of insincerity, although falsely implicating falls short of lying.

Again, Searlean Orthodoxy fails to predict this result. To be sure, it is not entirely clear whether we will want to say that, in cases of false implicature, the assertion *itself* is insincere. Searlean Orthodoxy for Assertions may be correct in predicting that asserting something one believes to be true is sufficient for the assertion itself to be not insincere, even if one does so in order to implicate something one believes to be false. However, there is a clear sense in which the utterance is insincere in such cases, and this should be explained by a general account of the insincerity conditions for utterances of declarative sentences.

The upshot is, then, that while Searlean Orthodoxy may be correct for assertion, a more complete account will need a broader understanding of insincerity for declarative utterances. But moreover, it is arguable that Searlean Orthodoxy is incorrect even for the limited case of assertion due to the belief-condition it appeals to. This issue is what I turn to next.

8.3. Assertion and Self-Deception

It has been argued that counterexamples to Searlean Orthodoxy for Assertions can be found in cases involving subjects that have false second-order beliefs, that is, false beliefs about what they believe. Such cases are cases of opacity, and in particular, they are cases of Fallibility for beliefs.

One source of this kind of opacity is self-deception. To be sure, it is questionable whether having false second-order beliefs is either necessary or sufficient for self-deception. Some philosophers argue that self-deception is not to be analyzed in terms of beliefs at all, but rather in terms of desires.[6] I will not attempt to provide an analysis of self-deception. It should be uncontroversial that having false second-order beliefs is, at least sometimes, an instance of self-deception.[7]

Here is an example that Michael Ridge (2006) gives:

> Bob believes that he believes his mother loves him but actually does not believe that she loves him. In fact, Bob believes his mother hates him. [. . .] Suppose we ask Bob whether his mother loves him and he says, "Yes, of course she does". [. . .] So according to Searle's view, Bob's answer is insincere. However, this is simply not correct. Bob's speech-act reflects delusion rather than insincerity.
>
> (Ridge, 2006, 488–9)

More schematically, this is a case in which a speaker asserts that p, believes that she believes that p, but does not in fact believe that p. Ridge's verdict on the case is that the assertion is not insincere. This I take to be correct. In other words, this is a counterexample to the right-to-left direction of Searlean Orthodoxy for Assertions.

What about the other direction? As Timothy Chan and Guy Kahane (2011) have observed, counterexamples arise from the kind of situation described in this example given by Christopher Peacocke (1998):

> Someone may judge that undergraduate degrees from countries other than her own are of an equal standard to her own, and excellent reasons may be operative in her assertions to that effect. All the same, it may be quite clear, in decisions she makes on hiring, or in making recommendations, that she does not really have this belief at all. (Peacocke, 1998, 90)

Now consider Chan's and Kahane's case:

> Suppose the professor, a Briton, is asked in a newspaper interview about how the best American universities compare with the best British ones. In order to help oppose proposed cuts in British government higher education funding, she

---

[6] See, e.g. Bach (1981).

[7] For relevant discussion, see Bach (1981), (2009), McLaughlin (1988), Johnston (1988).

answers, 'British universities are the best in the world,' even though she thinks this is not what an impartial and informed observer would say.

(Chan and Kahane, 2011, 219)

In this case a speaker asserts that p, believes that she does not believe that p, but in fact does believe that p. Yet, as Chan and Kahane point out, the assertion is insincere. Hence, this is a counterexample to the left-to-right direction of Searlean Orthodoxy for Assertions.

The conclusion to draw from this is that insincerity should not be characterized in terms of mere first-order belief.

8.4. Higher-Order Beliefs and Mental Assent

If first-order belief is not the right attitude to focus on, then what is? One suggestion is that what the cases we have looked at show is that, as we might put it in sloganized form, insincerity tracks the highest-order belief. That is, when there is a conflict between the speaker's first-order beliefs and her higher-order beliefs, then whether or not she is being insincere depends on the beliefs of the highest order.

Yet there is a further complication here. The highest-order belief in this sense need not be a conscious belief. One may have a belief that p but have an unconscious belief about this belief. For example, suppose that Michael consciously believes that there is no god but has a suppressed belief that this belief is sinful and false. (If one believes that the belief that p is false, one believes that p is false. In this case, therefore, Michael arguably also has a suppressed belief that there is no god.) Further, imagine that Michael is interviewed for a job in a religious institution. Trying to convince the interviewers of his hireability, Michael asserts:

(3)   There is a god.

Since he is conscious of believing that what he is saying is false, Michael's assertion is insincere. And yet, what is asserted corresponds to the highest-order belief that Michael has about that content.

So while the cases we looked at earlier showed that when a speaker has unconscious first-order beliefs and conscious higher-order beliefs, whether she speaks insincerely is determined by her conscious higher-order beliefs, this case shows that when a speaker has unconscious higher-order beliefs and conscious first-order beliefs, whether she speaks insincerely is determined by her conscious first-order beliefs.

In light of this it might be suggested that insincerity tracks the highest-order conscious belief. This would handle the cases we have examined above. In fact, however, this suggestion can be seen to be inadequate. Counterexamples arise from considering what is often called *judgment* or *assent*. (For the most part, I will stick to the latter term.)

Following Sydney Shoemaker (1998 [1996]), we can distinguish between *linguistic* and *mental* assent. In the former sense, one assents to a proposition "if one asserts it or answers affirmatively to a question whether it is true." (1998 [1996], 78) As such, linguistic assent is the expression of mental assent. The notion of mental assent is the relevant one here, and in what follows I will mean mental assent by "assent."[8] Mental assent, in this sense, is the mental action of judging as the result of having consciously considered a thought or issue and as such is always conscious.

As Chan and Kahane point out, assent and second-order belief may come apart. They cite the following of Shoemaker's examples:

[S]uppose that a psychiatrist tells me that I have the repressed belief that I was adopted as an infant. In fact, the psychiatrist has confused me with another patient (he has been reading the wrong case history), and has no good grounds for this belief attribution. But I accept it on his authority. It seems compatible with this that when I consider the proposition I am supposed to believe, that I was adopted, I find no evidence in its support, and am disposed to deny it.

(Shoemaker, 1998 [1996], 89–90)

What the patient assents to (that he was not adopted) here diverges from what he consciously believes he believes (that he was adopted.) Now suppose the patient is asked about his parentage and in reply asserts:

(4) I was adopted.

In this case the speaker asserts what he does not assent to, although he consciously believes he believes it. But nevertheless, the assertion is

---

[8] Note that, as Shoemaker (1998 [1996], 78) understood the notions, linguistic assent can be sincere or insincere, while mental assent cannot be insincere. By definition, one cannot mentally assent to a proposition half-heartedly, or in jest, or despite (consciously) not really accepting it. So if linguistic insincerity is characterized in terms of mental assent, as in the account I defend in this chapter, there is no sense in which the problem has been pushed back to a question of the insincerity conditions for a mental state. Cf. also Shoemaker who maintains that "When linguistic assent is sincere, it involves mental assent." (1998 [1996], 78).

insincere. So, insincerity is not always determined by the highest-order conscious beliefs.

The more plausible general condition on insincere assertion, then, involves the active, conscious attitude of mental assent rather than higher-order belief. I think this is the right idea. Next, I turn to a potential argument against it.

8.5. Huckleberry Finn

Although Chan and Kahane note that an account of insincerity in terms of assent makes the right predictions in cases like the one involving the psychiatric patient's utterance of (4), they argue that ultimately insincerity should not be analyzed in terms of assent. Their argument turns on the case of Huckleberry Finn who, although superficially endorsing the racist morals of his time, finds himself aiding a run-away slave in his attempt to escape pursuers.[9] Chan and Kahane describe a twist on the story involving self-deception:

Huck knows that search parties are on their trail. Whenever Huck is troubled by the fact that he is doing something (he takes to be) wrong, he tells himself that the following day he will deliberately lead Jim into the pursuers' likely path. But each time he either forgets about the plan, or delays it under some flimsy pretext, while continuing on the path to safety. One night Huck tells himself that there is still time to carry out his scheme, but in fact (though he wouldn't admit it) he possesses enough information to know that they have left the pursuers behind. When Jim anxiously asks, "Do you think we have shaken off the search parties?" Huck answers, "Yes, we have indeed shaken them off," taking himself to be lying in order to keep Jim at his side until he turns him in. Jim feels reassured, and Huck finds himself strangely satisfied and relieved.   (Chan and Kahane, 2011, 225–6)

Chan and Kahane conclude:

Huck assents to the proposition "We have [not] shaken off the search parties" yet asserts its negation. Nevertheless, his assertion seems to us clearly sincere.

(Chan and Kahane, 2011, 226)

---

[9] See Twain (1884). For more, relevant discussion of Huckleberry Finn, see Bennett (1974), Arpaly and Schroeder (1999).

According to Chan and Kahane, then, the case of Huckleberry Finn shows that sincerely asserting is compatible with not assenting to what is asserted.

I think this conclusion should be rejected. There are two reasons for this. The first is that Huck's assertion is made with the intention of deceiving Jim into thinking something he himself does not, that is, that they have escaped. This is evident from Chan's and Kahane's description of the case. The second is that Huck is arguably lying. Although Chan and Kahane do not explicitly present this judgment, it is nevertheless strongly suggested by the example. In particular, Chan and Kahane are explicit that Huck is "taking himself to be lying," and that he would not admit that he has enough evidence to realize that what he says is in fact true.

These features of Huck's assertion should be sufficient to judge it as insincere. In particular, if Chan and Kahane are right, one can consciously lie and intend to deceive while not being insincere. Both of these consequences are counterintuitive. Hence, I think the right thing to say about the case of Huck is that his utterance is insincere.

So since there are compelling reasons to reject Chan's and Kahane's argument, we may continue to assume that the right account of insincere assertion should be couched in terms of mental assent. The challenge now is to spell out such an account in more detail.

9

Shallow Insincerity

In the last chapter we considered the contrast between what I called "deep" vs. "shallow" conceptions of insincerity. We saw that Chan's and Kahane's (2011) account of insincerity is an instance of a "deep" conception of insincerity, as seen from their discussion of the case of Huckleberry Finn. On their view what matters for whether an assertion is insincere is the underlying motivations with which it is made, even if they are unconscious. As they say:

we might be insincere even when, from the inside, it appears to us that we are doing our best to present things just as we take them to be.

(Chan and Kahane, 2011, 233)

As foreshadowed, I disagree with this general outlook. I argued that Huck's intention to deceive Jim by lying to him is sufficient to count his assertion as insincere, even though this intention is, in part, motivated by Huck's unconscious desire to facilitate Jim's escape. Hence, my view can be described as one on which insincerity is shallow, in the sense that, in cases of conflict like this one, what matters for whether someone speaks insincerely is her conscious mental attitudes concerning what she communicates.[1] In this chapter I begin to map out a shallow conception of insincerity along these lines.

9.1. Conscious Intentions

Although I disagree with Chan's and Kahane's deep conception of insincerity, I agree with them that an adequate account of insincerity must be sensitive to what they call "the conative dimension." (Chan and

---

[1] Similarly, Sorensen (2011) argues that lying turns on what he calls "shallow belief," by which he means, roughly, a disposition to assent to a particular sentence.

Kahane, 2011, 228) Whether an utterance is insincere or not depends not only on the speaker's attitudes and their relation to the relevant content that is communicated, but also on, broadly speaking, the speaker's aims in making the utterance. But whereas, for Chan and Kahane, what counts here are the speaker's deep, underlying motivations, I think insincerity turns on the speaker's conscious aims.

I propose to represent the conative dimension of insincerity in speech by the speaker's *intentions*. Specifically, I will argue that insincerity in speech turns on the speaker *lacking* particular *conscious* intentions. As I said in Chapter 8, I assume that intentions are part of the opaque part of the self. Hence, I assume that No Self-Intimation and Fallibility are true for intentions. Not only may one be unconscious of one's intentions; even if one has formed an opinion of what they are, one may be mistaken about them.

Some think that, even though intentions satisfy at least No Self-Intimation, intentions nevertheless differ from other parts of the opaque self such as beliefs and desires in that intentions are characteristically accessible to consciousness. Chan and Kahane write:

An agent's intention [. . .] is akin to the disposition to assent in that it is accessible to awareness, even when it is not actually conscious.

(Chan and Kahane, 2011, 228)

I assume that what they have in mind is that intentions are accessible to awareness by way of introspection. But, as we noted earlier, even if a mental feature is accessible through introspection, it may still satisfy both No Self-Intimation and Fallibility.

Another reason to be cautious about the claim that intentions may be opaque might arise from the well-known thought that when one acts intentionally one knows what one is doing. According to Elizabeth Anscombe's (1963) influential account, one's intentional actions belong to a category of things of which one has knowledge "without observation," in the sense that, according to Anscombe, one knows the position of one's limbs without observation. On this view, roughly, if one is intentionally ϕ'ing, one knows that one is ϕ'ing.[2]

---

[2] Philosophers who agree, with a great deal of variation, include Velleman (1989), Moran (2004), Setiya (2007), (2011).

A more precise version of the view would need to take into account that, as Anscombe (1963, 11) points out, "a man may know that he is doing a thing under one description, and not under another."[3] As she puts it:

> the statement that a man knows he is doing X does not imply the statement that, concerning anything which is also his doing X, he knows that he is doing that thing. So to say that a man knows he is doing X is to give a description of what he is doing *under which* he knows it. (1963, 11)

So, on an Anscombian view, when one ϕ's intentionally, there is a description under which one knows, without observation, that one is ϕ'ing.

This thesis does not entail, without further argument, that if one is intentionally ϕ'ing, one knows what one's intention in ϕ'ing is. However, it is crucial to note that, even if one thinks there is a plausible additional claim of this kind, Anscombian views are compatible with the idea that either knowledge of one's intentional actions or knowledge of one's intentions may be opaque. Indeed, many Anscombians agree that the view must be qualified in this respect. For example, Kieran Setiya argues that, even if one accepts the view that "what we do intentionally, we do knowingly":

> This is not to say that one must consciously attend to whatever one is doing intentionally. It can be said of me as I sleep that I am writing a paper on *Intention*, and that I know I am, just as I know who my parents are and where I was born.
> (Setiya, 2011, 171)

One way in which one can reject the claim that an Anscombian view of intentional action is incompatible with No Self-Intimation, then, is to accept that the knowledge that invariably attends intentional action may be unconscious.[4] Similarly, one might think that even if we should accept that when one intentionally ϕ's, one knows what one's intention in ϕ'ing is, such knowledge itself may be opaque. Given a view of this kind, then, even though what one does intentionally, one does knowingly, both what one is doing intentionally and one's intentions in doing it may be unconscious.

There are more complications and qualifications here.[5] But for our purposes it is sufficient to note that there are good reasons to take the view that intentions may be opaque to be the consensus. However, since I think

---

[3] Cf. Velleman (1989, 15–16).   [4] Cf. Velleman (1989, 17).
[5] For an overview, see Setiya (2014).

insincerity turns on whether the speaker has certain conscious intentions, it will not be a threat to my view if it turns out that intentions are not part of the opaque self. Still, it remains plausible that intentions satisfy at least No Self-Intimation, that is, that one might be unaware of one's intentions. So I will not assume that intentions are always conscious.

Granting that intentions may be unconscious, then, I want to argue that insincerity in speech turns on the speaker lacking a conscious intention to speak in accordance with what she assents to. Along these lines, a simple proposal is that an utterance is insincere when it is not consciously intended to communicate something the speaker assents to. In terms of the Stalnakerian picture of communication, it might be proposed that insincerity is a matter of speaking without a conscious intention to make common ground information one assents to.[6] We will see later that this proposal needs to be refined in certain ways, but it is worth beginning by considering the core idea.

The first thing to note is that this idea relies on a particular way of understanding what an utterance is. I will postpone elaborating on this until Chapter 10, where I will comment on the broader issue of communicating and expressing one's attitudes in language. But we should note here that merely tokening a sentence of a language, even a language one can speak and understands, is not sufficient for making an utterance, in this sense. Suppose, for example, that in my sleep I say, "I'm French." I do not have a conscious intention to communicate anything, when I do so—let alone a conscious intention to communicate something I assent to. But my speech, in this kind of case, is not insincere. Nor is it sincere. It does not qualify as evaluable as sincere or insincere at all.

Again, I postpone until Chapter 10 further discussion of how to distinguish this kind of speech from the kind that is evaluable for sincerity and insincerity. In the rest of this chapter, as I have done so far in this book, I assume that the examples under discussion all fall within the category of speech that is evaluable for sincerity and insincerity.

9.2. Thinking while Speaking

Even if we screen off things like talking in one's sleep, however, an immediate challenge is that it may look like people often say things without

---

[6] Cf. Stokke (2014).

consciously intending to communicate something they assent to. And in many of these kinds of situations, the speaker is not being insincere. In particular, we often speak spontaneously and without premeditation. But we are not always insincere when we do so. Here is an example of a familiar kind:

Spontaneous Helpfulness
I walk past two tourists on the street, and I overhear them discussing where the museum is. Without thinking much about it, as I walk past, I tell them:

(1)   It's two blocks south of here.

There are two ways in which this kind of example might be thought to present a challenge to the view we are considering. First, it might be argued that, given the impulsive character of my utterance, I cannot be said to have a conscious intention to communicate something to the tourists in this example. And second, one might think that I cannot be said to assent to what I say, in the sense of consciously endorsing it.

However, on considering this kind of example further, we can see that neither of these claims hold up. The problem with the first complaint is that it is not ultimately plausible to say that this kind of spontaneous speaker lacks a conscious intention to communicate what she says. In the example above it is true that I might not have gone through the process of mentally asking myself, "Am I going to help them out?" and hence, I might not actually have tokened a thought like, "I'm going to tell them where the museum is." Yet this kind of mental process cannot of course be a constraint on intention-formation in general. If it were, we would not have many intentions. Indeed, it seems natural to ascribe to me a conscious intention to tell the tourists where the museum is. I am clearly aware of what I am doing. I am conscious of my action of telling the tourists the way to the museum. This action is an intentional action. And moreover, I am also aware of my reason for doing it, namely that I want to help them out.

Many philosophers of action hold that ϕ'ing intentionally does not always involve acting with an intention to ϕ.[7] This kind of distinction was made prominent by Michael Bratman's (1987) influential treatment.

---

[7] For discussion of this relevant to lying, see also Pepp (forthcoming).

To take Bratman's (1987, 123) well-known example, if I intend to run a marathon I might also believe that I will thereby wear down my sneakers. But when I run the marathon, according to Bratman, while I am intentionally wearing down my sneakers, I am not running the marathon with an intention to wear down my sneakers. For Bratman, acting with an intention to ϕ involves *endeavoring* to ϕ, where this means that "other things equal, I will be prepared to make adjustments in what I am doing in response to indications of my success or failure [...]" (Bratman, 1987, 129)

We can note that, given a distinction like Bratman's between intentionally doing something and doing something with an intention of doing it, my utterance in the Spontaneous Helpfulness example is most naturally seen as uttering with an intention of telling the tourists where the museum is. Indeed, in Bratman's terminology, I can be described as endeavoring to tell them where the museum is. I would be prepared to make adjustments in what I am doing in response to indications of failure. Suppose, for example, that while I am speaking, I realize that the wind is too strong, and they cannot hear me. I might take a step back, raise my voice, and repeat what I said. Or if I realize that they do not speak English, I might try another language, or I might point instead.

Indeed, it seems natural to say that if one thinks of variations of the example where I am not prepared to make such adjustments, it becomes more plausible to think of my utterance as insincere. Of course, as Bratman specifies, this has to be taken "other things equal." That is, if there are other circumstances that override my making these kinds of adjustments—perhaps I am in a hurry or I am on the phone—this does not mean that the relevant intention cannot be attributed to me. Still, if I am making no more than a half-hearted attempt, and I would not really care if I found out that the tourists could not hear me, I am not endeavoring, in Bratman's sense, and I cannot be said to make my utterance with an intention of communicating. Correspondingly, it is natural to say that, in such cases, my utterance is insincere. Yet, in the original case, where I am genuinely trying to help the tourists, it is plausible to describe what I am doing as making an utterance with an intention of communicating what I say.[8]

---

[8] The kind of spontaneous action exemplified by Spontaneous Helpfulness should be distinguished from mere reflex behavior, such as Bratman (1987, 126) describes with an

The second challenge was that, even if it is plausible to argue that, in cases like the Spontaneous Helpfulness example, there is a conscious intention to communicate, it may still be thought implausible to say that what is said is something the speaker assents to. Even though I know that the museum is two blocks south of where we are, and I would be able to bring this knowledge to mind, I may not have actively mentally assented to this proposition in Shoemaker's sense of having asked myself the question and answered affirmatively. Indeed, the Spontaneous Helpfulness example brings out that just because the speaker has not gone through the process of mentally assenting to what she says, this does not make her utterance insincere.

There is, however, a natural way of describing this kind of case, which is in line with the proposal on the table. Namely, even though I have not actively assented to the proposition that the museum is two blocks south of where we are *prior* to making the utterance, there is still a straightforward sense in which I am saying something I assent to. In particular, in this kind of case, I assent to what is said *as I say it*. The act of saying that the museum is two blocks south of here can be described as the external manifestation of the mental assent to that proposition, which takes place just as I say it.[9] Indeed, a great deal of our talk is characterized by this kind of simultaneity between outward utterance and mental assent or, as we might put it, thinking while speaking. We think as we talk, but that does not mean our talk is insincere. We are able to consciously endorse what we say, as we say it.

9.3. Speaking without Thinking

A different class of examples concern speaking without thinking. The type of account we are considering has the resources for explaining a range

example of catching a ball. Bratman rightly notes that such actions may best be characterized as neither intentional nor unintentional, or as manifestations of long-term intentions or plans. Either way, there is no corresponding sense in which my utterance in Spontaneous Helpfulness is unreflective in the sense of being a mere reflex.

[9] This does not mean that, in these kinds of cases, one's utterance is also always an instance of linguistic assent, in Shoemaker's (1998 [1996]) sense. The latter is the act of uttering an affirmation to a question that is asked explicitly. Rather, what I am claiming is that, in cases like the one discussed here, an assertoric utterance is the external manifestation of an act of mental assent. To be sure, such an utterance may also be an instance of linguistic assent, but it may also just be a declarative utterance in its own right.

of these. Consider first the following situation described by Jessica Pepp (forthcoming):

Anxious Dinner Host

Consider an anxious dinner host who has been informed that one of his guests, Isaac, is a vegetarian. He doesn't know Isaac well, so one of the primary ways in which he thinks of Isaac is as a vegetarian. Being the anxious type when it comes to entertaining, he's worked hard to ensure there are sufficient vegetarian options at the dinner. He's highly sensitive to the feelings of his guests and wants everyone to feel welcome. As a result, upon noticing that the other guests keep on neglecting to pass the steak to Isaac, he says, "Isaac might like some meat." (Pepp, forthcoming)

According to Pepp's description of the case, "The host is disposed to dissent from what he says [. . .]. But he is anxious and addled, and doesn't perform the needed bit of reasoning. Still, his assertion is not untruthful." (Pepp, forthcoming)

Given this description of the example, the host says that p (that Isaac might like some meat), even though he is disposed to assent to not-p. And moreover, it is plausible to think of the host as consciously intending to communicate that p, and correspondingly as not consciously intending to communicate that not-p. If Pepp is right, therefore, that the host is not insincere, this case might look like a potential problem for our suggestion that insincerity is a matter of lacking conscious intentions to communicate something one assents to.

We should agree that the host is not insincere. However, it is important to note that, as Pepp describes the example, the host is merely said to be *disposed* to assent to not-p. Hence, he is not obviously saying something he does not assent to. Indeed, it is not unnatural to think that the host is not actually assenting to not-p, as he says what he does. Perhaps he is even actually assenting to p, when he says it. Pepp uses this example to illustrate, as she says, that "people do not always do what they are disposed to do." (Pepp, forthcoming) This might suggest seeing the host as assenting to something he is not disposed to assent to. But if so, then our proposal will not count him as being insincere, since he says something he assents to, even if his utterance does not reflect his more general dispositions.

On the other hand, Pepp leaves some room for doubting this kind of reaction to the case:

This might even be a case in which the host is *actually* dissenting from what he says [. . .]. He may be actively reminding himself that Isaac is a vegetarian, Isaac does not want any meat, while at the very same time his desire for the food to be doled out fairly to all leads him to ascribe being a candidate for wanting meat to Isaac, both mentally and out loud in language. Here he consciously mentally dissents from what he says [. . .]. Still, his assertion is not untruthful.

(Pepp, forthcoming)

To the extent that this is a realistic variation of the case, it is one in which the host both assents to *p* and assents to not-*p*, while saying that *p*. As Pepp says, the host is "actively reminding himself" that Isaac does not want meat, and at the same time thinking of Isaac as a candidate for wanting meat, "both mentally and out loud in language." But if this is right, then our view will correctly count the host as not being insincere. The host has a conscious intention to communicate something he assents to, namely that Isaac might like some meat. Hence, it is not the case that the host lacks a conscious intention to communicate something he does not assent to.

Both the Spontaneous Helpfulness and the Anxious Dinner Host examples illustrate that we are often not insincere when we speak without premeditation. It is worth noting that we can also be insincere in these kinds of spontaneous ways. One can tell lies or be insincere in other ways without premeditation. I might, purely on the spur of the moment, tell the tourists a lie about where the museum is, without having first gone through a process of consciously deciding to do so. Yet, as before, the spontaneity of my utterance does not mean that it is unintentional. There is no reason to doubt that I have a conscious intention to communicate what I say. So, when I spontaneously lie to the tourists, I lack a conscious intention to communicate something I assent to.

Sometimes one may even be surprised not only to find oneself lying, but at the very spontaneity with which one does so. When the narrator of Iris Murdoch's novel *A Severed Head* is confronted with the news that his mistress is going to marry his brother, he overflows with insincere congratulations and assurances of his happiness at this turn of events. Describing the scene, the narrator says, "With a fluency that amazed me lies and treachery streamed from my lips." (Murdoch, 2001 [1961], 160) One may be surprised to find that one is lying. Since it it is hard to see how one could be surprised to find oneself lying if one's lying was premeditated, surprise of this kind signals a lack of premeditation. But, as I have been arguing, spontaneity and lack of premeditation does not mean that one does not have a conscious intention to communicate what one is saying, when one says it. Murdoch's narrator clearly intends to communicate his congratulations to his brother and mistress, even though he is surprised to find himself doing so.

9.4. Insincerity and Questions under Discussion

We have been exploring the idea that insincerity is a matter of speaking without a conscious intention to communicate something one assents to. This proposal has the consequence that an utterance that is consciously intended to communicate something the speaker assents to cannot be insincere. Yet, as we saw in Chapter 6, bullshitting is compatible with intentionally asserting things one assents to. Take, for example, Carson's Careful Exam Taker, who is mindful of asserting only things she believes to be true (and, we may assume, assents to), even though she is completely aware of bullshitting with respect to the exam question. The student's utterances are clearly intended to communicate things she assents to, but since she is bullshitting, we want to say that she is speaking insincerely.

This suggests that, just like our account of what is said and hence of lying and misleading, and our account of bullshitting, our account of what it is to speak insincerely more generally should be sensitive to discourse-structure, and in particular, to the stage of inquiry that the utterance is a contribution to. In other words our account of insincerity in speech should be relativized to QUDs.

Perhaps the most simple proposal of this kind is that to speak insincerely is to have a conscious intention to answer one or more QUDs with information one does not assent to. Yet we can see immediately that this idea is too narrow. When people engage in bullshitting, they are typically not concerned with answering QUDs at all. This indifference results in some bullshitters saying things they *do* assent to. For instance, the Careful Exam Taker says things she thinks are true, even though she is not concerned with answering the QUDs, that is, the exam questions. Similarly, Frankfurt's 4th of July Orator might very well assent to the things he says. On the other hand, bullshitting is compatible with saying things one does not assent to. Take, for instance, Lisa's wishful assertion about the fishing at Lake Mountain View in the Fishing Trip case from Chapter 6. Even though Lisa hopes that what she says is true, she most likely does not assent to it. (At least we can easily imagine versions of the example where she does not.) But still, when she says that the fishing at Lake Mountain View is outstanding, she does not have a conscious intention to answer a QUD with this information. Like most other bullshitters, she is not concerned with answering a QUD at all.

One might try to weaken the proposal by suggesting that to speak insincerely is to lack a conscious intention to answer one or more QUDs with information one assents to. This does capture the bullshitters above. It is also a true characterization of both Augustinian real liars and ordinary liars. None of them have conscious intentions to contribute truthful answers to QUDs. And moreover, it is likewise true of speakers, like Abraham, who walk the tightrope between lying and misleading, that they lack such an intention of truthfulness at least with respect to the QUD that they are trying to mislead about. In Abraham's case, he lacks an intention to contribute truthfully to the question of whether Sarah is his wife.

However, there are forms of insincere speech that do not fit this pattern, in particular, some of the ways of using presuppositions for misleading purposes. We have noted (in Chapter 3 and Chapter 5) that speakers sometimes presuppose things they know (consciously) to be false. This can be done with the aim of making their interlocutors accommodate false information. In those cases there is arguably an intention on the part of the speaker to answer QUDs (or, ultimately, the Big Question) untruthfully.

But what about the cases in which an utterance goes along with a presupposition the speaker recognizes to be false, either with the aim of allowing the other participants to persist in false beliefs, or simply for the sake of expediting smooth communication? Such ways of speaking are ways of speaking insincerely. Yet there need not be a QUD, in these cases, toward which the speaker lacks an intention of providing a truthful answer. One example of this is the case of our modern-day Saint Athanasius, Nathan, and his use of the third person to refer to himself in the case of Nathan and the Henchman from Chapter 5, repeated here.

Nathan and the Henchman
Nathan is sitting in the office, when suddenly a henchman of a loan shark he owes money to bursts in. As he questions him, Nathan realizes that the henchman does not know that he is Nathan.

(2)   **Henchman.** Where's Nathan?
      Nathan. He's not far away.

Nathan's use of the third person to refer to himself is not aimed at contributing untruthful information as an answer to a QUD. Since it is already common ground that he is not Nathan, there is no QUD about whether he is Nathan or not. As we observed, this is omissive, positive deception *secundum quid*, in Chisholm's and Feehan's (1977) sense (see also Chapter 1).

In other words, being untruthful with respect to QUDs is not the only way of speaking insincerely. Rather, the panoply of examples of insincere speech we have examined so far suggests that to speak *sincerely* is to consciously intend to truthfully answer QUDs *while avoiding communicating false information in the process.* Conversely, we can see insincerity as lacking a conscious intention to contribute truthful answers to QUDs while not communicating false information in the process. To make this precise, I propose to characterize the broad category of insincere speech for declarative utterances as follows:

Declarative Insincerity
A declarative utterance u by a speaker A is insincere with respect to a QUD q if and only if, in making u, A does not consciously intend to:

(I1)   communicate an answer p to q such that A mentally assents to p, and

(I2)   not communicate some proposition p' such that A does not assent to p'.

Below I briefly summarize how this proposal captures some of the different kinds of insincere speech we have looked at. I will then turn to discussing some potential problems for it and some other types of examples. In the next chapter we will see that this proposal does not translate directly to non-declarative utterances due to the way non-declaratives relate to the pursuit of inquiry.

Irony. When I say ironically that *Titanic* is a great movie, I am addressing a QUD concerning whether *Titanic* is a good movie. My utterance is consciously intended to communicate the answer that *Titanic* is not a good movie, which I assent to. So my utterance is not insincere, since it does not satisfy (I1). The fact that I also *say* something I do not mentally assent to—that *Titanic* is a great movie—does not mean that my utterance satisfies (I2), because I do not do so with the aim of communicating that information.

But, as we noted, ironic utterances can be insincere; for example, when they are intended to deceive. If I do in fact like the movie, I am consciously intending to communicate an answer I do not assent to. So I make my utterance without having a conscious intention to answer the QUD with something I assent to. Hence, when it is intended to deceive, irony is a form of insincerity, in the sense of satisfying (I1).

Lying. In the majority of cases not involving self-deception or other forms of opacity, both the ordinary liar and the Augustinian real liar have a conscious intention to answer a QUD with a proposition the negation of which they assent to. The ordinary liar's intention to do so is driven by her goal of communicating that particular proposition, whereas the real liar's intention is driven by her goal of communicating something false. Yet both types of lies satisfy (I1), and so both types of lies are insincere, on my view.

Misleading. When a speaker asserts something she assents to while thereby aiming to mislead by implicating something she does not assent to, she speaks insincerely. For example, Abraham speaks insincerely, because he consciously intends to communicate an answer to the QUD "Is Sarah your wife?" which he does not assent to. So with respect to this question, his utterance satisfies (I1).

Of course, Abraham also intends to communicate an answer to "Is Sarah your sister?" which he does assent to, and so he does have a conscious intention to communicate a truthful answer to a QUD. Hence, with respect to the latter question, his utterance does not satisfy (I1). But it nevertheless still satisfies (I2), since he does not intend to communicate a truthful answer to "Is Sarah your sister?" while avoiding communicating something he does not assent to in the process.

This means that, on my view, Abraham speaks insincerely with respect to both these questions. This is not surprising when it comes to the question "Is Sarah your wife?" since his aim is to mislead the king into thinking that she is not. But I also think he speaks insincerely with respect to the question "Is Sarah your sister?" even though he does provide the true answer that she is. It is not enough to simply deliver some truth; if the aim with doing so is to mislead by implicating a falsehood, one's way of addressing the issue with respect to which one carefully confines oneself to speaking the truth is still a form of insincerity.

Bullshitting. In standard cases of Frankfurtian bullshitting, a speaker, like the 4th of July Orator, makes an assertion while not caring about whether it is true or false. As we argued, in such cases, the speaker makes her assertion without being concerned with providing a true or a false answer to a QUD. So, in such cases, the speaker lacks a conscious intention to contribute an answer to a QUD that she assents to. Even if she does assent to what she is asserting, she is not making her assertion because she wants to influence a particular subinquiry. So, in these cases, the bullshitter does not satisfy (I1).

Analogously, consider ignorant bullshitting, as in the Umbrella case, in which Thelma tells Tom that it is raining in Chicago, even though she has no idea whether this is true or not, just to be able to sell him the umbrella. Thelma does not have a conscious intention to contribute an answer to the QUD which she assents to. So her utterance is insincere with respect to the QUD about the weather in Chicago.

The Careful Exam Taker has the conscious intention to communicate things she assents to. What is characteristic of this kind of bullshitting is precisely the lack of a corresponding intention to communicate answers to the relevant QUDs. In other words, this type of bullshitter is insincere with respect to the local QUDs; in this case the exam questions. However, it is worth noting that the the Careful Exam Taker is not being insincere with respect to the Big Question. She does intend to communicate true answers to the Big Question, and at the same time avoid communicating false information. On the other hand, while she does not speak insincerely relative to the Big Question, it is part of the complexity of this case that the same utterance is simultaneously insincere relative to the local QUDs.

Lisa's assertion about the fishing at Lake Mountain View is not made with an intention of answering either the local QUD about the fishing or the Big Question. So she is being insincere with respect to both. This gives us a way of distinguishing between this kind of bullshitting and the kind exhibited by the Careful Exam Taker. The latter differs by not being insincere with respect to the Big Question.

Presuppositions. Nathan's use of the third person to refer to himself triggers the presupposition that he is not Nathan. His utterance is therefore insincere in the sense of (I2). Nathan lacks a conscious intention not to communicate something he does not assent to. And this is so, even though he also does have a conscious intention to communicate an answer to the QUD "Where is Nathan?" that he does assent to, that is, that he is not far away. In this way a true assertion can be part of an insincere utterance, when it simultaneously carries an untruthful presupposition.

Similarly, recall Stalnaker's examples of saying something true while presupposing something false. In the Martini story from Chapter 3, Alice uses "the man drinking a martini" to refer to someone she knows is not drinking a martini in order to tell Bob he is a philosopher. Even though Alice is not lying in this case, she is speaking insincerely in the broader sense. Correspondingly, while Alice's utterance does not satisfy (I1), since she is concerned with communicating a true answer to a QUD such as, "Is that man a philosopher?" her utterance is insincere in the sense of (I2), since it is made in the absence of a conscious intention not to communicate untruthful information.

The same happens in the case of referring to Mary's partner as "her husband" from Chapter 5. Moreover, this kind of insincerity is involved both in cases where untruthful presuppositions are offered for accommodation and in cases where the speaker is going along with such presuppositions already present in the common ground. Even though, in the latter type of case, the presuppositions do not represent new information, and hence the speaker is not intending that they *become* common ground, they are still communicated by the relevant utterance.

Opacity. Consider Ridge's self-deceived asserter, Bob, who believes that he believes his mother loves him, but in fact does not believe his mother loves him. We assume that Bob also assents to the claim that his mother loves him. Hence, when Bob asserts that his mother loves him, he has a conscious intention to contribute an answer to a QUD that he assents to. His utterance is therefore not insincere, according to (I1).

Similarly, Peacocke's professor asserts that British universities are the best in the world, even though she believes she does not believe that British universities are the best in the world, while in fact she does believe that. Assuming that the professor does not assent to the claim that British universities are the best in the world (or even assents to its negation), her assertion is not made with a conscious intention to communicate an answer to the QUD, "How do the best British universities compare with the best American ones?" that she assents to. Hence, her assertion is insincere in the sense of (I1).

Yet, as we saw, higher-order beliefs, even when conscious, and assent can come apart, as in the case of Shoemaker's patient, who assents to the claim that he was not adopted, while consciously believing that he believes he was. Still, when the patient asserts that he was adopted, he has a conscious intention to convey an answer to a QUD such as "Were you adopted?" the negation of which he assents to. So he does not have a conscious intention to convey an answer that he assents to, and his assertion is therefore insincere.

Finally, Huck Finn consciously intends to deceive Jim by lying. In other words, he has the conscious intention to contribute an answer to a QUD such as, "Have we escaped?" the negation of which he assents to. So Huck does not have a conscious intention to communicate something he assents to, and his assertion is therefore insincere, on my view. To be sure, Huck has an unconscious *desire* to tell the truth, and moreover, this unconscious desire is at least part of the motivation for his assertion. Further, one can agree with Chan and Kahane (2011, 226) who maintain that "this desire expresses an aspect of his self that is more central than his feeble conscious endorsement of the contrary aim," and still not think that Huck has an *intention*—even an unconscious one—to tell the truth. But note that, even if one does think that Huck has an unconscious intention to tell the truth, this is unquestionably not an intention to communicate something he assents to. What he assents to—that they have not escaped—is the opposite of what he unconsciously believes to be the truth.

9.5. Speaking against One's Intentions

Before closing this chapter, I want to comment briefly on a more complex kind of phenomenon in order to show how our account is able to make sense of it, but equally to remind us of the admittedly dizzying depths that lurk just under the surface which we have been scratching.

The phenomenon I have in mind has to do with finding oneself speaking contrary to one's prior intentions. In particular, people sometimes have conscious intentions of telling the truth, but more or less unwittingly end up lying. A striking example of this is found in an episode in *War and Peace*. Tolstoy describes how the young Pétya Rostóv, when asked by his friends to tell the story of how he was wounded in battle, unwittingly slips into lying:

Rostóv's War Time Story

Rostóv was a truthful young man and would on no account have told a deliberate lie. He began his story meaning to tell everything just as it happened, but imperceptibly, involuntarily, and inevitably he lapsed into falsehood. [. . .] to tell everything as it really happened, it would have been necessary to make an effort of will to tell only what happened. [. . .] His hearers expected a story of how beside himself and all aflame with excitement, he had flown like a storm at the square, cut his way in, slashed right and left, how his saber had tasted flesh and he had fallen exhausted, and so on. And so he told them all that.

(Tolstoy, 2007 [1869], vol. I, book III, ch. 7, p. 258)

According to this description, Rostóv intends to tell the truth when he starts telling his story. This reflects the sense in which Rostóv might be said to be a truthful person, who "would on no account have told a deliberate lie." Still, we have the sense that his utterances, that is, those that are lies, are insincere in that they are voluntary utterances of things he knows to be false aimed at communicating those things to his audience. Suppose, for simplicity, that one of the things he says during his story is (3).

(3) I stormed the square.

Rostóv clearly assents to the negation of what is said by this utterance. Hence, it is a lie. In particular, our account will explain this by noting that his utterance addresses a QUD such as, "Did you storm the square?" without a conscious intention to communicate an answer that he assents to. Yet, depending on how we understand Rostóv's mindset further, we can imagine at least two possible scenarios.

In the first scenario the prior intention to tell the truth Tolstoy ascribes to Rostóv remains conscious. On this reading, Rostóv resembles, to some extent, the Careful Exam Taker, who has a general goal of saying true things, albeit with the difference that Rostóv fails to do so. However, this prior intention to be truthful while he is still insincere with respect to particular QUDs is an apt explanation of the sense that he is speaking against his intention, or more precisely, that he is being insincere (that is, with respect to particular QUDs) while he is still to be seen as a truthful person.

In the second and more complex scenario, Rostóv in fact has a specific prior intention to tell the truth about whether he stormed the square or not. So when he utters (3) he has a conscious intention to communicate an answer that he assents to. But he also intends to communicate what he says. And the latter is an answer he does not assent to.

10

Communicating Attitudes
Beyond the Declarative Realm

While discussing the lying–misleading distinction in Chapter 5, we noted in passing that declarative utterances are not the only ones that can be used for misleading purposes. Even though non-declarative utterances cannot be used to say, and hence assert, things—since they do not express minimal contents—they nevertheless often interact with common ground information in ways that can be exploited for misleading purposes. As examples, we looked briefly at the interrogatives and imperatives in (1)–(2).

(1)   a. Will Ronny ever stop stealing candy bars from the store?
         b. Ronny, stop stealing candy bars from the store!

(2)   a. Did you see the fake Eiffel Tower when you were in Las Vegas?
         b. When you're in Las Vegas, go see the fake Eiffel Tower!

We saw that, at least in ordinary circumstances, these non-declarative sentences carry the presuppositions of their declarative counterparts. So, for example, both (1a) and (1b) presuppose (among other things) that Ronny has been stealing candy bars from the store. As such, these sentences can be used to mislead in such ways as one can exploit presuppositions for misleading purposes in general. When utterances of questions and imperatives are used to mislead, they are insincere.

Yet exploiting presuppositions carried by non-declaratives as in the simple examples above is not the only way one can use non-declaratives insincerely. And moreover, there are other kinds of non-declarative utterances than interrogatives and imperatives to take into account. In this chapter I will look more generally at how utterances of non-declaratives can be insincere.

I will argue that non-declarative utterances typically communicate things about the speaker's attitudes. But as we will see, corresponding to what I argued for declarative utterances in the last chapter, whether one speaks insincerely when uttering a non-declarative depends on one's conscious state of mind. Hence, my account of insincerity in the non-declarative realm is a shallow one, parallel to the shallow conception of insincerity for declarative utterances I have argued for.

10.1. Interrogatives, Exclamatives, Imperatives, and Beyond

According to a standard taxonomic scheme, there are four main clause types (also sometimes called "sentence types") in English, as well as a wide range of other languages:[1]

Declarative.   He is nice.

Interrogative.   Is he nice?

Exclamative.   How nice he is!

Imperative.   Be nice!

Paradigmatically, each of these clause types is used for a particular type of speech act. Declarative clauses are canonically used for making assertions, interrogative clauses for asking questions, exclamative clauses for making exclamations, and imperative clauses for issuing requests, where the latter broadly encompasses orders, suggestions, invitations, wishes, and perhaps more.[2]

As is routinely observed, however, the correspondence between clause types and speech act types is not one–one. Complications arise due to the phenomenon of what Searle (1979 [1975]) called *indirect speech acts*.

---

[1] For discussion of clause type systems, in English and cross-linguistically, see, e.g. Sadock and Zwicky (1985), Zanuttini and Portner (2003), Portner (2004). Huddleston and Pullum (2002, 853) further distinguish between two types of interrogative clause types corresponding to what in this book is referred to as wh-questions vs. polar questions (see Chapter 4.) I have no quarrel with a system in which these two kinds of interrogatives are distinguished as clause types, as well, but for simplicity I refrain from doing so here. See also Krifka (2011) for discussion.

[2] See, e.g. Portner (2007).

For instance, Searle noted that one can issue a request by uttering an interrogative, as in (3), or by uttering a declarative, as in (4).[3]

(3) a. Can you reach the salt?
    b. Could you be a little more quiet?
(4) a. You could be a little more quiet.
    b. I would appreciate it if you would get off my foot.

Similarly, a question can be asked in a variety of different ways, beyond simply uttering a suitable interrogative sentence. For example, in the right setting, the following can all be used to ask where Mark is.[4]

(5) a. I need to know where Mark is.
    b. I'm wondering where Mark is.
    c. I'm trying to find out where Mark is.

I will comment on the issues raised by indirect speech acts toward the end of this chapter. We will see that the account of non-declarative insincerity I offer is able to capture the ways one may be insincere when engaging in indirect speech acts. However, for the main part I will confine myself to discussing examples in which clause types are used with their paradigmatic function.

What I want to note here is that, even though various clause types can be used to perform speech acts different from those associated with their characteristic uses, it remains true that no non-declarative clause type can be used to make an assertion, and hence that no non-declarative clause type can be used to lie. As I will argue in this chapter, and as foreshadowed already, the reason is that non-declarative clause types do not express minimal contents. That is, whatever their compositional meaning, it is not a minimal content.

At the same time, it is sometimes observed that non-declaratives can be used to communicate propositional information. David Braun gives the following example:[5]

---

[3] Examples from Searle (1979 [1975]).
[4] For discussion, see, e.g. Braun (2011), Schoubye and Stokke (2016).
[5] Example numbering altered.

Speakers sometimes ask a question and thereby imply a proposition. Suppose, for instance, that Alice observes Betty taking Carol's mobile phone from Carol's purse, and reading Carol's text messages. Suppose Alice then utters (6) while addressing Betty.

(6)   Do you really think that it's OK for you to do that?

Alice thereby implies (the proposition) that it is not OK for Betty to read Carol's text messages.   (Braun, 2011, 574)

I agree that interrogative sentences can be used to communicate propositional information in this way. Indeed, we have already seen that non-declaratives often carry presuppositions. As we noted in Chapter 5, presuppositions can be used to communicate new information, for example when offered with the expectation of being accommodated by the interlocutors. Even so, one cannot use a non-declarative to *assert* propositional information. Again, the reason is that no non-declarative sentence can be used to *say* anything. Even though one can mislead in cases like Braun's, or in other ways by uttering non-declaratives, one cannot lie in doing so, since lying requires making an assertion.

As a final preliminary I want to note that, according to the way I intend to speak of non-declarative utterances, such utterances are not necessarily utterances of one of the three non-declarative clause types. Non-declarative utterances include non-sentential exclamations and interjections, either of meaningful words, as in (7), or of non-meaningful sounds, as in (8).

(7)   a. Damn!
       b. Jesus!
       c. Thanks!
       d. Shit!

(8)   a. Aargh!
       b. Oops!
       c. Wow!
       d. Sh!

Note that the latter category is intended to include inarticulate sounds, like (8a), but also sounds that are conventionally used in particular situations and for particular communicative purposes, like (8b–d). I include such utterances as non-declarative utterances.

According to the shallow conception of declarative insincerity I argued for in the last chapter, an insincere declarative utterance is an utterance made in the absence of an intention to communicate something that corresponds to the speaker's conscious attitudes while avoiding communicating information that does not match the speaker's conscious attitudes in the process. We will see that something similar, although slightly more broad, applies to non-declarative utterances.

In the next section, I begin by considering the involvement of conscious attitudes. As before, it is useful to start by considering Searlean Orthodoxy. I will look at this view as it applies to orders and questions.

10.2. Questions, Orders, and Opacity

On Searle's (1969) classic view, a variety of speech act types serve to express attitudes. Here is the statement of this view we quoted in Chapter 7:

to assert, affirm, or state that p counts as *an expression of belief* (that p). To require, ask, order, entreat, enjoin, pray, or command (that A be done) counts *as an expression of a wish or desire* (that A be done). To promise, vow, threaten, or pledge (that A) counts as *an expression of intention* (to do A). To thank, welcome, or congratulate counts as an *expression of gratitude, pleasure* (at H's arrival), *or pleasure* (at H's good fortune).   (Searle, 1969, 65)

Moreover, Searle thought that these attitudes figure directly in the sincerity conditions for the relevant speech acts. In the last chapter we examined this view as it relates to assertion, that is, the claim that an assertion is insincere when the speaker does not believe what is asserted.

Since Searle took assertions to be expressions of beliefs, his account of non-declaratives is parallel to his account of insincerity for assertions. So, for example, utterances of questions and orders are insincere, according to Searlean Orthodoxy, when the speaker lacks the corresponding attitudes:[6]

Searlean Orthodoxy for Questions
A question whether *p* uttered by a speaker *S* is insincere if and only if *S* does not want to know whether *p*.

---

[6] See Searle (1969, 66–7).

Searlean Orthodoxy for Orders

An order to ϕ uttered by a speaker S to a hearer H is insincere if and only if S does not want H to ϕ.

In accordance with what I said in the last chapter, I assume that Opacity is true for the attitudes that Searle associated with non-declaratives. For interrogatives and imperatives the attitude is one of desiring some reaction, for example, that of the hearer's telling the speaker something, or performing a particular action. For other non-declaratives, the associated attitudes are emotions such as gratitude, pleasure, resentment, anger, etc.[7]

I take it to be largely uncontroversial that one may be in these kinds of states without believing that one is, and that one might mistakenly believe one is in such states. That is, I assume that the kinds of desires and emotions that are expressed by non-declaratives such as interrogatives, imperatives, and exclamatives are opaque in that they satsify No Self-Intimation and Fallibility. So it should not be surprising that problems arise for Searle's view of the insincerity conditions of non-declaratives mirroring those we considered for his account of assertion.

In particular, cases involving self-deception present counterexamples to Searlean Orthodoxy for questions and orders. For both types of non-declarative utterances, it is neither necessary nor sufficient for insincerity that the speaker fails to have the attitude she expresses. Rather, such utterances are insincere depending on whether the speaker consciously has the attitude expressed, regardless of any unconscious configuration that may be in play.

Consider the following example:

Literary History Class

Julie is a student in a literary history class. While her professor regularly emphasizes the importance of biographical information for the appreciation of a writer's authorship, Julie is steeped in modernist criticism and takes herself to be a firm believer in the doctrine that biographical information is irrelevant. Julie nevertheless wants to make

---

[7] I use the term "attitude" as a neutral label for the broad category of mental states I am concerned with, that is, as encompassing (at least) beliefs, desires, emotions, and intentions. Even though one might argue that some of the emotional states expressed by certain non-declaratives are also propositional attitudes, I do not want to commit myself to a view on this matter, and hence I use "attitude" as one might use "mental states," or the like.

a good impression on her professor, and so during a class on Proust, she poses as keenly interested in the professor's biographical explanations, and asks her:

(9)   Did Proust feel inferior to his brother?

Yet, at the same time, although she does not realize it, Julie is unconsciously fascinated by the lurid details of Proust's biography.

In this example the speaker does not consciously have the attitude expressed, that is, that of wanting to know whether Proust felt inferior to his brother. Yet she unconsciously does have that attitude. Nevertheless, her utterance is clearly insincere.

Hence, this case is a counterexample to the left-to-right direction of Searlean Orthodoxy for Questions. I take it to be clear that there are cases that are equally damaging to the other direction. (For example, imagine that Julie is consciously as interested as the professor in Proust's biography but deep down feels guilty about this.)

Here is a similar example involving an order:

Window Ledge
James is trying to impress Donna by feigning a devil-may-care disposition. Their friend, Bobby, is standing on a window ledge high above the street having second thoughts on whether he can make the jump and land safely on the ledge of the opposite building. James knows that Bobby will do anything he tells him. So he shouts:

(10)   Jump!

Wanting to display to Donna both his power over Bobby as well as his supposed recklessness. As a matter of fact James is as faint-hearted as most people and consciously hopes that Bobby will call off the dangerous feat. However, unconsciously, without realizing it, James harbors the desire that Bobby *will* jump because of a repressed wish to see him plummet to his demise.

As in the previous example, the speaker does not consciously have the attitude expressed, that is, that of wanting Bobby to jump. Yet he unconsciously does have that attitude. But since the utterance is clearly insincere, this case falsifies the left-to-right direction of Searlean Orthodoxy for Orders. Again, analogous examples will be counterexamples to the other direction.

Similarly to what I argued for the case of declarative utterances in Chapter 7, this suggests that insincerity for non-declarative utterances turns not just on whether the speaker has the Searlean attitude associated with her utterance, but on whether the speaker consciously has the relevant attitude.

10.3. Communicating Attitudes

One idea, therefore, is to propose that a non-declarative utterance is insincere when the speaker lacks a conscious attitude that is expressed by her utterance. However, in order for such a proposal to be informative, we need to understand what is meant by the claim that an utterance *expresses* an attitude. Many different theories on this matter have been proposed, and I will not try to do justice to them here.[8]

Instead, I want to point out that, regardless of how one characterizes expressing attitudes, we can observe that non-declarative utterances *communicate* attitudes. In particular, an utterance of a non-declarative sentence typically has the effect of making it common ground that the speaker has a particular attitude. We will see that this makes it possible to understand the ways in which non-declarative utterances can be insincere in a way that is parallel to the account of insincerity for declarative utterances I proposed in the last chapter.

The feature of non-declarative utterances that Searle observed interacts with common ground information, in the sense that non-declaratives contribute information to the common ground ascribing to the speaker the attitude that Searle identified as expressed by the type of non-declarative utterance in question.

For example, if you ask the question in (11), you propose to make it common ground that you want to know how the tomato sauce is made.

(11)   How is the tomato sauce made?

As with assertions, your interlocutors can reject your proposal. For example, they might reply with (12).

(12)   Oh, come on! You don't care about the sauce, you're just trying to flatter the host!

---

[8] See, e.g. Searle (1969), Davis (2003), Bar-On (2004), Ridge (2006), Green (2007b), Eriksson (2011b).

In such a case it will not become common ground that you want to know how the tomato sauce is made.

Similarly, if you tell someone the imperative in (13), you propose to make it common ground that you want them to go clean up their room.

(13)   Go clean up your room!

Unless it is rejected, (13) has the effect of making it common ground that you want the addressee to go clean up their room.

I think the claim that non-declaratives involve proposals to make common ground the kind of expressive information Searle identified is intuitively plausible. But there are also more explicit kinds of evidence for it. Here I will look at two of these.

First, note that, subsequent to a non-declarative utterance having been made, the information that the speaker has the relevant attitude can be felicitously presupposed. To illustrate this, I will use the so-called "Hey, wait a minute" test introduced by Kai von Fintel (2004).[9] Suppose Ken asks Amy the question in (11), but Amy does not hear him. Then consider the following dialogue between two bystanders, Paul and Emma, both of whom clearly heard the question and knows that the other one heard it, knows that the other one knows this, etc.:

(14)   **Paul.** Amy doesn't realize that Ken wants to know how the tomato sauce is made.

Emma. #Hey, wait a minute, I had no idea that Ken wants to know how the tomato sauce is made.

Paul's utterance presupposes that Ken wants to know how the tomato sauce is made.[10] The utterance is perfectly felicitous. So this is evidence that this information is established in the common ground by Ken's question. Correspondingly, it is infelicitous to challenge this information, as Emma's utterance tries to do. Again, this supports the claim that the information that Ken wants to know the answer to his question is common ground subsequent to his asking it.

---

[9] von Fintel (2004, 316, n. 3) cites Shannon (1976) as inspiration.

[10] *Realize* is a factive verb that presupposes its propositional complement, as seen from the fact that the information in the complement projects from under negation. See Levinson (1983, ch. 4), Geurts (1999, ch. 1). For an account of the presuppositions of factive verbs in terms of the common ground framework, see Stalnaker (1999 [1974]).

Next, suppose Lou utters the imperative in (13) to his son, David, but David does not hear him. Then consider the following dialogue between two bystanders, Nellie and Willa, both of whom clearly heard the utterance and knows that the other one heard it, knows that the other one knows this, etc.:

(15) **Nellie.** David doesn't realize that Lou wants him to go clean up his room.

      Willa. #Hey, wait a minute, I had no idea that Lou wanted David to go clean up his room.

Again, since Willa's utterance felicitously presupposes that Lou wants David to go clean up his room, this information can be seen to be common ground. Correspondingly, it is infelicitous to question this information, as in Willa's utterance.

Second, the suggestion that non-declaratives contribute to common ground information can be further supported in the following way. In normal situations, one cannot felicitously assert a declarative, and then subsequently assert its negation, as illustrated by (16).

(16) It's raining. #It's not raining.

This is readily explained as the infelicity of adding a proposition to the common ground and subsequently proposing to add its negation. Orders and questions exhibit the analogous pattern:

(17) a. How is the tomato sauce made? #I don't want to know how the tomato sauce is made.
      b. Go clean up your room! #I don't want you to go clean up your room.

Our suggestion explains this pattern. In each case uttering the first sentence adds a proposition to the common ground the negation of which is then asserted by the second sentence. Hence, the infelicity of the utterances in (17a–b) is parallel to that of (16).

Of course, utterances such as those in (17) are not infelicitous in all circumstances. The speaker may change her mind, for example. (Note that, tellingly, in such a case it is natural to prefix the retracting utterance with *actually* or *come to think of it*, or the like.) But significantly that is again completely parallel to (16). One may of course discover that one was wrong and therefore want to adjust the common ground accordingly. The fact that, in both the declarative and the non-declarative case, the follow-up counts as a form of retraction supports our suggestion that the antecedent utterance involves a bid to make the relevant information common ground.

So far we have confined ourselves to two types of non-declarative utterances, interrogatives and imperatives. Yet, as we have seen, there are other kinds of utterances that do not serve to set forth declarative pronouncements. One example concerns utterances of thanks, congratulations, and the like. As seen from the passage quoted earlier, Searle (1969) thought that thanking someone counts as an expression of gratitude or appreciation, and that to congratulate someone is to express pleasure at someone's good fortune.

We can see that the observations concerning common ground interaction we made concerning interrogatives and imperatives apply to these cases, too. This is illustrated by (18)–(21).

(18)   **Martha to Burt who doesn't hear her.** Hey, thanks for telling my daughter to do her homework!

   Cheryl to Marty. They both heard Martha's utterance. Burt doesn't realize that Martha appreciates that he told her daughter to do her homework.

   Marty. #Hey, wait a minute, I had no idea that Martha appreciates that Burt told her daughter to do her homework.

(19)   Hey, thanks for telling my daughter to do her homework! #I don't appreciate that you told my daughter to do her homework.

(20)   **Susie to Mick who doesn't hear her.** Hey, congratulations on getting engaged!

   Hannah to Fred. They both heard Susie's utterance. Mick doesn't realize that Susie is happy for him because he got engaged.

   Fred. #Hey, wait a minute, I had no idea that Susie's happy for Mick because he got engaged.

(21)   Hey, congratulations on getting engaged! #I'm not happy for you because you got engaged.

Finally, the same effects occur with utterances of exclamations like *sh* and *wow*, as illustrated by (22)–(25).

(22) **Denise to Oscar who doesn't hear her. Sh!**
Liza to Tim. They both heard Denise's utterance. Oscar doesn't realize that Denise wants him to be quiet.
Tim. #Hey, wait a minute, I had no idea that Denise wants Oscar to be quiet.

(23) Sh! #I don't want you to be quiet.

(24) **Carol to Larry who doesn't hear her. Wow!**
Anna to Morty. They both heard Carol's utterance. Larry doesn't realize that Carol is impressed.
Morty. #Hey, wait a minute, I had no idea that Carol's impressed.

(25) Wow! #I'm not impressed.

There is evidence, then, for thinking that one effect of non-declarative utterances is to propose for common ground uptake the information that the speaker has the attitude associated with the relevant type of utterance. That is to say, non-declaratives communicate attitudes.

Moreover, I take it to be clear that what I argued concerning the Searlean view of insincere orders and questions carries over to the other non-declarative utterances mentioned above. In other words, in all these cases, non-declarative insincerity turns on whether the speaker consciously has the attitude in question, and not on whether she has that attitude *tout court*. Take, for instance, (18). Suppose Martha consciously believes that she appreciates Burt's telling her daughter to do her homework, but at a deep, unconscious level she resents him for interfering with her efforts to take charge of her child's education. Even so, given that these feelings of resentment are genuinely absent from her conscious mind, her utterance of thanks in (18) is not insincere. The same applies, *mutatis mutandis*, to our other examples.

10.4. Ironic Non-Declaratives

We have seen that there are two main ways in which non-declaratives interact with common ground. On the one hand, a non-declarative utterance communicates something about the speaker's attitudes. In particular, uttering a non-declarative involves a bid to make it common ground that one has the attitude associated with the relevant type of speech act, that is, the kind of attitude that Searle identified. For ease of reference, let us call this the *expressive content* of non-declaratives. On the other hand, just like declarative utterances, non-declaratives carry presuppositions, and can be used to implicate things.

The latter kind of contribution made by non-declarative utterances should be distinguished from their expressive content for at least the following reason. Presuppositions and implicatures of non-declaratives do not necessarily concern attitudes, let alone the speaker's attitudes. Of course, they may do so, as in (26).

(26)   Why do I want my son to clean up his room?

The interrogative in (26) arguably presupposes that I want my son to clean up his room. Hence, this presupposition of (26) is the same as the expressive content of (13), when uttered by me to my son.

(13)   Go clean up your room!

But (26) also has an expressive content. Namely, it conveys that I want to know why I want my son to go clean up his room. The same considerations apply to other non-declaratives.

We should not infer from this, however, that one cannot utter a non-declarative without conveying the associated expressive content. In Chapter 3 we noted that one can avoid making assertions when uttering declarative sentences, and thereby saying something by making it clear that one is not speaking in earnest, for example, by winking or the like. Correspondingly, if I utter (13) while winking, I do not communicate that I want my son to go clean up his room. One can utter non-declaratives in an ironic tone of voice with similar results. Consider, for example, (27).

(27)   [Ironically] Thanks a lot for telling my daughter to do her homework!

In this case the speaker does not communicate that she is grateful to the hearer for telling her daughter to do her homework. Indeed, just as for ironic utterances of declaratives, the result is the opposite. What is communicated by (27) is that the speaker is *not* grateful for this act.

Unsurprisingly, the possibilities for insincerity also parallel those we have already examined for declarative utterances in these kinds of cases. When uttering (27), the speaker is not insincere if she consciously is not grateful to the addressee for telling her daughter to do her homework. Still, one can use non-declaratives ironically and be insincere, for example, if one's goal in doing so is to mislead about one's own attitudes. Suppose, for example, that the speaker of (27) in fact *is* consciously grateful to the addressee, but that she wants to be perceived as resentful of the act because she wants to appear as caring about being in control of her child's education. In that case the ironic exclamative is arguably insincere.

10.5. Insinuating Disclosure and Surreptitious Probing

Given the two communicative dimensions of non-declaratives we have identified, it is plausible to think that to characterize insincerity for non-declarative utterances, we will need to take into account each of them. Indeed, one immediate reason is that speakers' attitudes toward expressive and non-expressive content may come apart.

On the one hand one can utter a non-declarative sentence and thereby communicate an expressive content that does not match one's conscious attitudes, while at the same time presupposing something one assents to. This can happen with utterances like that in our example of (1a) from above:

Insinuating Disclosure
Clarence is talking to Ronny's mother. Clarence knows that she has no idea that Ronny has been stealing candy bars from the store. But Clarence wants to expose Ronny to his mother without directly ratting him out. So he sighs and says,

(28)   Will Ronny ever stop stealing candy bars from the store?

Clarence is not really interested in whether Ronny will stop stealing candy bars from the store. Instead he is uttering (28) in order to let Ronny's mother know that he has been doing so. So, while the expressive content of Clarence's utterance does not match his conscious attitudes, what he is presupposing does, that is, it is something he mentally assents to. Nevertheless, his utterance is insincere.

In other cases the expressive content may be matched while some other contribution is not. For example, consider a variation on Braun's (2011) example quoted earlier:

Surreptitious Probing

Alice sees Betty reading Carol's phone messages. Alice does not really think it is wrong for someone to read other people's phone messages; in fact, she has often done so herself. Still, she wants to be perceived as considering that kind of action objectionable. At the same time, however, Alice has a desire to know what Betty thinks about the matter. So, she puts on a shocked air and says in a concerned tone of voice:

(29)   Do you really think that it's OK for you to do that?

In this kind of case the expressive content of the utterance is matched by the speaker's conscious attitudes. Alice consciously wants to know whether Betty thinks it is OK for her to read Carol's messages. But at the same time, the utterance implicates something the speaker does not mentally assent to, namely that it is not OK for Betty to read Carol's messages. For this reason, Alice's utterance is arguably insincere.

10.6. Bullshitting with Non-Declaratives

Given this, one thought is that to utter a non-declarative insincerely is to make the utterance while not consciously intending to communicate something that matches one's conscious attitudes. Yet, this proposal is too weak. In the example of Insinuating Disclosure above, Clarence intends to communicate truthfully that Ronny has been stealing candy bars. But still, he is being insincere by asking the questions while not really caring about the answer. So we might think of suggesting that insincerity for non-declaratives is a matter of consciously intending to communicate some proposition that does not match one's attitudes.

The reason this kind of proposal was not suitable for characterizing insincerity for declarative utterances was that when one is bullshitting, one does not necessarily have an intention to communicate something one does not assent to. One can bullshit with non-declaratives, as well. Here is an example:

Dinner Party
During a dinner party, Jeff asks the host:

(30) How is the tomato sauce made?

But he isn't interested in the answer. Nor is he interested in making people think he's interested in the answer. He's simply trying to keep the conversation going. In fact, he's so desperate to avoid an uncomfortable silence that he doesn't care what people think about his interest in how the tomato sauce is made.

While people sometimes utter non-declaratives in order to mislead, Jeff is not asking his question because he wants to communicate misleading information. For example, Julie's question in the Literary History Class example is intended to deceive the professor into thinking that she is interested in the answer. By contrast, Jeff is asking his question without really caring about whether he thereby contributes misleading or truthful information. As such, it is natural to describe him as bullshitting.

10.7. Shallow Non-Declarative Insincerity

On a shallow conception insincerity depends on the speaker's conscious state of mind. This kind of view is opposed to accounts like Chan and Kahane's (2011), according to which speakers such as Huckleberry Finn are not insincere because their deep, unconscious motivations are morally praiseworthy. Moreover, we saw that what characterizes the general phenomenon of insincere utterances of declaratives is not the *presence* of particular intentions toward contributing truthfully to the conversation. Rather, what the different types of insincerity had in common was the *absence* of conscious intentions to contribute truthfully to the conversation.

On our account of Declarative Insincerity from Chapter 9, there were two components to this. We said that insincerity, in the declarative realm, is a matter of speaking without conscious intentions to, first, contribute an answer to a QUD that one assents to, and second, to avoid contributing information one does not assent to in the process. I suggest that the insincerity in the non-declarative realm is likewise a matter of lacking particular conscious intentions. In particular, corresponding to the second component of the way we understood Declarative Insincerity, I propose to characterize insincerity for non-declarative utterances as follows:

Non-Declarative Insincerity

A non-declarative utterance u by a speaker A is insincere if and only if, in making u, A does not consciously intend to not communicate some proposition p such that p does not match A's conscious attitudes.

More intuitively, to speak insincerely when making non-declarative utterances, according to this proposal, is to lack a conscious intention to avoid communicating things that do not correspond to one's conscious state of mind. Conversely, as this suggests, sincerity in the non-declarative realm can be understood as speaking with a conscious intention to avoid communicating information that does not match one's conscious attitudes.

Giving someone an order while being conscious of not wanting them to carry it out, as in the Window Ledge example, is a way of being insincere on this view. Since one is communicating that one wants the order to be carried out, one is lacking a conscious intention to avoid communicating something one is conscious of not agreeing with. Similarly, asking a question while being conscious of not caring about the answer, as in the Literary History Class example, is a way of being insincere, since when asking a question, one communicates that one wants to know the answer.

In cases where the speaker's, conscious attitudes toward the expressive and the non-expressive content of her utterance come apart, the speaker lacks an intention to avoid contributing information that does not match her conscious attitudes. For example, in the Insinuating Disclosure case Clarence's aim in asking his question is to let Ronny's mother know that Ronny has been stealing. But since he is not interested in the answer to the question, he lacks an intention to avoid communicating something that does not correspond to his conscious state of mind. In the Surreptitious Probing case Alice wants to know whether Betty thinks it is OK for her to read Carol's messages, but she also implies that it is not OK to do so, while this does not correspond to her own conscious opinions. So, again, this is an utterance made in the absence of the kind of intention I have been highlighting.

In the case of Jeff's bullshit question in the Dinner Party example, he contributes the information that he wants to know how the tomato sauce is made. But regardless of whether he in fact does or not, he is not making his utterance in order to get that content across. Like other bullshitters, Jeff is indifferent toward whether he makes a truthful or untruthful contribution. Hence, he does not have an intention to avoid contributing untruthful information.

10.8. Indirect Speech Acts

Having set out the proposal above, I want to comment briefly on its consequences for how to understand the phenomenon of indirect speech acts.

In cases of indirect speech acts, the speaker communicates information corresponding to the indirect act. Call this the *indirect content* of such utterances. For example, when someone utters (4a), in the right situation, they communicate the indirect content that they want the addressee to be more quiet.

(4) a. You could be a little more quiet.

Our account predicts that if an indirect speech act is made, while the indirect content conveyed in this way does not correspond to the speaker's conscious attitudes, this constitutes a form of insincerity. For example, if one utters (4a), while being conscious of not wanting the addressee to be more quiet—perhaps one is simply making the request in order to make oneself appear a certain way to a third party, or the like—one is being insincere.

Similarly, consider again Searle's example of (3a).

(3) a. Can you reach the salt?

Even though this particular case may be a slightly odd example, I take it we want to say that someone uttering (3a), in the appropriate situation, while being conscious of not wanting the addressee to pass the salt, is being insincere. We are able to capture this by accepting that, in the relevant setting, (3a) communicates that the speaker wants the addressee to pass the salt.

However, there is a potential problem here. According to what we have supposed about non-declaratives, interrogative clauses such as (3a) communicate that the speaker wants to know the answer. Call this the *direct content*. But it is not clear that we want to say that an utterance of (3a), in the relevant setting, is insincere if the speaker is not interested in whether the addressee can reach the salt, but simply wants the addressee to pass the salt. Indeed, it might even be thought strange, if not inconsistent, to request that someone pass the salt if one does not already think that they are able to do so. If one is attracted to this line of thinking, one might suggest that when (3a) is used indirectly, the speaker must already be presupposing the positive answer to the question, or else the indirect request would be hard to make sense of. Consequently, it might look plausible to suggest that (3a), when used in this way, does not function as a question at all.

As I will explain in more detail below, I think something along these lines is right. In particular, we do not want to say that the direct content of utterances used to perform indirect speech acts is communicated, at least not in the sense that it makes a difference for whether the speaker is being insincere or not.

There are broadly speaking three ways of thinking of indirect speech acts. First, some writers hold that, in such cases, two speech acts are being performed (see, for example, Searle, 1979 [1975]). Second, some think that only the direct speech act is being performed (see, for example, Bertolet, 1994). Third, some think that only the indirect speech act is being performed (see, for example, Potts, 2005, Lepore and Stone, 2015). There is no space here for assessing each of these alternatives. Instead, I will briefly describe the one I find most plausible. As foreshadowed above, this is a version of the third type of view.

Christopher Potts (2005) argues that indirect speech acts are instances of conversational implicatures. Potts argues for this view by noting that indirect speech acts share well-known Gricean characteristics of standard cases of (particularized) conversational implicatures. These are non-detachability, calculability by maxims, and cancellability.

Concerning the first characteristic, Potts notes (2005, 26–7) that the request issued by (3a) is, in the right setting, likewise associated with the utterances in (31).

(31) a. Are you able to reach the salt?
 b. I could sure use the salt.
 c. My dish could use a salting.
 d. Could you send the salt my way?

This observation generalizes to other cases of indirect speech acts. Hence, Potts concludes that "The unifying feature of all these cases is not a linguistic matter. Rather, we arrive at it by way of the maxims [...]." (2005, 27).

It is worth reproducing Potts's sketch of how the implicature (that is, the indirect content) of a case such as (3a) is calculated:

a. Cooperative agents do not request information they already possess. Such requests do not increase the collective knowledge of the discourse participants and so always fail to qualify as informative, relevant, and sufficiently brief. b. If the addressee is not near the salt, then the speaker already knows that the answer to the literal readings of [(3a), (31a), (31d)] is 'no'. c. If the addressee is near the salt, then the speaker already knows that the answer to literal readings of [(3a), (31a), (31d)] is 'yes'. d. Hence, [(3a), (31a), (31d)] must not be questions at all. e. Some reflection on our current context suggests to the speaker that [(3a), (31a), (31d)] must be indirect ways of asking for the salt.   (Potts, 2005, 27)

As Potts notes, the first premise relies on maxims of quantity, relevance, and brevity. Moreover, the next two premises are observations about the discourse. The fact that, if they are removed, the implicature is not inferred is what shows that the implicature is cancellable.

I take Potts's view to be a plausible one. However, we need to specify a further component of these kinds of cases. In particular, as we have seen repeatedly in Part I of this book, when it comes to standard conversational implicatures, both the "literal" content and the implicature are communicated, that is, offered for the common ground. Yet, as noted above, this is not a comfortable conclusion to draw in the case of indirect speech acts. We do not want to say that the "literal" meaning of such utterances is offered for the common ground, since its status vis-à-vis the speaker's attitudes has no bearing on the insincerity of the utterance.

Yet we have seen many times already that there are cases of conversational implicatures where the literal content is not offered up for the common ground. This is what happens in cases of irony. In particular, it is a feature of ironic utterances that part of the inference-process that hearers undertake is to observe that the literal meaning cannot be what the speaker wanted to convey.

This is analogous to what goes on in Potts's premises b–d above. Indeed, Potts's premise d is tantamount to the claim that hearers do not consider the literal meaning as on offer for common ground uptake in these cases.

To be sure, just as in the case of irony, this does not mean that hearers cannot use the fact that the speaker uttered the literal content in their reasoning. It is just that they note that, while they did so, they did not thereby propose that it be added to the common ground. In the case of declaratives, such as (4a), (31b), (31c), we can characterize this, as we did for ironic utterances, by suggesting that the literal meaning is said but not asserted. For non-declaratives, we do not have an analogous distinction in place, but it is arguable that the parallel phenomenon is occurring.

So, on the view I am sketching here, in the case of indirect speech acts, as in the case of ironic utterances, while a direct content is uttered and is used in the reasoning process that leads hearers to the indirect content, only the latter is communicated in the sense of being proposed for the common ground. As for ironic utterances, this means that if the direct content does not match the speaker's attitudes, this does not make the utterance insincere. Rather, only the indirect content is relevant for evaluating the utterance as insincere or not.

We cannot here defend this idea in more detail. Still, I want to mention one potential objection to it. It is not unnatural to think that this suggestion will not work for all cases of indirect speech acts. For example, take Searle's (4b).

(4) b. I would appreciate it if you would get off my foot.

Arguably, there is a sense in which an utterance of (4b)—when used to convey its associated indirect content—is insincere if the speaker would not appreciate if the addressee would get off her foot. However, it is arguable that, in cases like this, the direct and indirect content are closely related in such a way that, even if only the indirect content is communicated, as we have suggested, its role suffices to explain the effect just observed. Bluntly, if the speaker does not want the addressee to get off her foot, she would not appreciate it if she did.

In conclusion, I take it that the kind of view I have outlined, on which cases of indirect speech acts are cases of conversational implicature where the literal content is not proposed for the common ground, has the potential for being a plausible view. If so, it should be clear that the proposal for how to understand insincerity in the non-declarative realm I have argued for extends to cases involving indirect speech acts.

10.9. Phonetic, Phatic, and Rhetic Acts

As we noted in the beginning of this chapter, the range of non-declarative utterances extends beyond utterances of non-declarative sentences, that is, interrogative, exclamative, or imperative sentences. In particular, we included utterances of mere sounds, such as *aargh*, *oops*, *wow*, and *sh*, as well as utterances of words like *damn*, *Jesus*, *thanks*, and *shit*. To clarify how our account applies to these kinds of utterances, it is useful to speak in terms of J. L. Austin's (1962) well-known distinction between three different aspects of speech, namely, what he called *phonetic*, *phatic*, and *rhetic* acts, respectively.[11]

For Austin, a phonetic act is the mere production of sound. All our ordinary talk therefore involves phonetic acts, even though ordinary talk is much more than just production of sound. But we can also engage in *merely* phonetic acts. For example, crying out "Aargh!" upon burning one's hand is a case of a merely phonetic act. Further, if one performs a phonetic act while knowing that the sounds produced are meaningful in some language, one has performed what Austin called a *phatic* act.[12]

Ordinary talk involves phatic (and hence phonetic) acts, even though ordinary talk is much more than just production of sounds that one knows to be meaningful in some language. Still, one can also perform *merely* phatic acts. In particular, performing a phatic act, for Austin, is compatible with having no idea *which* meaning attaches to the sounds one is producing. This kind of situation is illustrated by a well-known example given by Searle (1969, 44):

Captured Soldier
An American soldier is captured by Italian troops during World War II. The soldier wants to make his capturers think he is German. So he recites the line,

(32)   Kennst du das land, wo die Zitronen blühn,

which he knows by heart, while being ignorant of its meaning.

---

[11]   See in particular, Lecture VIII in Austin (1962).

[12]   Complications arise due to issues concerning what counts as a way of manifesting words of a given language, as well as what counts as words or meaningful part of a language. For some relevant discussion, see, e.g. Kaplan (1990), Cappelen and Lepore (2007, ch. 12).

Given Austin's taxonomy, the Captured Soldier has performed a phatic act (we assume the soldier knows the line is meaningful in German), even though he does not know the meaning of his words.

When one performs a phatic act, while in addition knowing which meaning attaches to the sounds one is producing and while attending to getting that meaning across, one is performing what Austin called a *rhetic* act. François Recanati describes the distinctive traits of rhetic acts as follows:

I do not perform a rhetic act simply by uttering a sentence that I know to have a meaning; I must also know *which* meaning the sentence has, and I must utter the sentence as having *this* meaning. But this is still not sufficient for there to be a rhetic act. To perform a rhetic act is to *mean something* by uttering a sentence: The speaker must have something definite in mind that he intends to get across.

(Recanati, 1987, 239)

I take it that the distinction between phonetic, phatic, and rhetic aspects of speech acts applies not merely to communication that is made by means of sounds—let alone to communication made by means of sounds produced by a human voice—but also to communication by means of, for example, written marks or symbols. For example, we might distinguish between the mere production of marks, producing marks that one knows to be meaningful in some language, and producing marks with the full range of involvement that characterizes rhetic acts. As we have done for the most part so far, however, we will confine ourselves to oral communication here.

10.10. Communicative Acts

Given this distinction between phonetic, phatic, and rhetic acts, at each level, we can further distinguish between what I will call *communicative* vs. *non-communicative* acts. By a communicative act I mean an act of communicating some content. According to the Stalnakerian account of communication I have been defending, to communicate that p is (at least) to propose that p become common ground.

A merely phonetic act can be an act of communicating some particular information. For example, one might deliberately scream "Aargh!" in order to attract help. Depending on the details of the case, one can be described as performing a merely phonetic act that involves a proposal to make it common ground that one needs help. Even more quotidian cases involve exclamations of familiar sounds such as *wow*, *oops*, or *sh*. The latter, for example, is typically produced in order to communicate, roughly, that one wants someone to be quiet. One can also perform merely phonetic acts without any communicative goals. This happens, for instance, when one involuntarily cries out, "Aargh!" upon burning one's hand. In such a case, one performs a merely phonetic act, but one is not communicating anything to anyone. (Note that, even though such an exclamation may, and typically does, *result* in certain information becoming common ground, it is not made as a proposal to this effect.)

The Captured Soldier example is a case of a communicative, merely phatic act. The soldier is performing a merely phatic act, in that he is uttering a string of sounds that he knows to be meaningful in German, even though he does not know which meaning it has. And moreover, he is clearly doing so in order to communicate a particular piece of information, namely that he is German. But one can also perform merely phatic acts without communicating. For example, suppose you have been told by a reliable source that *strålende* is a meaningful expression in Danish, which is often used as an exclamation, even though you do not know which meaning it has.[13] We can imagine a case in which you involuntarily blurt out, "Strålende!" upon burning your hand. This would be a case of a merely phatic act that is not a communicative act.

Finally, we should also distinguish between communicative acts that satisfy all the conditions on rhetic acts, and non-communicative acts that satisfy all but the last condition on rhetic acts. Fully fledged rhetic acts are standard cases of utterances, that is, productions of sounds that one knows are meaningful, and for which one knows which meaning they have, uttered in order to communicate a particular content to one's audience. Yet, one can also produce sounds that one knows are meaningful, and for which one knows which meaning they have, but without communicating anything. For example, Mitchell Green writes:

testing a microphone—as Ronald Reagan once did, in preparing for a news conference—with the words, "The bombing of Russia begins in five minutes," is not a speech act because, thankfully, there was no question of Reagan's meaning what he said. (Green, 2010, 83)

---

[13] *Strålende* in Danish means "radiant" and can be used as an exclamation in roughly the same situations in which one can use *fantastic* as an exclamation in English.

Given Austin's taxonomy, Reagan was not performing a rhetic act, since he did not propose to communicate what he said. Yet he was performing slightly more than a merely phatic act, since he not only knew that his sentence was meaningful, but moreover knew which meaning it had. But regardless, he was not performing a communicative act.

10.11. Utterances as Communicative Acts

We can now make good on our promissory note from Chapter 9. By an "utterance," in both the characterization of Declarative Insincerity from Chapter 9 and the account of Non-Declarative Insincerity above, I mean a communicative act. This means that my account of insincerity does not apply to phonetic and phatic acts that are not communicative acts. This reflects the fact that such acts are arguably not evaluable as insincere or not (nor as sincere or not.) Consider my involuntary cry of an inarticulate sound on being frightened. If someone were to ask whether I was being insincere or not in doing so, we would consider such a question misguided. Similarly, even when my act is a phatic one, that is, the sound I let out is a meaningful word or sentence, still it seems inappropriate to even raise the question of whether I was being insincere, if it is not also a communicative act. Since such acts are not utterances, therefore, our account does not classify them either as insincere or not insincere.

And moreover, given that Reagan was not trying to communicate anything when he was testing the microphone, it makes no sense to ask whether his utterance was insincere or not. The same applies to the example we mentioned in Chapter 9, namely that of talking in one's sleep. When I say, "I'm French," in my sleep, I arguably perform the same kind of act that is slightly more than a phatic act but not a fully fledged rhetic act as in the Reagan example. I utter a sentence, for which I know not only that it is meaningful but also which meaning it has. But I am not doing so with the aim of getting anything across, and hence my act is not an utterance, in our sense. Correspondingly, it not evaluable as insincere or not.

By contrast, it is completely natural to ask whether I am being insincere or not in the case of my deliberately screaming in order to attract help, that is, in the case of a communicative, merely phonetic act. Similarly for communicative, merely phatic acts. There is a clear sense in which Searle's soldier is evaluable as being insincere or not. Indeed, he is clearly being insincere when he is trying to mislead his capturers by making them think he is German.

In Searle's original example the soldier in fact utters a non-declarative (that is, interrogative) German sentence.[14] So, given what I have said above, this utterance falls under our account of Non-Declarative Insincerity. The soldier is performing a communicative, merely phatic act, which is a non-declarative utterance. The account gives the right result, since the soldier proposes to make common ground a proposition that does not match his conscious attitudes, and hence he is making his utterance in the absence of conscious intentions to avoid conveying information that does not match his conscious attitudes. In particular, the soldier communicates the proposition that he is German, which is a proposition he does not mentally assent to.

Alternatively, we can imagine a version of Searle's example in which the soldier utters a declarative sentence, which he knows to be a meaningful sentence in German, even though he does not know what it means. In such a case the soldier's utterance would fall under our account of Declarative Insincerity. But we still get the right result. In this case the soldier proposes to make common ground an answer to a QUD he does not assent to, namely the answer "I am German" to the QUD, "Is he German?" or "Is he an enemy?" or the like.

So even though insincerity is characterized in terms of the absence of certain conscious intention to contribute truthfully to the conversation, my account is restricted to communicative acts in the sense just described. In other words, an insincere utterance is a communicative act, but one that is made without a conscious intention not to convey untruthful information. In particular, note that even the bullshitter (declarative or non-declarative) is performing a communicative act. That is, the bullshitter is not like someone who cries out merely by reflex, even if the cry is a meaningful part of a language. The bullshitter, just like all the other speakers we are considering, is communicating a particular content.

---

[14] The fact that it is only part of a longer interrogative sentence in the poem does not mean that (32) is not a grammatical interrogative sentence.

10.12. Why You Can't Lie with Non-Declaratives

Despite the variety of ways in which one can be insincere while uttering non-declaratives, as noted earlier, it is intuitive to say that no non-declarative can be used to lie.[15] If one asks a question while consciously one does not care about the answer, one has not lied, even if one's goal was to deceive the listener concerning one's attitudes. If one makes a suggestion, or issues an order, while not wanting it to be carried out, one has not lied, even if one's goal was to mislead or deceive. Even for exclamations, we do not think of insincerity in terms of lying. If one exclaims *thanks*, *wow*, *sh*, or the like to someone while consciously lacking the attitudes one thereby communicates that one has, one is not lying, even though one is being misleading. And similarly, one does not lie if one exclaims, "How nice he is!" about someone one thinks is not nice.

As I suggested earlier, given the view of lying I argued for in Part I of this book, what is needed in order to account for the fact that non-declaratives cannot be used to lie is the claim that they cannot be used to make assertions. Since assertion requires saying something, in the technical sense of what is said I argued for in Chapter 4, if it is plausible that non-declaratives cannot be used to say things, this would explain why they cannot be used to make assertions, and hence cannot be used to lie.

According to our account of what is said, to say something is to utter a declarative sentence whose minimal content interacts with the space of answers to a QUD in the specific way we defined. The minimal content associated with declarative sentences was identified with compositional meaning, that is, the content that is determined by the lexical meaning of the constituents and their syntactic mode of combination.

Many philosophers and linguists think that, although non-declarative clause types—for instance, interrogatives, imperatives, and exclamatives—do have compositional semantic properties, their compositional contents differ from those of declarative sentences. For each non-declarative clause type, the literature contains many different views of this kind. But note

---

[15] Exceptions arise when non-declaratives convey conventional implicatures. See Stokke (2017a) for discussion.

that, for each non-declarative clause type, as long as some view of this kind is right, we will be in a position to explain why non-declaratives do not serve to make assertions.

However, some of the existing theories of the semantics and pragmatics of non-declaratives are more congenial to the rest of the framework I have been developing than others. Below I will briefly outline what I take to be a promising picture of interrogatives, imperatives, and exclamatives. In addition to the reservations made above, though, I stress that in providing this sketch, I do not pretend to supply anything like adequate motivation for the claims in question. I gloss these views, hoping that the motivations their original proponents provide for them will suffice. My goal is merely to introduce them in order to show how adopting them fits with the rest of the picture presented in this book.

10.13. Questions under Discussion, To-Do Lists, and Widening

When spelling out my account of what is said, in Chapter 4, I endorsed the view that the compositional meanings of interrogatives are not the same kind of object as the compositional meaning of declaratives. Instead, following Roberts (2012), I adopted the semantics for questions developed by Hamblin (1973), Karttunen (1977), Groenendijk and Stokhof (1984), and others, according to which interrogatives denote sets of propositions. For example, we ascribed denotations like the one in (33), where the ellipsis is meant to indicate that the set of propositions (intuitively, of potential answers) extends to all the relevant individuals in the domain.

(33) $[\![$Who is working?$]\!]$ = {{w: Mary is working in w}, {w: Kelly is working in w}, {w: Jim is working in w} ...}

On the Stalnaker–Roberts view of discourse structure I subscribe to, the denotations of interrogatives interact with the set of QUDs in the context. The usual effect of uttering an interrogative is to update the set of QUDs, so that the question asked is accepted as being under discussion.

Yet, it is important to note that, even though interrogatives are seen as targeting a discourse component different from the common ground, the claim I have made in this chapter—that asking a question involves a proposal to update the common ground with the information that one wants to know the answer—is not incompatible with this theory. Indeed, Roberts allows that accepting a question may influence the common ground. In particular, she plausibly suggests that:

When interlocutors accept a question, they form an intention to answer it, which intention is entered into the common ground.   (Roberts, 2002, 4)

My suggestion, which I take to be equally plausible, is that when a speaker asks a question, her desire to know the answer is entered into the common ground—or at least it is proposed for the common ground. That claim is not incompatible with seeing questions as updating the set of QUDs.

Analogously to this analysis of interrogatives, Zanuttini and Portner (2003), Portner (2004), (2007), and others, argue that the other non-declarative clause types—for instance, imperatives and exclamatives—likewise denote non-declarative denotations, which in turn interact with other elements of discourse structure.

First, a number of semanticists (for example, Ninan, 2005, Portner, 2007) have argued that utterances of imperative sentences do not function to update the common ground of a conversation but rather serve to impose obligations.[16] To repeat, I will refrain from reviewing the arguments for this view here. Instead, I want to focus on the consequences of it for our more immediate purposes. To implement this view of imperatives, Portner (2004), (2007) follows Hausser (1980) in proposing that imperatives denote properties. In turn, the function of imperatives to impose obligations is modelled by letting this kind of imperative meaning interact with an appropriate discourse element that Portner calls the *to-do list* function, that is, a function that assigns properties (representing actions) to individuals of the context.

---

[16] This view is similar to views, such as that of Pagin (2004), on which the intended effects of non-declaratives are part of what such utterances communicate. For instance, on Pagin's view, an order not only imposes an obligation, but this effect is part of what is communicated by the utterance. Pagin argues that this feature of non-declaratives marks the distinction between assertions and other speech acts, in that the latter, although they have social effects, do not communicate such effects as part of their linguistic function. A technical implementation of a view like Pagin's might naturally make use of different discourse components targeted by declaratives and different kinds of non-declaratives, respectively, analogously to proposals such as those in Ninan (2005) and Portner (2007) for imperatives.

Here is a (grossly over-simplified) illustration of this view.[17] The imperative (34) is seen as denoting the property of being nice.

(34) Be nice!

More particularly, (34) will denote a property that can only be true of the addressee. This is represented by the denotation in (35).[18]

(35) $[\![(34)]\!]^c = [\lambda w \lambda x : x = \text{the addressee of } c. \; x \text{ is nice in } w.]$

As usual the condition between the ":" and the " . " in this notation is a condition on the domain of the function. In other words, (34) denotes a property that applies to an individual if and only if that individual is the addressee of c, and is true of that individual at a world w if and only if she is nice in w. In turn, on this view, the function of (34) is not to add information to the common ground but to place the act of being nice on the to-do list of the addressee. Technically, that is, the to-do list function of the context is updated so that it will assign the property of being nice to the addressee.

So, on this view, the compositional meaning of imperatives are not minimal contents like those denoted by declaratives, and correspondingly they do not interact with QUDs. Hence, if this is right, no imperative can be used to say anything. But moreover, we can note that this view of the semantics and discourse function of imperatives is completely compatible with also seeing them as interacting with common ground. In particular, we have seen that typically an imperative has the effect of making it common ground that the speaker wants the relevant action to be carried out.

One can accept that the right analysis of the semantics of imperatives is one that sees them as adding non-propositional information to a special discourse component distinct from the common ground and still maintain that imperative utterances, in addition, increment the common ground with a particular piece of propositional information. It might be that the right analysis of the semantics of imperatives will turn out to be one that takes imposing obligations to be their chief semantic feature; and this might then in turn be analyzed in terms of

---

[17] For full details, see Portner (2004, Sec. 3).

[18] See Portner (2004, 240). I suppress some details from this denotation concerning the world of evaluation, which are not relevant for my purposes here.

non-propositional to-do lists. Indeed, it seems undeniable that orders do impose obligations, in some way or other. But I think it is equally evident that orders also communicate information about the desires of the speaker.

Let us now turn briefy to the case of the exclamative clause type. Corresponding to the analyses of interrogatives and imperatives we have outlined, Zanuttini and Portner (2003) have proposed that, like interrogatives, exclamatives denote sets of propositions. But unlike interrogatives, they do not interact with the set of QUDs in a context. Rather, Zanuttini and Portner suggest that the discourse function of exclamatives involves an operation of *widening*, which is modelled as the expansion of a domain of quantification.

Again simplifying for present purposes, the basic idea of this proposal is that an exclamative such as (36) serves to widen a previously expected range of possibilities.

(36)   How nice he is!

In particular, (36), on this view, serves to convey that the niceness of the referent of *he* exceeds the range of previously expected possibilities. Hence, the widening effect of (36) is to add possibilities to the relevant domain.

As for the case of interrogatives and imperatives, therefore, this view has the consequence that exclamatives do not denote compositional contents that can interact with QUDs in the way that declaratives do, and therefore they cannot be used to say things. But at the same time, there is nothing to prevent us from accepting that—as we have seen—exclamations have the effect of making particular propositional information common ground.

Bibliography

Adler, J. (1997). Lying, deceiving, or falsely implicating. *Journal of Philosophy, 94* 435–52.

Alston, W. (1971). Varieties of privileged access. *American Philosophical Quarterly 8*(3), 223–41.

Anscombe, G. (1963). *Intention* (2nd ed.). Oxford: Blackwell.

Aquinas, T. (1922 [1265–74]). Of lying. In *Summa theologica* (Vol. XII, pp. 85–98). London: Burns, Oates, and Washbourne.

Arpaly, N. and T. Schroeder (1999). Praise, blame and the whole self. *Philosophical Studies 93*(2), 161–88.

Audi, R. (1973). Intending. *Journal of Philosophy 70*(13), 387–403.

Augustine. (1952 [395]a). Against lying. In R. Deferrari (ed.), *Treaties on various subjects* (Vol. 16, pp. 125–79). Washington, DC: Catholic University of America Press.

Augustine. (1952 [395]b). Lying. In R. Deferrari (ed.), *Treaties on various subjects* (Vol. 16, pp. 53–120). Washington, DC: Catholic University of America Press.

Austin, J. (1962). *How to do things with words.* Oxford: Oxford University Press.

Bach, K. (1981). An analysis of self-deception. *Philosophy and Phenomenological Research 41*(3), 351–70.

Bach, K. (1994). Conversational impliciture. *Mind and Language 9*, 124–52.

Bach, K. (2001). You don't say? *Synthese 128*, 15–44.

Bach, K. (2009). Self-deception. In B. McLaughlin, A. Beckermann, and S. Walter (eds), *The Oxford handbook of philosophy of mind* (pp. 781–97). Oxford/New York: Oxford University Press.

Barker, C. (1995). *Possessive descriptions.* Stanford, CA: CSLI Publications.

Barnes, J. (1994). *A pack of lies: Towards a sociology of lying.* Cambridge: Cambridge University Press.

Bar-On, D. (2004). *Speaking my mind: Expression and self-knowledge.* Oxford: Clarendon Press.

Bennett, J. (1974). The conscience of Huckleberry Finn. *Philosophy 49*, 123–34.

Bertolet, R. (1994). Are there indirect speech acts? In S. Tsohatzidis (ed.), *Foundations of speech act theory: Philosophical and linguistic perspectives* (pp. 335–49). London: Routledge.

Bezuidenhout, A. (2001). Metaphor and what is said. *Midwest Studies in Philosophy 25*, 156–86.

Black, M. (1983). The prevalence of humbug. In *The prevalence of humbug and other essays* (pp. 115–46). Ithaca, NY: Cornell University Press.

Bok, S. (1978). *Lying: Moral choice in private and public life*. New York: Random House.

Borg, E. (2004). *Minimal semantics*. Oxford: Oxford University Press.

Bratman, M. (1987). *Intention, plans, and practical reasoning*. Cambridge, MA: Harvard University Press.

Braun, D. (2011). Implicating questions. *Mind and Language 26*(5), 574–95.

Burge, T. (1988). Individualism and self-knowledge. *Journal of Philosophy 85*, 649–63.

Burge, T. (1996). Our entitlement to self-knowledge. *Proceedings of the Aristotelian Society 96*, 91–116.

Byrne, A. (2005). Introspection. *Philosophical Topics 33*(1), 79–104.

Camp, E. (2011). Sarcasm, pretense, and the semantics/pragmatics distinction. *Noûs 46*(4), 587–634.

Cappelen, H. and E. Lepore (2004). *Insensitive semantics—a defense of semantic minimalism and speech act pluralism*. Oxford: Blackwell.

Cappelen, H. and E. Lepore (2007). *Language turned on itself*. Oxford/New York: Oxford University Press.

Carlson, L. (1982). *Dialogue games: An approach to discourse analysis*. Dordrecht: Reidel.

Carson, T. (2006). The definition of lying. *Noûs 40*, 284–306.

Carson, T. (2010). *Lying and deception: Theory and practice*. Oxford/New York: Oxford University Press.

Carson, T. (forthcoming). *What's wrong with lying?* In E. Michaelson and A. Stokke (eds), *Lying: Language, Knowledge, Ethics, Politics*. Oxford: Oxford University Press.

Carston, R. (1998). Informativeness, relevance, and scalar implicatures. In R. Carston and S. Uchida (eds), *Relevance theory—applications and implications* (Vol. 37, pp. 179–235). Amsterdam: John Benjaminis.

Carston, R. (2002). *Thoughts and utterances*. Oxford: Blackwell.

Chan, T. and Kahane, G. (2011). The trouble with being sincere. *Canadian Journal of Philosophy 41*(2), 215–34.

Chisholm, R. and T. Feehan (1977). The intent to deceive. *Journal of Philosophy 74*, 143–59.

Cohen, G. (2002). Deeper into bullshit. In S. Buss and L. Overton (eds), *Contours of agency: Essays on themes from Harry Frankfurt* (pp. 321–39). London/Cambridge, MA: MIT Press.

Cohen, L. (1989). Belief and acceptance. *Mind 98*(391), 367–89.

Cooper, R. (1983). *Quantification and syntactic theory*. Dordrecht: Reidel.

Cowen, T. (2017). *Why Trump's staff is lying*. *Bloomberg*, January 23, 2017. Retrieved from https://www.bloomberg.com/view/articles/2017-01-23/why-trump-s-staff-is-lying.

Davidson, D. (1985). Deception and division. In J. Elster (ed.), *The multiple self* (pp. 79–92). Cambridge/New York: Cambridge University Press.

Davidson, D. (1986). A nice derangement of epitaphs. In E. Lepore (ed.), *Truth and interpretation: Perspectives on the philosophy of Donald Davidson* (pp. 161–80). New York: Basil Blackwell.

Davidson, D. (1989 [1978]). Intending. In *Essays on actions and events* (pp. 83–102). Oxford: Clarendon Press.

Davis, W. (2003). *Meaning, expression, and thought.* Cambridge/New York: Cambridge University Press.

Davis, W. (2010). Implicature. *Stanford Encyclopedia of Philosophy.* https://plato.stanford.edu/archives/fall2014/entries/implicature/.

DeRose, K. (2002). Review of T. Williamson, *Knowledge and Its Limits. British Journal for Philosophy of Science 53*, 573–7.

Donnellan, K. (1966). Reference and definite descriptions. *Philosophical Review 75*, 281–304.

Dynel, M. (2011). A web of deceit: A neo-Gricean view on types of verbal deception. *International Review of Pragmatics 3*, 139–67.

Egan, A. (2007). Epistemic modals, relativism and assertion. *Philosophical Studies 133*, 1–22.

Eriksson, J. (2011a). Defining lying: In defense of the falsity condition. In R. Sliwinski & F. Svensson (eds), *Neither/nor: Philosophical papers dedicated to Erik Carlson on the occasion of his fiftieth birthday* (pp. 69–78). Uppsala: Uppsala University.

Eriksson, J. (2011b). Straight talk: conceptions of sincerity in speech. *Philosophical Studies 153*, 213–34.

Fallis, D. (2009). What is lying? *Journal of Philosophy 106*, 29–56.

Fallis, D. (2010). Lying and deception. *Philosophers' Imprint 10*, 1–22.

Fallis, D. (2012). Lying as a violation of Grice's first maxim of quality. *Dialectica 66*(4), 563–81.

Fallis, D. (2013). Davidson was almost right about lying. *Australasian Journal of Philosophy 91*(2), 337–53.

Fallis, D. (2014a). Are bald-faced lies deceptive after all? *Ratio 28*(1), 81–96.

Fallis, D. (2014b). Review of *Lying, Misleading, and What Is Said: An Exploration in Philosophy of Language and in Ethics,* by Jennifer Mather Saul. *European Journal of Philosophy 22*(S1), e17–e22.

Fallis, D. (2015). Frankfurt wasn't bullshitting! *Southwestern Journal of Philosophy 37*, 11–20.

Faulkner, P. (2007). What is wrong with lying? *Philosophy and Phenomenological Research 75*, 535–57.

Faulkner, P. (2013). Lying and deceit. In H. LaFollette (ed.), *International encyclopedia of ethics.* Hoboken, NJ: Wiley.

von Fintel, K. (2004). Would you believe it? The King of France is back! (Presuppositions and truth-value intuitions). In M. Reimer and A. Bezuidenhout (eds), *Descriptions and beyond* (pp. 315–41). Oxford/New York: Oxford University Press.

von Fintel, K. (2008). What is presupposition accommodation, again? *Philosophical Perspectives 22*, 137–70.

Frankfurt, H. (1988). *The importance of what we care about*. Cambridge: Cambridge University Press.

Frankfurt, H. (2005 [1986]). *On bullshit*. Princeton, NJ: Princeton University Press.

Gauker, C. (2012). What Tipper is ready for: A semantics for incomplete predicates. *Noûs 46*(1), 61–85.

Geurts, B. (1999). *Presuppositions and pronouns*. Amsterdam: Elsevier.

Gibbard, A. (1990). *Wise choices, apt feelings: A theory of normative judgement*. Oxford/New York: Oxford University Press.

Ginzburg, J. (1995a). Resolving questions I. *Linguistics and Philosophy 18*(5), 459–527.

Ginzburg, J. (1995b). Resolving questions II. *Linguistics and Philosophy 18*(5), 567–609.

Glanzberg, M. (2002). Context and discourse. *Mind and Language 17*, 333–75.

Green, M. (2007a). How do speech acts express psychological states? In S. Tsohatzidis (ed.), *John Searle's philosophy of language: Force, meaning, and mind* (pp. 267–84). Cambridge/New York: Cambridge University Press.

Green, M. (2007b). *Self-expression*. Oxford/New York: Oxford University Press.

Green, M. (2010). Speech acts. In T. O'Connor and C. Sandis (eds), *A companion to the philosophy of action* (pp. 58–66). Oxford: Wiley Blackwell.

Greenough, P. (2012). Discrimination and self-knowledge. In D. Smithies and D. Stoljar (eds), *Introspection and consciousness*. Oxford/New York: Oxford University Press.

Grice, H. (1973). Intention and uncertainty. *Proceedings of the British Academy 57*, 263–79.

Grice, H. (1975). Logic and conversation. In *Studies in the way of words* (pp. 22–40). Cambridge, MA: Harvard University Press, 1989.

Grice, H. (1989). *Studies in the way of words*. Cambridge, MA: Harvard University Press.

Griffiths, P. (2001). *Lying: An Augustinian Theology of Duplicity*. Eugene, OR: Wipf & Stock.

Groenendijk, J. and F. Roelofsen (2011, April). *Inquisitive semantics and pragmatics*. MS. Retrieved from http://www.illc.uva.nl/inquisitive-semantics.

Groenendijk, J. and M. Stokhof (1984). *Studies on the semantics of questions and the pragmatics of answers*. PhD thesis, University of Amsterdam. Retrieved from http://dare.uva.nl/record/123669.

Hamblin, C. (1973). Questions in Montague English. *Foundations of Language 10*, 41–53.

Hausser, R. (1980). Surface compositionality and the semantics of mood. In M. Bierwisch, F. Kiefer, and J. Searle (eds), *Speech act theory and pragmatics* (pp. 71–96). Dordrecht: Reidel.

Hawthorne, J. and O. Magidor (2009). Assertion, context, and epistemic accessibility. *Mind, 118*, 377–97.

Heim, I. (1992). Presupposition projection and the semantics of attitude verbs. *Journal of Semantics 9*, 183–221.

Heim, I. (2008). Features on bound pronouns. In D. Harbor, D. Adger, and S. Bèjar (eds), *Phi-theory: Phi-features across modules and interfaces* (pp. 35–57). Oxford/New York: Oxford University Press.

Heim, I. and A. Kratzer (1998). *Semantics in generative grammar*. Oxford: Blackwell.

Huddleston, R. and G. Pullum (2002). *The Cambridge grammar of the English language*. Cambridge/New York: Cambridge University Press.

Huvenes, T. and A. Stokke (2016). Information centrism and the nature of contexts. *Australasian Journal of Philosophy 94*(2), 301–14.

Isenberg, A. (1964). Deontology and the ethics of lying. *Philosophy and Phenomenological Research 24*, 465–80.

Johnston, M. (1988). Self-deception and the nature of mind. In B. McLaughlin and A. O. Rorty (eds), *Perspectives on self-deception* (pp. 63–91). Berkeley, CA: University of California Press.

Kant, I. (1997 [1784–5]). Of ethical duties towards others, and especially truthfulness. In P. Heath and J. Schneewind (eds), *Lectures on ethics* (pp. 200–9). Cambridge/New York: Cambridge University Press. (Lecture notes taken by Georg Ludwig Collins, Königsberg, 1784–5).

Kaplan, D. (1989). Demonstratives. In J. Almog, J. Perry, and H. Wettstein (eds), *Themes from Kaplan* (pp. 481–563). Oxford/New York: Oxford University Press.

Kaplan, D. (1990). Words. *Proceedings of the Aristotelian Society Supplementary Volume, LXIV*.

Karttunen, L. (1977). Syntax and semantics of questions. *Linguistics and Philosophy 1*, 3–44.

Keiser, J. (2015). Bald-faced lies: How to make a move in a language game without making a move in a conversation. *Philosophical Studies 173*(2), 461–77.

Kim, J. (1998). *Philosophy of mind* (3rd edn). Boulder, CO: Westview Press.

Kimbrough, S. (2006). On letting it slide. In G. Hardcastle and G. Reich (eds), *Bullshit and philosophy* (pp. 3–18). Chicago, IL: Open Court.

Kissine, M. (2013). *From utterances to speech acts*. Cambridge/New York: Cambridge University Press.

Korsgaard, C. (1986). The right to lie: Kant on dealing with evil. *Philosophy and Public Affairs 15*, 325–49.

Krifka, M. (2011). Questions. In K. von Heusinger, C. Maienborn, and P. Portner (eds), *An international handbook of natural language meaning* (Vol. 2, pp. 1742–85). Berlin/Boston, MA: de Gruyter.

Kripke, S. (2009). Presupposition and anaphora: Remarks on the formulation of the projection problem. *Linguistic Inquiry 40*, 367–386. (Edited transcript of a talk given in 1990).

Kumon-Nakamura, S., S. Glucksberg, and M. Brown (2007). How about another piece of pie: The allusional pretense theory of discourse irony. In R. Gibbs Jr. and H. Colston (eds), *Irony in language and thought: A cognitive science reader* (pp. 57–96). New York/London: Lawrence Erlbaum Associates.

Kupfer, J. (1982). The moral presumption against lying. *Review of Metaphysics 36*, 103–26.

Lackey, J. (2008). *Learning from words.* Oxford/New York: Oxford University Press.

Lackey, J. (2013). Lies and deception: An unhappy divorce. *Analysis 73*(2), 236–48.

Lear, J. (1998). *Open-minded.* Cambridge, MA: Harvard University Press.

Lepore, E. and M. Stone (2015). *Imagination and convention: Distinguishing grammar and inference in language.* Oxford/New York: Oxford University Press.

Levinson, S. (1983). *Pragmatics.* Cambridge: Cambridge University Press.

Levinson, S. (2000). *Presumptive meanings—the theory of generalized conversational implicature.* Cambridge, MA: MIT Press.

Lewis, D. (1978). Truth in fiction. *American Philosophical Quarterly 15*, 37–46.

Lewis, D. (1979). Scorekeeping in a language game. *Journal of Philosophical Logic 8*, 339–59.

Lincoln, A. (1953 [1865]). To James M. Ashley. In R. Basler (ed.), *Collected works* (Vol. 8). New Brunswick, NJ: Rutgers University Press. Retrieved from http://name.umdl.umich.edu/lincoln8.

Ludlow, P. (2013). *The real war on reality. New York Times*, June 14, 2013. Retrieved from http://opinionator.blogs.nytimes.com/2013/06/14/the-real-war-on-reality.

Lycan, W. (2006). On the Gettier problem. In S. Hetherington (ed.), *Epistemology futures* (pp. 148–68). Oxford/New York: Oxford University Press.

MacFarlane, J. (2010). What is assertion? In H. Cappelen and J. Brown (eds), *Assertion—new philosophical essays* (pp. 79–96). Oxford/New York: Oxford University Press.

MacIntyre, A. (1995). Truthfulness, lies, and moral philosophers: What can we learn from Mill and Kant? *The Tanner Lectures on Human Values, 16*, 307–61.

Mahon, J. (2006). Kant and the perfect duty to others not to lie. *British Journal for the History of Philosophy 14*, 653–85.

Mahon, J. (2009). The truth about Kant on lies. In C. Martin (ed.), *The philosophy of deception* (pp. 201–24). Oxford/New York: Oxford University Press.

Mahon, J. (2011). Review of *Lying and Deception* by Thomas L. Carson. *Notre Dame Philosophical Reviews* 2011.01.13 https://ndpr.nd.edu/news/lying-and-deception-theory-and-practice/.

Mahon, J. (2015). The definition of lying and deception. *Stanford Encyclopedia of Philosophy*, https://plato.stanford.edu/archives/win2016/entries/lying-definition/.

McLaughlin, B. (1988). Exploring the possibility of self-deception in belief. In B. McLaughlin and A. O. Rorty (eds), *Perspectives on self-deception* (pp. 29–62). Berkeley, CA: University of California Press.

Meibauer, J. (2005). Lying and falsely implicating. *Journal of Pragmatics 37*, 1373–99.

Meibauer, J. (2011). On lying: Intentionality, implicature, and imprecision. *Intercultural Pragmatics 8*, 277–92.

Meibauer, J. (2014). Bald-faced lies as acts of verbal agression. *Journal of Verbal Agression 2*(1), 127–50.

Mele, A. (2010). Intention. In T. O'Connor and C. Sandis (eds), *A companion to the philosophy of action* (pp. 108–13). Oxford: Wiley Blackwell.

Michaelson, E. and A. Stokke (forthcoming). *Introduction*. In E. Michaelson and A. Stokke (eds) *Lying: Language, Knowledge, Ethics, Politics*. Oxford: Oxford University Press.

Moran, R. (2001). *Authority and estrangement*. Princeton, NJ: Princeton University Press.

Moran, R. (2004). Anscombe on 'practical knowledge'. In J. Hyman and H. Steward (eds), *Agency and action* (pp. 43–68). Cambridge: Cambridge University Press.

Murdoch, I. (2001 [1961]). *A severed head*. London: Vintage Books.

Neale, S. (1992). Paul Grice and the philosophy of language. *Linguistics and Philosophy 15*, 509–59.

Neale, S. (2005). Pragmatics and binding. In Z. G. Szabó (ed.), *Semantics versus pragmatics* (pp. 165–285). Oxford/New York: Oxford University Press.

Ninan, D. (2005). *Two puzzles about deontic necessity*. In J. Gajewski, V. Hacquard, B. Nickel, and S. Yalcin (eds), *New work on modality*, Vol. 51 of *MIT Working Papers in Linguistics* (pp. 149–78). Cambridge, MA: MITWP.

Owens, D. (2006). Testimony and assertion. *Philosophical Studies 130*, 105–29.

Pagin, P. (2004). Is assertion social? *Journal of Pragmatics 36*, 833–59.

Paton, H. (1954). An alleged right to lie: A problem in Kantian ethics. *Kant-Studien 45*, 190–203.

Peacocke, C. (1998). Conscious attitudes, attention and self-knowledge. In C. Wright, B. Smith, and C. MacDonald (eds), *Knowing our own minds* (pp. 63–98). Oxford/New York: Oxford University Press.

Pepp, J. (forthcoming). *Truth serum, liar serum, and some problems about saying what you think is false*. In E. Michaelson and A. Stokke (eds), *Lying*. Oxford: Oxford University Press.

Portner, P. (2004). The semantics of imperatives within a theory of clause types. *Proceedings of SALT XIV*, 235–52.

Portner, P. (2007). Imperatives and modals. *Natural Language Semantics 15*, 351–83.

Potts, C. (2005). *The logic of conventional implicatures*. Oxford/New York: Oxford University Press.

Predelli, S. (2005). *Contexts: Meaning, truth and the use of language*. Oxford: Clarendon Press.

Pruss, A. (2012). Sincerely asserting what you do not believe. *Australasian Journal of Philosophy 90*, 541–6.

Recanati, F. (1987). *Meaning and force: The pragmatics of performative utterances*. Cambridge/New York: Cambridge University Press.

Recanati, F. (1989). The pragmatics of what is said. *Mind and Language 4*(4), 295–329.

Recanati, F. (1993). *Direct reference—from language to thought*. Oxford: Blackwell.

Recanati, F. (2000). *Oratio obliqua, oratio recta: An essay on metarepresentation*. Cambridge, MA: MIT Press.

Recanati, F. (2004). *Literal meaning*. Cambridge: Cambridge University Press.

Recanati, F. (2010). *Truth-conditional pragmatics*. Oxford/New York: Oxford University Press.

Reimer, M. (2004). What malapropisms mean: A reply to Donald Davidson. *Erkenntnis 60*(3), 317–34.

Ridge, M. (2006). Sincerity and expressivism. *Philosophical Studies 131*, 478–510.

Roberts, C. (2004). Context in dynamic interpretation. In L. Horn and G. Ward (eds), *The handbook of pragmatics* (pp. 197–220). Oxford: Blackwell.

Roberts, C. (2012). Information structure in discourse: Towards an integrated formal theory of pragmatics. *Semantics and Pragmatics 5*, 1–69.

van Rooij, R. and K. Schultz (2004). Exhaustive interpretation in complex sentences. *Journal of Logic, Language and Information 13*, 491–519.

Ross, W. (2002 [1930]). *The right and the good*, P. Stratton-Lake (ed.). Oxford/New York: Oxford University Press.

Rutschmann, R. and A. Wiegmann (2017). No need for an intention to deceive? challenging the traditional definition of lying. *Philosophical Psychology, 30*(4), 438–57.

Sacks, O. (2013). *Speak, memory*. New York Review of Books, February 21, 2013. Retrieved from http://www.nybooks.com/articles/archives/2013/feb/21/speak-memory/.

Sadock, J. and A. Zwicky (1985). Speech act distinctions in syntax. In T. Shopen (ed.), *Language typology and syntactic description* (pp. 155–96). Cambridge: Cambridge University Press.

Sauerland, U. (2004). Scalar implicatures in complex sentences. *Linguistics and Philosophy 27*, 367–91.

Sauerland, U. (2008). On the semantic markedness of phi features. In D. Harbour, D. Adger, and S. Bèjar (eds), *Phi-theory: Phi-features across modules and inter-faces* (pp. 57–83). Oxford/New York: Oxford University Press.

Saul, J. (2012). *Lying, misleading, and what is said: An exploration in philosophy of language and in ethics*. Oxford/New York: Oxford University Press.

Schoubye, A. and A. Stokke (2016). What is said? *Noûs 50*(4), 759–93.

Schwitzgebel, E. (2014). Introspection. *Stanford Encyclopedia of Philosophy*, https://plato.stanford.edu/archives/win2016/entries/introspection/.

Searle, J. (1969). *Speech acts: An essay in the philosophy of language*. Oxford: Oxford University Press.

Searle, J. (1979 [1975]). Indirect speech acts. In *Expression and meaning: Studies in the theory of speech acts* (pp. 30–57). Cambridge: Cambridge University Press.

Setiya, K. (2007). *Reasons without rationalism*. Princeton, NJ: Princeton University Press.

Setiya, K. (2011). Knowledge of intention. In A. Ford, J. Hornsby, and F. Stoutland (eds), *Essays on Anscombe's Intention* (pp. 170–97). Cambridge, MA: Harvard University Press.

Setiya, K. (2014). Intention. *Stanford Encyclopedia of Philosophy*, https://plato.stanford.edu/archives/sum2015/entries/intention/.

Shannon, B. (1976). On the two kinds of presuppositions in natural language. *Foundations of Language 14*, 247–9.

Shiffrin, S. (2014). *Speech matters: On lying, morality, and the law*. Princeton, NJ: Princeton University Press.

Shoemaker, S. (1998 [1990]). First-person access. In *The first-person perspective: And other essays* (pp. 50–73). Cambridge/New York: Cambridge University Press.

Shoemaker, S. (1998 [1996]). Moore's paradox and self-knowledge. In *The first-person perspective: And other essays* (pp. 74–93). Cambridge/New York: Cambridge University Press.

Simpson, D. (1992). Lying, liars and language. *Philosophy and Phenomenological Research 52*(3), 623–39.

Soames, S. (2008). Drawing the line between meaning and implicature—and relating both to assertion. *Noûs 42*, 440–65.

Solan, L. and P. Tiersma (2005). *Speaking of crime: The language of criminal justice*. Chicago, IL: University of Chicago Press.

Sorensen, R. (2007). Bald-faced lies! Lying without the intent to deceive. *Pacific Philosophical Quarterly 88*, 251–64.

Sorensen, R. (2011). What lies behind misspeaking. *American Philosophical Quarterly 48*(4), 399–409.

Spector, B. (2007). Scalar implicatures: Exhaustivity and Gricean reasoning. In M. Aloni, A. Butler, and P. Dekker (eds), *Questions in dynamic semantics*, (pp. 225–50). Amsterdam: Elsevier. http://www.semanticsarchive.net/Archive/WU2MGJkN/.

Sperber, D. and D. Wilson (1981). Irony and the use-mention distinction. In P. Cole (ed.), *Radical pragmatics* (pp. 295–318). New York: Academic Press.

Sperber, D. and D. Wilson (1986). *Relevance: Communication and cognition*. Oxford: Blackwell.

Stalnaker, R. (1984). *Inquiry*. Cambridge, MA: MIT Press.

Stalnaker, R. (1999). Introduction. In *Context and content* (pp. 1–28). Oxford/New York: Oxford University Press.

Stalnaker, R. (1999 [1970]). Pragmatics. In *Context and content* (pp. 31–46). Oxford/New York: Oxford University Press.

Stalnaker, R. (1999 [1974]). Pragmatic presuppositions. In *Context and content* (pp. 47–62). Oxford/New York: Oxford University Press.

Stalnaker, R. (1999 [1978]). Assertion. In *Context and content* (pp. 78–95). Oxford/New York: Oxford University Press.

Stalnaker, R. (1999 [1998]). On the representation of context. In *Context and content* (pp. 96–114). Oxford/New York: Oxford University Press.

Stalnaker, R. (2002). Common ground. *Linguistics and Philosophy 25*, 701–21.

Stalnaker, R. (2009). On Hawthorne and Magidor on assertion, context, and epistemic accessibility. *Mind 118*, 399–409.

Stalnaker, R. (2014). *Context*. Oxford/New York: Oxford University Press.

Stanley, J. (2007 [2000]). Context and logical form. In *Language in context—selected essays* (pp. 30–68). Oxford: Clarendon Press.

Stanley, J. and Z. G. Szabó (2000). On quantifier domain restriction. In *Language in context—selected essays* (pp. 69–110). Oxford: Clarendon Press, 2007.

Stern, J. (2000). *Metaphor in context*. Cambridge, MA: MIT Press.

Stokke, A. (2010). Intention-sensitive semantics. *Synthese 175*, 383–404.

Stokke, A. (2013). Lying and asserting. *Journal of Philosophy CX*(1), 33–60.

Stokke, A. (2014). Insincerity. *Noûs 48*(3), 496–520.

Stokke, A. (2016a). Lying and misleading in discourse. *Philosophical Review 125*(1), 83–134.

Stokke, A. (2016b). *Proposing, pretending, and propriety: A response to Don Fallis*. Forthcoming in *Australasian Journal of Philosophy*.

Stokke, A. (2016c). Truthfulness and Gricean cooperation. *Grazer Philosophische Studien 93*(3), 489–510.

Stokke, A. (2017a). Conventional implicature, presupposition, and lying. *Proceedings of the Aristotelian Society Supplementary Volume 91*, 127–47.

Stokke, A. (2017b). *Lies, harm, and practical interests*. Forthcoming in *Philosophy and Phenomenological Research*.

Stokke, A. and D. Fallis (2017). Bullshitting, lying, and indifference toward truth. *Ergo 4*(10), 277–309.

Tolstoy, L. (2007 [1869]). *War and peace*. London/New York: Penguin Books.

Travis, C. (1985). On what is strictly speaking true. *Canadian Journal of Philosophy 15*(2), 187–229.

Turri, J. and A. Turri (2015). The truth about lying. *Cognition 138*, 161–8.

Twain, M. (1884). *The adventures of Huckleberry Finn*. London: Chatto & Windus.

Velleman, J. (1989). *Practical reflection*. Princeton, NJ: Princeton University Press.

Vogel, J. (2010). Luminosity and indiscriminability. *Philosophical Perspectives, 24* 547–72.

Weatherson, B. (2004). Luminous margins. *Australasian Journal of Philosophy 82*, 373–83.

Webber, J. (2013). Liar! *Analysis 73*(4), 651–9.

Williams, B. (2002). *Truth and truthfulness: An essay in genealogy*. Princeton, NJ: Princeton University Press.

Williamson, T. (2000). *Knowledge and its limits*. Oxford: Oxford University Press.

Wilson, D. (1995). Is there a maxim of truthfulness? *UCL Working Papers in Linguistics 7*, 197–212.

Wilson, D. and D. Sperber (2002). Truthfulness and relevance. *Mind 111*(443), 583–632.

Wood, A. (2008). *Kantian ethics*. Cambridge/New York: Cambridge University Press.

Wreen, M. (2013). A P.S. on B.S.: Some remarks on humbug and bullshit. *Metaphilosophy 44*, 105–15.

Yglesias, M. (2017). *The bullshitter in chief. Vox.com* May 30, 2017. Retrieved from https://www.vox.com/policy-and-politics/2017/5/30/15631710/trump-bullshit.

Zanuttini, R. and P. Portner (2003). Exclamative clauses: At the syntax-semantics interface. *Language 79*(1), 39–81.

Zardini, E. (2013). Luminosity and determinacy. *Philosophical Studies 165*(3), 765–86.

Index